COACHING ON THE AXIS

The Professional Coaching Series
Series Editor: David Lane

Other titles in the series

The Art of Inspired Living: Coach Yourself with Positive Psychology
  Sarah Corrie

Integrated Experiential Coaching: Becoming an Executive Coach
  Lloyd Chapman, with contributing author Sunny Stout Rostron

Coaching in the Family Owned Business: A Path to Growth
  edited by Manfusa Shams and David A. Lane

Coaching in Education: Getting Better Results for Students, Educators, and Parents
  edited by Christian van Nieuwerburgh

Internal Coaching: The Inside Story
  Katharine St John-Brooks

Business Coaching International: Transforming Individuals and Organizations (Second Edition)
  Sunny Stout-Rostron

Swings and Roundabouts: A Self-Coaching Workbook for Parents and Those Considering Becoming Parents
  Anna Golawski, Agnes Bamford, and Irvine Gersch

COACHING ON THE AXIS
Working with Complexity in Business and Executive Coaching

Marc Simon Kahn

Routledge
Taylor & Francis Group

LONDON AND NEW YORK

First published 2014 by Karnac Books Ltd.

Published 2018 by Routledge
2 Park Square, Milton Park, Abingdon, Oxon OX14 4RN
711 Third Avenue, New York, NY 10017, USA

Routledge is an imprint of the Taylor & Francis Group, an informa business

British Library Cataloguing in Publication Data

A C.I.P. for this book is available from the British Library

ISBN-13: 9781780491363 (pbk)

Typeset by V Publishing Solutions Pvt Ltd., Chennai, India

CONTENTS

ACKNOWLEDGEMENTS   ix

ABOUT THE AUTHOR   xi

SERIES EDITOR'S FOREWORD   xiii
by David A. Lane

INTRODUCTION   xvii

CHAPTER ONE
The complexity of client   1
    Who is the client?   1
    Understanding the duality of client 5
    Systems thinking   7
    Holism   10
    Circular causality   11
    Homeostasis   14
    Valence   17

CHAPTER TWO
The complexity of culture   21
    What is culture?   22
    How culture emerges   23
    Organisational culture   26
    Leadership and organisational culture   29
    Attributes or typologies of organisational culture   30
    Coaching business culture   34
    A word on creating a "coaching culture" in organisations   42

CHAPTER THREE
The complexity of theory   45
    Business culture and the underlying assumptions of science   46
    Integrative and eclectic approaches to theory   48
    The modern scientist-practitioner   50

CHAPTER FOUR
Introduction to the Coaching on the Axis framework   55
    The Coaching on the Axis tree   56

CHAPTER FIVE
The environmental dimension   59
    The environment below and above the surface   64
    Uncovering the individual's relational system   66
    Environmental goals and expectations   68
    Environmental sources of data   70
    Feedback is not just data   71
    The trouble with anonymous feedback   72
    Coaching using open feedback   76
    Creating a relational map with the client   78
    Environmental sources of theory   80

CHAPTER SIX
The individual dimension   83
    The individual below and above the surface   83
    Accessing the individual's story   85
    The roots of an individual's social and cultural identity   87
    Helping individuals manage power relations and rank   90
    Business coaching at the existential level   95
    Individual goals and expectations   99

Individual sources of data   101
A caution on using psychometrics in business coaching   102
Individual sources of theory   105

CHAPTER SEVEN
The coaching relationship   107
Working with purpose in the coaching relationship   108
Goals are compasses not destinations   113
Reflexive awareness—an axial imperative   114
The axis connects coaching with business reality   115
The axis helps avoid pathology-based orientations   117
The coaching relationship below and above the surface   122
Transference and countertransference   123
Creating an axial coaching contract   129
Evaluating success and wrapping up on the axis   134
Coaching ethics on the axis   136
A word on supervision   141
Theory informing the coaching relationship   142

CHAPTER EIGHT
Coaching on the Axis: technique   143
The story of imagination   144
Story as formulation   145
Working thematically   147
Story as iterative and emergent learning   149
Never-ending stories   151

CHAPTER NINE
Case study   155
The first meeting   155
Contracting   157
Gathering data from the dimensions   158
Des's journey in themes   161
Conclusion   166

REFERENCES   167

INDEX   181

ENDORSEMENTS   191

ACKNOWLEDGEMENTS

This book would not have been possible without the support, input, and guidance of many people. There have been so many individuals who influenced and guided me over the last twenty-five years that it would take a book in itself just to acknowledge them properly. Of course, I do not have that latitude here, and must therefore constrain my acknowledgements to those who most immediately contributed to this work.

First, I would like to express my deep gratitude to my coaching clients, especially those who gave permission to use their stories in this work. Thank you also to the coaches, consultants, and students with whom I have worked over the years, and especially those who have been in supervision with me. Without all of you, there simply would be nothing to say.

I would like to acknowledge Professor David Lane of the Professional Development Foundation and Middlesex University in London, who encouraged me to write this book in the first place, provided important ongoing feedback throughout its creation, and kindly wrote the Foreword.

A professional, but also very personal, thank you to Dr Allen Zimbler of Investec, a rare master of organisation development. He has influenced an inordinate amount of my thinking and he generously provided critical feedback on this book.

A special thank you to: Professor Frans Cilliers of the University of South Africa, Dr Salome van Coller of the University of Stellenbosch Business School, Dr Sunny Stout-Rostron of the Institute of Coaching at Harvard/McLean Medical School, Dr Paddy Pampallis Paisley of the Coaching Centre, and Dr Caryn Solomon of the London School of Economics and Investec. You all provided valuable feedback that helped shape the book into its current form.

Sincere thanks also go to the following people who were sounding boards for parts or all of the text and whose feedback or input resulted in meaningful additions, changes, or important confirmations: Lesley-Ann Gatter, Toni Gaddie, Edwin Edelstein, Justin Cohen, Matthew Shelley, Brett Morris, Alon Davidov, Barbara Walsh, Adam Bulkin, Steven Sachs, Paul Haupt, Raymond Goss and Dr Henk Struwig.

I also wish to acknowledge my colleagues and friends at Investec, especially those in the incredible OD and HR divisions, as well as to Investec's remarkable leaders. Much of the wisdom offered in this book comes from my experience and learning with so many of you.

Finally, I take a moment here to stop, and offer a private appreciation to my amazing wife Kelly and my wonderful children Laila, Sage, Judah, and Sierra. You are my light, my heart … my home.

ABOUT THE AUTHOR

Marc Simon Kahn is a Chartered Business Coach™ with the Worldwide Association of Business Coaches (WABC), a clinical psychologist with registrations in both South Africa and Australia, and a seasoned management and organisation development consultant.

He is currently head of human resources and organisation development for Investec Ltd, a listed financial services corporation. Prior to this, he was managing director of a management consultancy that specialised in large-scale learning and development solutions, competency-based assessments, and coaching programmes in both the private and public sectors. He began his career as a clinical psychologist in private practice, where for nine years he focused on adult psychotherapy as well as psychological assessments for medico-legal cases, for which he regularly gave evidence as an expert witness in the High Court of South Africa.

Marc has been consulting to organisations for twenty years, having worked at scale across the coaching industry as a provider, teacher, supervisor, and corporate procurer of business and executive coaching services. Marc was one of the early developers of coaching in South Africa. He led the establishment of the first Code of Ethics for COMENSA (Coaches and Mentors of South Africa) in 2004 and was its first Chair of Ethics. He also sat on the Worldwide Association of Business Coaches International Certification Program Expert Panel in 2005 and 2006. Marc lectures at universities and business schools, has published several papers in peer-reviewed academic journals on the subjects of coaching and psychology, and has appeared regularly as an expert guest on radio and television.

Marc's initial interest in coaching began in the 1980s when he studied martial arts under a renowned teacher and discovered the transformative power of a coaching relationship. Marc holds two black belts in Chinese and Japanese martial arts, and ran a school for many years.

Marc Kahn can be contacted via email on marcsimonkahn@gmail.com.

SERIES EDITOR'S FOREWORD

I am delighted to introduce this latest edition of our Professional Coaching Series. It is all I hoped it would be when it was commissioned. It weaves important insights from a range of literatures, both psychological and from business science, to produce a tapestry of useful ideas. It tells us stories in a way that captivates us but leads through to applications in the complex contexts we face in this field.

The Professional Coaching Series aims to provide core reading on issues important to the field of coaching. It also uniquely creates opportunities for specialist areas of practice to receive due attention. It is based on a core belief that we need practical resources that are fully underpinned by research. The author fulfills our mission for this series by providing a theoretically informed yet useful book, which can be applied to the realities of coaching in organisations.

One of the most rapidly growing areas of practice is that of business and executive coaching. We have in this series provided coverage through our books on international business coaching, (Stout Rostron, 2009, 2014) integrated experiential coaching, (Chapman, 2010), coaching in the family business, (Shams and Lane, 2011) and, our most recent offer, internal coaching, (St John-Brooks, 2014). One area that has received less attention in the literature has been how to bring business and executive coaching in line with marketplace reality and organisational culture. Marc Kahn is ideally suited to attempt this task, as he combines both insider knowledge of organisational development with wide coaching and consulting experience.

He sets out to address the complex nature of the relationship between coach, the person being coached, and the organisation commissioning the work. As he demonstrates, each party brings their own expectations. The coach has to find a way for each to see that their objectives are being met. The literature that is the primary source of information to many in the field lies in psychology, yet, as Marc Kahn observes, the business sciences also have much to contribute. Yet, they have not been a major influence on coaching practice. We have to do much more than adapt a psychological model from a therapeutic origin to coaching a single individual. This book addresses this by aligning the psychology with business and marketplace realities. The business is focused on wealth creation. It asks the coach, in working with a client, to make a difference to the business through generating changes that make sense for the individual in the context of the organisation. Aligning these perspectives is complex and an essentially relational process. It is different from individual centric healthcare or wellness approaches. Business coaching does not seek to fix the unhealthy but rather promotes business success for both the individual and the organisation.

The coaching relationship provides a narrative bridge to connect the individual's story and those operating within the organisation. Marc Kahn offers a well-researched yet practical and engaging framework to assist the coach. The coaching axis is offered as a way to manage the complexity. As he argues, at one end sits the individual with his or her stories of personal career goals, competence, history, and personality. At the other, we have the market and organisational needs with its narratives of strategy, culture, and business objectives.

Thus, the purpose of business coaching becomes one of bringing the individual's story into a better relationship with those of the organisation. The aim is for them to be equally appreciated and thereby create an improved relationship to deliver business results. Marc Kahn argues that coaches need to acknowledge the unique context of business and align their service to its culture. He implores coaches to become theoretically unrestricted and seek to provide "the most viable intervention that presents the greatest prospect for achieving outcomes that truly result in the promotion of success at all levels of the organisation".

The task is a hard one. However, this author has the ability to stay close to the concerns and realities of the business, grapple with a difficult and patchy literature, and, through the stories told, present a clear path forward. He offers his readers some building blocks on which to base their process for understanding the client's world, systems theory, and the application of these to organisational life. He then elaborates on the relationship between notions of culture and organisation. The final building block is that of three core theoretical frameworks that are culturally aligned to the context of business.

These foundations provide a way of understanding how coaching interfaces with personal, interpersonal, and organisational realities. The coaching on the axis framework links these elements together in a practical conversational process to track themes arising across the axis. The narrative methodology he presents is underpinned by a systemic, integrative, yet culturally sensitive orientation. Coaches who take on board the approach will be able to ensure that they deliver an effective service.

Finally, he offers a detailed case study to enable the reader to pull together the understanding in a coherent way. This framework practically assists coaches in effectively delivering a service properly aligned with business, honouring the culture from which this work derives its legitimacy and sanction, and significantly increasing the likelihood of its success.

Marc Kahn has succeeded in his task, to embed coaching within both a psychological and business frame. Although the task is hard, he has succeeded admirably and, in doing so, has produced an exceptional book. It is authoritative, practical, and thoughtful and, unusually, will appeal to coaches of many different orientations. There is a place for all coaches to draw out of the insights explored ways to inform their own practice. He does not duck the challenges or seek to offer simplistic solutions. Rather, he grapples with the reality of coaching on the axis between the individual and the organisational agenda.

Coaches, their senior business clients, organisations, and organisational development consultants will find that this is the book for which they have been waiting. It is a resource of immense value. I highly recommend it to you.

Professor David A. Lane
Professional Development Foundation

INTRODUCTION

Coaching is an interdisciplinary and eclectic field with many influences. Today, its practitioners come from a myriad of backgrounds including psychology, business, law, teaching, human resources, and sports, and there are no regulated barriers to entry into practice, anyone can be a coach (American Management Association (AMA), 2008; International Coach Federation (ICF), 2012).

The last decade has witnessed a remarkable surge of this service. By 2012, there were an estimated 41,300 active coaches worldwide, and the industry generated about $2 billion in that year, with the average practitioner earning $47,900 for coaching interventions in addition to other services they might offer (ICF, 2012). There has been similar dramatic growth in the number of publications devoted to coaching this century, and the focus placed on coaching research by academia has rapidly swelled (AMA, 2008). Also, the number of organisations that offer training to coaches has simply exploded (ibid.). All indications are that continued growth of the coaching field globally is probable, particularly in emerging markets (AMA, 2008; ICF, 2012).

The American Management Association reports that historically coaching was an activity performed primarily by psychologists and organisation development (OD) professionals as part of their general practice, and the earliest form of coaching in organisations was called "developmental counselling" (AMA, 2008, p. 3; Kilburg & Diedrich, 2007, p. 17). Coaching has primarily drawn from the discipline of psychology, particularly the practice of counselling and psychotherapy, for its development (ibid.; Passmore et al., 2013; Peltier, 2001; Right Management, 2009), and its other major influences have also come from human sciences such as adult learning theory, neuroscience, and sports science (ibid.; Page & Rock, 2009; Ringleb & Rock, 2009; Stout-Rostron, 2009).

Although today's coaches come from a wide array of backgrounds other than psychology, the field of psychology remains a powerful influence for the coaching profession. The Chartered Institute of Personnel and Development, amongst others, explains that the influence of psychology on the field of coaching is so significant that it can be difficult to draw a clear distinction between the concepts of coaching and that of counselling because many of the theoretical underpinnings of coaching are drawn from models associated with counselling (CIPD, 2012; Gold et al., 2010). More recently, the profession of psychology began to formalise its position on coaching with the advent of a sub-discipline called coaching psychology. Indeed, coaching psychologists now form part of the British and Australian Psychological Societies, which have established peer-reviewed academic journals such as the *International Coaching Psychology Review* (Palmer & Cavanagh, 2006), first published in 2006. To illustrate the interest in coaching from the profession of psychology, the British Psychological Society (BPS) Special Group in Coaching Psychology "held its inaugural meeting on 15 December 2004 and by March 2005 it had become the third largest BPS subsystem with over 1600 Founder Members and by December 2005, it had almost 2000 members" (Palmer & Whybrow, 2006, p. 5).

Business and management academics have recently begun to take serious interest in coaching; however, when compared to the influence of the human sciences, business theory and practice has had rather limited participation in the theoretical emergence of coaching as a service to the business world. "What is lacking today is valid benchmarking and measurement of the value coaching brings to organisations, and its actual return on investment" (Stout-Rostron, 2009, p. 35) as there is "little evidence-based research that can prove a genuine ROI on impact" (Right Management, 2009, p. 2). This is despite the fact that a substantial component of the field of coaching is focused on helping individuals and organisations achieve business objectives and enable business performance (AMA, 2008; ICF, 2012; Right Management, 2009; Stout-Rostron, 2009). A survey by the Chartered Institute of Personnel and Development (CIPD) in 2011 found that coaching takes place in eighty-six per cent of organisations, is rated as one of the most popular learning and development tools available, and its procurement is steadily increasing (CIPD, 2011).

The Worldwide Association of Business Coaches (WABC), founded in 1997, was the first international professional association dedicated exclusively to business coaching and is regarded as a leader in the field. It broadly defines business or executive coaching as occurring within an organisational context with the goal of promoting success at all levels of the organisation by affecting the actions of those being coached (Worldwide Association of Business Coaches, 2007). This conception is widely embraced: for example, Right Management (2009) conducted a study of business and executive coaching practices amongst 28,000 employees in ten major industries across three continents and found that it "should be viewed as an organsational process driving systemic change and performance and seen not just as a one to one development event" (p. 10). Business and executive coaching is therefore distinct from life coaching or counselling in two specific ways. First, it is primarily focused on helping to achieve business outcomes, and second, both the individual being coached and the sponsoring organisation are simultaneously the client. This difference introduces enormous complexity into the service, requiring considerably greater theoretical and practical competence on the part of the coach.

Organisations pay coaches to help individuals transform themselves in a way that ultimately creates prosperity for the organisation. The organisation has its own goals for the coaching and provides direction and sanction for the process. Ultimately, the organisation decides whether or not success has been achieved and has the power to terminate or extend the coaching. At the same time, individuals being coached have their own perspective, and their individual reality is foundational in the coaching journey. In this sense, both the individual client and the organisational client, together, are equal meaning-making parties in the coaching process.

This means that coaches working with businesses manage a fundamental and complex duality manifesting in the relationship between two parties: the individual being coached and the organisation sanctioning the service. Each has a set of expectations of the other, each interprets deliverables in their own way, each brings their own history and memory to bear on their interactions, and both have their own perceptions and expectations of what coaching means and must deliver. The coach's job is to help the parties achieve a level of alignment where both are happy with the value and performance they receive from each other. The conduit through which this occurs is the coaching relationship, which acts as a narrative bridge between the organisation's and individual's stories.

This essentially relational view of business and executive coaching is differentiated from health-care or wellness approaches typical in human sciences, which tend to be "individual-centric" in orientation and healing or remedial in focus. Business coaching is not about curing or fixing an unhealthy or deviant individual; it's a business performance service focused on promoting business success for both the individual and the organisation as a whole. Unfortunately, many coaches have a tendency towards remedial courses as a result of the field's historical reliance on psychology, especially psychotherapy and counselling, which are focused on facilitating individual healing. The underlying cultural assumptions of these disciplines are different from those of business, which are driven by marketplace forces and focused on the creation of wealth. This is a real challenge for business coaching practice because many coaching offerings tend to be effective conversions from established psychotherapeutic approaches (Kahn, 2011; Passmore, 2007; Stout-Rostron, 2009) with "a focus on transferring a single model from its therapy origins to coaching" (Passmore, 2007, p. 68).

This book assists coaches in properly aligning their work to business culture and marketplace reality. It does this by explaining how to manage several challenges that the primary influence of the human sciences, particularly psychology, create for business coaching practice as follows. First, coaches need to release any bias in favour of the individual over the organisation, and adopt the notion of a duality of client. Second, they need to ensure they balance their theoretical focus in individual psychology with that of organisational and cultural theory. And finally, they need to shift from the health and well-being mindset that is typical of psychology into a relational mindset focused on business performance and financial success. Coaches who make these shifts adopt the underlying assumptions of business culture which then properly aligns their practice with the environment that ultimately sanctions and legitimates their service. Furthermore, it ensures that coaching is best positioned to deliver real value to the business world that is worth the substantial fees many coaches now request.

Building on this theoretical foundation, the latter chapters of this book offer an overarching framework for the work, called "Coaching on the Axis". This framework helps coaches manage the client duality of organisation and individual relationally by placing them on a hypothetical axis. On the one end of this axis appears the individual being coached with his or her specific deliverables, personal and career goals, competence, background and personality. On the other end sits the respective market, organisational context, and, where relevant, team, together termed "environment", with its strategy, institutional history, organisational culture, and business objectives. In the centre of this axis rests the coaching relationship, where coach and client ("client" here simultaneously referring to *both* the individual and the environment) explore their intersecting stories.

From this point of view, the purpose of business coaching is to bring the individual's story into better relationship with those of the environment, to the extent that both are equally appreciated and valued, and in so doing, create an improved relational state that delivers real business results. To achieve this, it is necessary for coaches to acknowledge and understand the unique context of business and align their service to its culture. In so doing, coaches will be unrestricted theoretically and practically in providing the most viable intervention that presents the greatest prospect for achieving outcomes that truly result in "the promotion of success at all levels of the organisation" (WABC, 2007).

Chapters One, Two, and Three of the book explore three interlocking theoretical discussions which help coaches properly orientate to the work. First, in managing the duality of client in business coaching practice, systems theory and its application to organisational life is explored. Second, in appreciating the culture of business, the notions of culture and organisational culture are unpacked, and the interface between the culture of business and the culture of coaching is discussed. Third, Chapter Three explores the theories that underlie coaching practice and considers their cultural alignment with the theoretical context of business.

Chapters Four to Eight describe the Coaching on the Axis framework. This framework demonstrates how by using the notion of a coaching "axis", coaches can manage a duality of client and align with the culture of business whilst employing almost any type of coaching model or technique. These chapters also outline a conversational process to track themes, elicit insights, and test actions along this axis using a narrative methodology that underpins a systemic, integrative, and culturally sensitive theoretical orientation.

Finally, Chapter Nine offers a detailed case study to illustrate the approach.

The Coaching on the Axis framework is ultimately an overall approach that assists coaches in effectively delivering a service properly aligned with business, honouring the culture from which this work derives its legitimacy and sanction, and significantly increasing its likelihood of success.

Note 1: *The difference between "business" and "executive" coaching*

The coaching fraternity espouses a wide range of definitions that differentiate between business and executive coaching. Unfortunately, these are not consistent and in some cases diverge to the extent that confuse rather than assist. This book adopts the Worldwide Association of Business Coaches framework which draws on the term "business coaching" as an overarching construct incorporating all forms of coaching involved in the promotion of success of a business or organisation. As such, I use the term "business coaching" to refer to both executive and business coaching from here on.

Note 2: *What constitutes an organisation?*

In this framework, an organisation can be as large as a multinational corporation or sovereign state or as small as a single person working alone, such as a writer, actor, consultant, or, for that matter, business coach. In the latter, the organisation is constituted in the relational field between the single person and his or her customers (readers, audience, or clients), colleagues (for example, fellow writers, actors, consultants, or coaches) who commonly participate together in some form of society, association, federation, or professional body, and any outsourced service providers (IT support, marketing or advertising, accounting, landlords, agents, attorneys/solicitors, advisors, etc.). In single-person businesses, it can, at first glance, appear that the organisation is not an equitable client to the individual. However, in working with the Coaching on the Axis framework, this should not be taken as the case. Rather, the organisation should be worked with *as if* it existed in the same way as a larger concern. Failure to do this will likely result in poor business outcomes that, ironically, ultimately negatively impact the individual.

Note 3: *Identity of clients and coaches mentioned in the text*

Throughout this book, many coaches' and clients' stories and comments are offered to illustrate the points being made. In most cases, including the final case study, these individuals requested that their identity not be revealed for a wide variety of reasons. As a result, where requested to do so, names have been changed or withheld, and significant facts about their stories have been altered, so as to make it almost impossible to recognise them. Also, in one or two cases, subjects' stories have been merged into a single vignette.

CHAPTER ONE

The complexity of client

Who is the client?

Many authors (e.g., Brunning, 2006; Cavanagh, 2006; De Haan, 2008; Huffington, 2006; Kahn, 2011; Kemp, 2008; Kets de Vries et al., 2007; Passmore, 2007) have established the theoretical and practical foundations for a relational approach to business coaching in which success derives from the quality of the coaching relationship and the degree to which it aligns with the sponsoring organisation. In this view, business coaching is an engagement of relatedness more so than any one particular method or skill.

Central to this relational perspective of business coaching is the fact that both the organisation and the individual being coached are clients. Business coaching has the challenge of "always having two clients to serve: the individual or team that they are directly engaging with, and the organisation that is employing them to do the work" (Hawkins & Schwenk, 2010, p. 204), and each may differ in their expectations of the coaching. Coaches therefore need to attend to both of these client requirements as well as the relationship between them at the same time. Huffington (2006) puts it that in business coaching "there is always an implicit external context in view, [which is] the organisation from which the client comes, in which she or he works, and which pays for the coaching" (p. 41). She calls for business coaches to engage in *dual listening* to both "the individual in the organisation" and "the organisation in the individual" (ibid., p. 44), and Kahn (2011) concludes that "successful approaches to business coaching incorporate significant consideration of the relational dynamics between the triad of coach, individual client and organisation, and focus on the coaching relationship and its systemic interface with the business environment" (p. 194).

This systemic perspective of business coaching is eloquently captured in The Worldwide Association of Business Coaches' original definition of the practice: "A process of engaging in meaningful communication with individuals in businesses, organisations, institutions or governments, with the goal of promoting success at all levels of the organisation by affecting the actions of those individuals." (Worldwide Association of Business Coaches, 2007). The idea that business coaching's ultimate purpose is the promotion of success *of the organisation at all levels* through the individual being coached is important. Notice how it is the organisation's success that is highlighted specifically, not only that of the individual. And many others (e.g., Huffington, 2006; Kahn, 2011; Kilburg, 2007; Right Management, 2009; Stout-Rostron, 2009) describe the practice similarly, for example: "Executive coaching is defined as a helping relationship formed between a client who has managerial authority and responsibility in an organisation and a consultant who uses a wide variety of behavioural techniques and methods to help the client achieve *a mutually identified set of goals* [i.e., between organisation and individual] to improve his or her professional performance and personal satisfaction and, consequently, to *improve the effectiveness of the client's organisation* within a formally defined coaching agreement" (Kilburg, 2007, p. 28). Right Management (2009) simply puts it that business coaching "needs to be regarded not only as an individual event but also as an organisational process driving systemic change" (p. 13).

This means that in business coaching there resides a deep complexity in that both the individual being coached and the sanctioning organisation are framed equally as clients. This differentiates business coaching from life coaching and counselling in a significant way. In the latter, the individual enjoys primacy as the client, and although associated others may form part of systemic considerations, the promotion of their success is at best secondary to that of the individual being coached or counselled. In business coaching, this is not the case. The primary goal is the success of the organisation and the individual's success is inherently tied to the organisation's success. It is not one over the other. In fact, if the individual were to enjoy success that has no benefit to the organisation or vice versa, the other party would feel the coaching has failed to add value and deliver a return on investment. Both must feel success has been achieved.

However, from a historical and theoretical perspective, coaching has drawn heavily from the human sciences, where the individual tends to enjoy primacy, such as in psychotherapy and counselling (Gold et al., 2010; Palmer & Whybrow, 2007; Passmore, 2007; Stout-Rostron, 2009). Business coaching's early influences came from psychology mainly because coaching formed part of the general practice of psychologists and psychologically trained human resource professionals who conducted what was referred to as workplace or developmental counselling, the forerunner to workplace coaching (AMA, 2008; Brock, 2008; Gold et al., 2010). Subsequent influence from adult learning theory, organisational theory, and management practices meant that coaching only later developed beyond a single source foundation in psychology and beyond its curative and remedial associations, into the realm of potential, growth, and workplace productivity (ibid.).

Today, business coaching is a widespread service industry, with a myriad of theoretical and practical influences, open to anyone with few, if any, barriers to entry. Nevertheless, the field of psychology remains the primary influence for the practice, as many coaching offerings tend to be effective conversions from established psychotherapeutic approaches with "a focus on transferring a single model from its therapy origins to coaching" (Passmore, 2007, p. 68). Stout-Rostron (2009) explains: "Coaching does not yet meet the requirements for a 'true profession.' It is here that psychology and psychotherapy research offer much insight into the complexity of human behaviour and organisational systems for the business coach" (pp. 21–22). She references Peltier (2001), adding that a range of psychotherapy phenomena positively correlate with coaching interventions such as "insight, awareness of the goal, self-examination, intra-personal understanding, talking about things ..., rapport building, and special relationship feedback from an impartial party within a confidential relationship" (p. 24), and this means that "the basic ingredients of the executive coaching relationship are based on a few common themes from the psychology literature" (ibid.).

Although extremely helpful, the formative influence of the human sciences, especially psychology, on the field of coaching presents important challenges for coaching in aligning its practice with the culture of business. Central to these challenges is the tendency for coaches to import the primacy of the individual, as opposed to the organisation, as the client, into the context of business. Seeing the individual as the primary client is an underlying assumption common to the culture of counselling and psychotherapy, with the possible exception of systemic family therapy (Becvar & Becvar, 1998). However, seeing the individual as primary over the group is foreign to the underlying practice of business.

When coaches import this "individual-centric" counselling notion into the workplace context, coaching can proceed with little dialogue with the organisation. In extreme cases, the individual being coached can be in session after session in the coaches' practice room (next to the quintessential pot plant, clock, and bookshelf—cultural icons of a counselling room) with only their fantasies about the business to work with, having not properly understood or aligned with business expectations or culture. When the individual is granted primary status over the organisation, the probability that business coaching will "promote success at all levels of the organisation" is significantly diminished. This is because, in such an arrangement, coaching occurs in a partial vacuum, standing outside of the organisational context, and ignoring the culture of business and the inherent complexity of client in business coaching practice.

This is not to say that the human sciences, especially psychology and counselling, are unhelpful to business coaches, on the contrary, they are critically important. First, they inform on human nature and behaviour and, second, provide a base of rich and deep theory and research from which coaching is able to draw and build. In many respects, it has been a true blessing that these fields preceded coaching and they continue to provide ongoing nourishment for understanding and progressing coaching practice. The point is that business coaching occurs within the culture of a marketplace not a counselling room or human science department, and thus business coaching should begin with business culture as the starting point informed by psychotherapy and other established fields, rather than the other way around (Kahn, 2011). What is required is a significantly more complex orientation to this work than simply transferring therapy practices to a workplace context.

Understanding the duality of client

The departure point for effective business coaching should therefore begin with the inherent duality constellated between the individual being coached and the organisation sanctioning the service. Each has a set of expectations of the other, both interpret deliverables in their own way and both bring their history and memory to bear on their interactions. This duality continuously needs to be processed in the emergent coaching dialogue. The business coach's job is simultaneously to help both the individual and the organisation achieve greater success, where the value they receive from each other is maximised and/or transformed. In this view, what an individual says or does and what this elicits in the coach, as she or he listens and observes, needs to always have reference to the organisation, which is omnipresent and sometimes hidden (Huffington, 2006).

This "duality of client" may be understood through the concept of an organisational "role", where business coaching aims "to further the effectiveness of the client [individual] in his or her role in the organisation" (Huffington, 2006, p. 41). In this notion, a person enters into a contract with an organisation to occupy a role. The role requires the individual to perform tasks and in so doing add value to the business, in return the organisation provides reward. The reward is obviously financial but also non-financial in the form of recognition, job satisfaction and a sense of meaning and purpose. The term "role" also describes less visible forms of organisational relations that are important in the coaching context. Role is a psychosocial concept and exists in both overt and covert ways. Overt roles are part of the conscious organisation; these are negotiated and given labels, while covert roles are psychological in nature and constellated in the group dynamic common to organisational life. In line with this perspective, the role-consultancy approach (Armstrong, 2005; Newton et al., 2006) defines a role as "an idea or conception in the mind through which one manages oneself and one's behaviour in relation to the system in which one has position, so as to further its aims" (Roberts & Jarrett, 2006, p. 20).

For example, a person working in a bank may for instance fulfill the overt role of investment banker. This label carries with it a set of tasks and responsibilities that are known and expected in relation to the activities of the overt organisation. The same person might also be the shoulder to cry on in the team or the one that challenges the status quo where others simply follow. These kinds of role boundaries are important phenomena because they demand time and energy from the individual and significantly impact the degree to which a person is able to exercise his or her talent in a given context (Struwig & Cilliers, 2012).

> Thus, a role is not merely *given* by the employing organisation; it is also *taken*—that is, the person in the role makes of it something personal, based on individual skills, ideals, beliefs, and their understanding of what is required. However, what one makes of the role is also influenced by the system, not only by tangible factors such as job descriptions, hierarchical position, and the resources one has access to, but also by other's expectations of the role and by the culture of the system. (Roberts & Jarrett, 2006, p. 20)

This means that the essential contract between a person and a company positions business coaching as a service that helps individuals take up overt roles and manage covert roles in the most effective way, thereby simultaneously promoting success for both them and their organisation. It is therefore useful to locate the focus point of business coaching at the *relational interface* constituted in an organisational role. This interface may be conceived of as an axis between the person being coached and his or her organisation, upon which rests the degree to which both the person and the organisation ultimately succeed or fail.

Figure 1 illustrates this *axial* notion, showing how business coaching is essentially a *relational engagement* focused on creating value by improving the relationship between the individual and his or her organisation. In this view, coaching interventions create relational bridges or *axes* between organisations and individuals which facilitate intersubjective story-making processes. These axes deliver value because they offer a unique place to co-create a shared success story; a story that emerges from a meeting of meaning between the individual and the organisation that is based in a sense of mutual responsibility for the business.

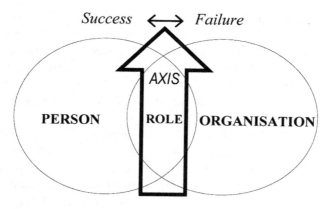

Figure 1. Coaching's *axial* orientation.
(Adapted from Brunning, 2006).

In this *axial* conception, the entire organisation is the client in as much a way as the individual being coached, and neither organisation (represented by manager, colleagues, stakeholders and customers) nor individual can be approached as completely separate entities. What is required is a way of working with all the parties in an interdependent web or matrix that is contemplated holistically without positioning one part as necessarily more important than another.

A philosophy that provides such a framework for business coaches can be found in the field of systems thinking and the remainder of this chapter offers an introduction to such with guidance for further learning.

Systems thinking

Systems thinking is not a single discipline but rather a gathering of a wide range of theories that share a set of underlying philosophical notions about reality. Systems thinking stretches from psychology and biology to engineering and ecology, and includes many theories that have been used to underpin services such as family therapy (e.g., Bowen, 1978; Minuchin, 1974), management consulting (e.g., Senge, 1990; Stapley, 2006) and coaching (e.g., Cavanagh, 2006; O'Neill, 2007). The field finds its origin in the study of biological systems. The biologist Ludwig von Bertalanffy developed his general systems theory from the 1920s to the 1960s in an attempt to counteract the limitations of reductionism in traditional science. Bertalanffy (1962, 1968) conceived the world as a whole and opposed atomistic or mechanical approaches to understanding. Thinking of this kind has been around since ancient times in Eastern philosophy (Allen et al., 2011), notably in the eternal Chinese text of the *Tao Te Ching* (Lao Tzu, 2002) and others such as the *Sun Tzu* or *Art of War* (Denma Translation Group, 2001), both written over two thousand years ago.

Simply put, a system "is a set of interacting units with relationships among them" and "in human systems these relations make the system self-organise into characteristic patterns of interaction" (Compernalle, 2007, p. 31). The whole system is different from the sum of its parts and a part of the system derives properties from the whole that it does not have in any other context (ibid., p. 32). Systems also compose subsystems as parts, and so, for example, a systemic view of an organisation allows us to zoom in and out to different levels of an organization, where each level is a subsystem of the next and suprasystem for the level below. As it says in the *Tao Te Ching*: "Man patterns himself on earth, earth patterns itself on heaven, heaven patterns itself on the Way, the Way patterns itself on nature" (Lao Tzu, Chapter Sixty-Two). To illustrate this, imagine zooming out from the biological level of the brain cell, to the brain, to the person, to the team, to the organisation, and then reversing the process by zooming back in (Compernalle, 2007). In systems thinking, "one is continually aware that different observations at each level lead to different theories, different hypotheses and different interventions" (ibid., p. 34).

Systems theory is seen to be particularly appropriate for any discipline that studies human interaction (Hanson, 1995). In systems thinking, the whole, in terms of the dynamic interplay of the parts, is the object of inquiry. When one sees in wholes, rather than in parts, patterns appear that simple linear cause-and-effect models of reality fail to reveal. A systemic view conceptualises the world in terms of "relational wholes", and "is an alternative to more reductionistic or mechanical models that encourage study through dissection, then reconstitution, as is traditional in classical biology and medicine" (ibid., p. 27).

In systems theory, the individual is therefore viewed as part of a whole, and the experience of the individual is inherently entangled with their relational field. As Stapley (2006) explains: "There is no such thing as 'just an individual' … From birth onwards, we are in a constant state of relatedness to various other individuals and groups" (p. 5). He adds that as children we are dependent on our mothers for our very survival and, on the other end, our mothers are deeply affected by us as they respond to our physical and psychological needs. This process of mutual influence between mother and child is the basic building block of relationship and continues with other people throughout our lives. "We may helpfully describe relatedness as the process of mutual influence between individual and individual, between individual and group, group and group, and group and organisation. Beyond that, we might consider the relatedness of organisation and the wider society ... the process of mutual influence between individuals is an on-going process that will have an effect on nearly everything we do" (p. 6).

To appreciate this relational notion of being, it might be useful to consider whether or not a person is capable of having a completely original thought? What would that be? If this thought was tested in terms of its origin it would, no doubt, be discovered that many other ideas heavily influenced its birth, and that these ideas arose through exposure to others views in the first place. In fact, what may be deemed to be original thought actually belongs to a combination of others views the "originator" has been in relationship with (virtual or real). As the famous advertising executive Leo Burnett once said: "The secret of all effective originality in advertising is not the creation of new and tricky words and pictures, but one of putting familiar words and pictures into new relationships" (Quotes & Poems.com, 2012). How do we know what we know? It turns out that everything we believe comes from others' influence. Even if we think the opposite to what we have been told, our belief is a reaction and therefore still in relationship with the original influence.

In systems theory, the idea that one exists as an individual outside of a system is thus untenable. "The self does not reside in the individual as a fixed entity but is co-created in the web of relationships between individuals and in the narratives created by the individual and by others about them" (Hawkins & Schwenk, 2010, pp. 204–205). In other words, individuals exist in a web of relatedness from conception to death and are never separate, or as Stacey (2001) puts it: "The human self-conscious mind is not an 'it' located and stored in an individual. Rather, individual mind arises continuously and transiently in relationships between people" (p. 5). In this sense, we cannot escape relatedness. "Even if, as adults, we sit alone in the isolation of our own homes contemplating some problem or issue, we are never alone in our minds. We are still linked to many others in a state of relatedness and this will have an effect on our contemplation" (Stapley, 2006, p. 7).

This means that one's experience of others is constituted in the context of the relationships one has in the world, and particularly the set of relationships most closely associated with others in that moment. For example in a corporation, "marketing may see human resources as bureaucratic and unhelpful. Should that be the case, then any relationship between representatives [individuals] of these departments is likely to be affected by the intergroup political system ... Each may be attributed the stereotype attached to his or her department" (ibid., p. 85). As Wilfred Bion (1961) put it: "In fact no individual, however isolated in time and space, should be regarded as outside of a group or lacking in active manifestations of group psychology" (p. 169).

Systems' thinking offers coaching a framework that allows for the conception of the component parts of a system (organisation) to be understood in the context of relationships with each other and with other systems, rather than in isolation (Allen et al., 2011). In so doing, from a theoretical point of view, it comfortably manages the complexity of a dual client in business coaching practice.

Holism

Common to all systemic approaches is that systems are holistic. The term "holism" was coined in 1926 by Jan Christiaan Smuts, a South African and British Commonwealth statesman, military leader, philosopher, and forefather of the United Nations, who defined it as: "The tendency in nature to form wholes that are greater than the sum of the parts through creative evolution" (Smuts, 1926, p. 88). This fundamental systemic concept means that in order to understand a system "one must stand back from the level of the particular, and examine a system in terms of what is created when the parts interact" (Cavanagh, 2006, p. 316). For example, a person cannot be understood as a collection of functioning organ systems without losing the essence of what it means to be human. A person is more than the sum of their functioning parts (ibid.). As discussed earlier, in organisational life an individual usually occupies a role that commonly predates the entry of that individual into the organisation. A systemic perspective allows for a view of that role and the individual in a holistic way, seeing them in a state of relatedness in the context of all the relationships of the system—which include the organisation's set of relations and history and also all those of the individual.

It is also not possible to predict the behaviour of the system only with knowledge of its individual units because an understanding of the interactions, or the relationships between the units, is an essential component to appreciating the nature of the system (Compernalle, 2007). For example, one cannot tell whether or not two people will make a good couple based on prior knowledge about them as individuals, as we know, individually excellent people can make totally dysfunctional couples and vice versa because "the behaviour of couples and individuals is governed by totally different rules" (ibid., p. 31). This is naturally also true for groups and teams, "the functioning of an executive team cannot be predicted only on the basis of information and hypotheses about the individual executives. Again and again executives are hired who, when screened individually, seem excellent choices, but who do not function well in a particular team" (p. 32). Unfortunately, this commonly results in a perception that the executive is not competent in some way. The executive in question might complain that it is the team that is dysfunctional and not themselves and cite prior success in other teams or organisations as evidence. This dynamic of blame is the same as a romantic couple blaming each other for the dysfunction in their relationship and citing prior romantic successes with other partners as evidence for the apportionment of blame. Clearly, a system (couple or team) is unique by virtue of the interrelatedness of its parts (e.g., partners or team members) which come together in a particular time and context (e.g., marketplace or organisational reality, geography, or family setting) and set it apart from all other systems.

In other words, seeing a system as a whole, as opposed to as a sum of its parts, is the only way to fully appreciate it. As Peter Senge (1990) explains in his classic *The Fifth Discipline*, individuals can influence their organisations if they can "make a shift of mind from seeing parts to seeing wholes" (p. 69).

Circular causality

By seeing in wholes, a systemic approach avoids problematic "blame-game" dynamics typical in more linear cause–effect perspectives of organisational life, and in so doing provides for some liberation from remedial coaching orientations. Systems thinking "resists identifying a single element or person in a system as the root cause of a problem" (O'Neill, 2007, p. 49), and offers the principle of *circular* or *reciprocal causality* (Hecker & Wetchler, 2003) as a means of appreciating cause. This principle views events as multicausal and reciprocal as opposed to *linear* (p. 49).

In other words, A does not simply cause B, but rather A and B are interrelated in a causal circle. For example, if a manager is described as disempowering and controlling by his staff, system thinkers will not accept this behaviour as causal on its own, they will want to understand the extent to which the interrelationship between the individuals gives rise to this behaviour. Perhaps they will find that staff are perceived by the manager as not fully competent or somewhat careless which in turn leads the manager to micromanage, which in turn results in staff not taking ownership of the tasks, which in turn results in poor task delivery, which in turn confirms the manager's original conceptions and reinforces the manager's controlling behaviour and so on, leading one to ask the question: Where is the original cause?

From a systemic perspective, a broader understanding of causality is possible which allows for solutions that are more sustainable and more likely to promote success for an organisation as a whole, but unfortunately as Senge (1990) says: "We tend to focus on snapshots of isolated parts of the system, and wonder why our deepest problems never seem to get solved. Systems thinking … makes patterns clearer, and helps us see how to change them effectively" (p. 7). He asserts that real leverage lies in understanding dynamic complexity, not detailed complexity. "Reality is made up of circles, but we see straight lines. Herein lies the beginning of our limitation as systems thinkers" (pp. 72–73).

So the call to business coaches is to approach their work with systemic eyes and see past the simplistic lens of linear causality. Unfortunately, as Cavanagh (2006) points out, "as coaches we are often asked to treat system members as if they are isolated units. This is particularly true in situations involving remedial coaching. It is not unusual for individuals to be referred for coaching in the hope that they will be 'fixed' and that their negative impact on team or group performance might be alleviated" (p. 325). The idea that a single individual is responsible for a systems lack of performance is often based in simple linear cause–effect thinking which is analogous to the old tales of "cursed" men being made to walk the plank on old sailing ships to bring back the wind. This is why teams can sometimes blame their poor performance on the poorest performing member, or their leader, and push the organisation to eject them, only to find themselves repeatedly having to do the same several times before realising that there is something systemic that they create together, as a team, that underpins their performance problems. Only once the team acknowledges a shared causal reality can it actually address the real business issues that are the source of its lacklustre. However, business coaches are often brought in to "deal with" the individual concerned before a systemic understanding is achieved, which, of course, is counterproductive for the business. Unfortunately, business coaches without a strong systemic orientation and influenced by the remedial culture of counselling and psychotherapy are prone to accepting a linear cause–effect contract without question.

This is not to say that a dysfunctional individual is never the cause of system problems, or for that matter that ejecting such a person from an organisation is not the right way to go. Sometimes replacing a poor leader with a good one is the most viable option for a system to address its failure to perform. Indeed, "individual actions within a system can have a significant impact, for good or ill, on the system as a whole" (Cavanagh, 2006, p. 325). Rather, it is important to understand why the system is failing or succeeding as a whole before assuming individual parts to be solely responsible.

To illustrate this using the previous example, irrespective of whether or not removal of a poor performer helps a team perform better, the team needs to understand and take responsibility for the extent to which it, as a system, creates conditions for poor performance that make it difficult for certain individuals to succeed. This will ensure that the next poor performer in the team does not experience the same attack, for if this occurs repeatedly the team may develop a culture in which it is not safe to "have a few bad days" which can result in dysfunctional overall team behaviour not conducive to productivity. Another example is when a company performs poorly and the board fires the CEO. In these cases, irrespective of whether or not it is actually necessary to change CEOs, the system needs to understand and own how it came to appoint such a leader in the first place and how it will not repeat the same again. It also needs to determine the veracity of the idea that the CEO was so powerful a figure as to have negatively impacted performance to such an extent or whether, once again, a person is being made to walk the plank to bring back the wind.

Unfortunately, the notion of a single person as the cause of a business wide problem or success can be reassuring for an organisation. This is because it gives people heroes and scapegoats and explains outcomes in a way that does not call for personal change on the part of others (Cavanagh, 2006). "While locating causality in the individual may protect system members from having to face their complicity in the outcome, in the long run it fails to address problematic system patterns. Colluding with this avoidance serves to undermine the coaching engagement and weaken both the client and the organisation" (p. 326).

Homeostasis

The tendency of individuals in a system to resist change does not usually stem from a malicious or ignorant predisposition on the part of the person. Self-regulating systems have a powerful tendency to create environments that drive individuals within them to protect the status quo and perpetuate the existing systemic reality. Systems thinkers call this phenomenon *homeostasis* (Hecker & Wetchler, 2003) and define it as the tendency for all systems to sustain predictable patterns of interaction over time so as to maintain system equilibrium (stability) and survive.

Imagine if organisations did not strive to sustain predictable patterns of interaction inside of a rapidly changing marketplace? One day the company targets a certain type of customer and the next day they ignore them in favour of another kind of customer? One day an employee is required to sell items in a shop front as part of her role and the next day the same employee is required to write software for the IT department. One day payments are processed electronically and the next day manually. Such a degree of unpredictability would cause chaos, create instability and threaten the survival of the business. Predictability and replication within a system result in system strength and ultimately underpin sustainability. However, an organisation must also simultaneously be sensitive to change as the environment around it changes. What if the customer base no longer supported the company product due to changes in society, in this case it would indeed be necessary for the survival of the company to target a new type of customer. What if a competitor introduces a superior product or service? Failure to continually adjust to environmental change also threatens the survival of an organisation. Homeostasis is therefore the balancing act between staying stable through creating predictable and replicating patterns and at the same time continually changing to adapt to dynamic environmental conditions. This balancing act reflects the degree to which a system is closed or open to feedback from other systems. The more open, the more receptive to feedback and adaptation, the more closed, the more resistant to feedback and therefore change.

Systems continually reestablish homeostasis, making repeated adjustments by interacting or communicating with each other through feedback. A simple example is the way a person maintains their balance whilst standing upright. This requires thousands of minor adjustments in muscles that counteract many environmental forces such as gravity, wind and obstacles. Other systems are also involved in this feedback process, for example the ear detects body position in relation to gravity. Patches of hair cells in the inner ear are attached to thousands of tiny spheres of calcium carbonate and are pulled downward by the force of gravity thereby providing the brain with feedback of any change in position such as a tilting of the head. The brain in turn instructs muscles to countermove accordingly and ensures balance is sustained (Schnupp et al., 2011). In this way, a continual process of feedback facilitates ongoing homeostasis.

However, it is important to understand that homeostasis is not synonymous with perfect health, functioning or comfort. Just because a system is homeostatic does not mean it is free from dysfunction, discomfort or pain. Figure 2 illustrates two physical homeostatic states of a person standing and maintaining balance. In both states,

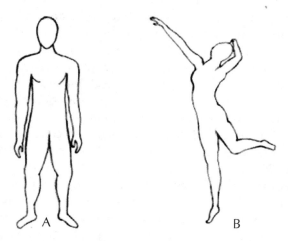

Figure 2. Posture's A and B.
(Images © K. Kahn).

the person is balancing, and many sub-systems are working together through feedback to maintain this balance. Posture A is comfortable and easier to maintain. Posture B is very difficult to maintain and strains the body, even though the dancer chooses and probably enjoys the position. Also, Posture A is a functional posture for everyday life, whereas Posture B is functional in the context of a dance but dysfunctional for everyday life. Repeated use of Posture B may result in physiological pain and dysfunction; nevertheless, the dancer may persist in using it and find ways to manage the biological suffering. Both physical postures reflect states of homeostasis. Posture B also illustrates that even when a system is experiencing pain or in a state of dysfunction, it may still work to sustain its current state and resist change.

There is a somewhat paradoxical reality to system homeostasis in that for a complex system to endure it must also adapt to a changing external environment. This is because the external environment is also a system—systems within systems—and feedback must also happen between the system in question and its supra-system. So in a sense, continuous adaptation to the supra-system may be seen as a form of on-going change for the system, but is itself another level of maintaining homeostasis.

For example, a business works hard to maintain consistent and predictable operations (as previously discussed), possibly mechanising or digitising them to ensure repeated accuracy and reliability in the way they communicate and interact with each other. This ensures a cost effective, reliable, and accurate service to the customer and in this sense is a form of homeostasis. However, when the market changes and competitors employ new and better technology, or a new generation of customer emerges that calls for new types of products or services, the operational homeostasis must change in order to service the new market differently. This type of homeostasis can be seen as a kind of second order change, sometimes referred to as *autopoiesis* (Maturana & Varela, 1987), in which a system repeatedly readjusts its internal homeostasis as necessary, reestablishing new boundaries to sustain itself within the suprasystem. "Firms can be regarded as *autopoietic* systems that continuously reproduce themselves … [through] continual learning and renewal in [a] changing business environment" (Maula, 2000, p. 157).

Valence

As previously discussed, business coaching is commonly employed to help an individual assume and manage overt and covert roles inside an organisation in the most successful way. From the individual's point of view, a systemic perspective enables the coach to work with the individual as part of the organisational system by facilitating awareness of the systemic roles that are at play in that person's relational field. The concept of *valence* is a powerful idea that coaches can use to understand this interplay.

The term *valence* was first used by the pioneer of social psychology, Kurt Lewin, in the 1930s. He offered the systemic equation: $B = f(P, E)$ (behaviour is a function of the person in his or her environment) and was one of the first psychologists to suggest that neither nature nor nurture drives behaviour, but that both interact in shaping human beings. Lewin wrote in 1931: "Only by the concrete whole which comprises the object and the situation, are vectors which determine the dynamics of the event defined" (in Sansone et al., 2003, p. 119). He used the term *valence* to refer to the intrinsic attraction (positive valence) or aversion (negative valence) of an event, object, or situation for a specific individual. For Lewin, valence "indicates that, for whatever reason, at the present time and for this specific individual, a tendency exists to act in direction toward this region [situation or object] or away from it" (Lewin, 1938, p. 88). In other words, valence is an unconscious predisposition or tendency for an individual to repeatedly choose to behave in particular ways when placed in provoking contexts.

The concept of valence was adopted by the influential British psychoanalyst Wilfred Bion (1961) who focused his work on understanding group dynamics. He was particularly interested in the way human beings manage anxiety in organisational contexts. His theories fathered the field known today as systems psychodynamics that emerged from the group relations programme of the Tavistock Institute in London (Fraher, 2004). Systems psychodynamics is based on the Institute's innovative work in bringing together open systems thinking and psychodynamic perspectives to the study of group and organisational processes (ibid.). More recently, it is being applied in business coaching (Brunning, 2006; Cilliers, 2005; Cilliers & Terblanche, 2010; de Vries et al., 2007).

> Systems psychodynamic coaching is a multi-factorial, multi-layered process that primarily addresses itself to the person-in-the-role and the multiple organizational and social fields that comprise the context in which work with the client takes place ... by virtue of working with and making links across person-role-system boundaries, this is a powerful, robust approach to the practice of executive coaching. (Brunning, 2006, pp. xxvii–xxviii)

In systems psychodynamics, Lewin's concept of valence is used to specifically refer to an individual's predisposition to reproduce particular patterns of behaviour in the form of roles in group contexts when presented with anxiety. For example, people tend to take up similar roles across different group contexts, where, for instance, they are regularly described as the "quiet one" or the "challenger" or the "mediator", and they can't help repeatedly and consistently repeating this behaviour in group after group. This is because they have valence for this role-based behaviour. One can say for example: "I have *valence* for taking up the role of a 'rescuer.' I often seem to be the first one to console or defend a group member in need and I do it without thinking, I just feel compelled." Such an individual is taking up the "rescuer role" despite themselves, so to speak, as a repeated and compulsive pattern of responding across group contexts in which they experience anxiety when they witness another member in a state of difficulty.

To help understand this, Bion (1961) explains that within every group there are two realities, the first is more conscious, metaphorically above the surface, which he called the *work group* and the second is more unconscious, metaphorically below the surface, which he called the *basic assumption group*. The work group is occupied with the primary task—the conscious and rational reason or aim of the group. In contrast, the basic assumption group is preoccupied with anxieties based on maladaptive assumptions about the group which are usually unconscious and interfere with the primary task the work group is trying to accomplish.

Bion (1961) identified three maladaptive basic assumptions: *dependency, fight–flight*, and *pairing*. He theorised that human beings tend to unconsciously adopt these basic assumptions in order to manage anxiety (basic assumption group), but this in turn tends to derail the group's primary work tasks (work group). He suggested that interpretation of the underlying assumptions for the group would create insight for the members, who would then be more able to effectively focus on the primary task. He postulated that lack of awareness of the underlying assumptions in a group generate off-task or anti-task behaviour which is generally unproductive and sometimes destructive (Green & Molenkamp, 2005; Rioch, 1970). "In a group taken over by basic assumption mentality, the formation and continuance of the group becomes an end in itself ... members ... are likely to lose their ability to think and act effectively ... as [they] become more absorbed with their relationship to the group than with their work task" (Stokes, 1994, p. 26). Bion (1961) explained his three basic assumptions as follows:

- *Dependency* refers to a dynamic where group members seek to attain security and protection from the group leader. In these contexts, members tend to be passive and idealise the leader as all-knowing or all-powerful, which ultimately sets the leader up for failure and the group for disappointment.
- *Fight–flight* refers to the underlying assumption that the group exists to ensure the preservation of its members at all costs. In these contexts, members believe that this is achieved by running away from, or fighting against, someone or something. Flight behaviour can be observed when the group members avoid the primary task through unproductive or disruptive behaviour, whereas fight behaviour often appears in the form of hostility and aggression where there is little tolerance for weakness. The leader in this group context is expected to inspire courage, self-sacrifice, and spearhead the metaphorical attack or retreat. In addition, the group often selects a scapegoat that becomes the object of attack.
- *Pairing* refers to the underlying assumption that the group exists to afford the opportunity for pairing between two of its members. Originally this was conceived as sexual for purposes of reproduction, but the theory was expanded to include more metaphorical applications and include same-sex pairs. Members tend to have a fantasy that a pair in the group will produce a member who will bring forth the realisation of all their projections and dreams. In the work context, this dynamic often manifests when "two individuals within a group are looked upon as the sole hope of creating a solution to the groups' problems" (Minahan & Hutton, 2004, p. 1).

Valence is then an individual's "propensity to take up a particular role in a group or *to adopt a particular basic assumption*" (Huffington et al., 2004, p. 229; italics added). From a business coaching point of view, it is therefore important to explore the degree to which individuals unconsciously participate in basic assumption mentality. In particular, an understanding of what they hold or contain for the group by virtue of their valence is seminal to promoting success for the organisation.

In summary, a systemically orientated business coaching dialogue explores the way the team or organisation "pulls" the individual, as a consequence of their valence, into roles (overt and covert) for the group (Cytrynbaum & Noumair, 2004), thereby derailing or delaying the delivery of primary business tasks. When this becomes conscious in the dialogue, options for action arise that may return the individual (and the group) towards focusing on the work task rather than cycling in the unproductive dynamic of one or other underlying assumption. Adopting this view enables the promotion of success for an organisation by affecting the actions of individuals. For a coach to work like this, he or she is required to manage the inherent and complex duality of client, and adopt a systemic appreciation of the organisational context. This means that causality is seen as circular inside of a holistic appreciation of the environment within which an individual exists. This also ensures a relational orientation, where the primacy of the individual as client, something core to the practice of counselling and psychotherapy, is avoided in business coaching practice.

CHAPTER TWO

The complexity of culture

The previous chapter introduced the notion that business exists within a unique and distinct cultural context characterised by marketplace forces. It further suggested that business coaches should begin with this cultural context as a starting point, informed by other fields, rather than the other way around. In order to do so, an understanding of the phenomenon of culture, and particularly corporate or organisational culture, is required.

Edgar Schein, MIT professor emeritus and early pioneer of the notion of corporate culture, explains that although culture is an abstraction, the social forces derived from culture are enormously powerful in influencing behaviour, and failure to understand the operation of these forces can result in people becoming victims to them. "Cultural forces are powerful because they operate outside of our awareness. We need to understand them not only because of their power but also because they help to explain many of our puzzling and frustrating experiences in social and organisational life. Most importantly, understanding cultural forces enables us to understand ourselves better" (Schein, 2010, p. 7).

What is culture?

The notion of culture has been widely explored in many subjects including anthropology, sociology, psychology, economics and history. In spite of this, it lacks a widely accepted common definition or shared theoretical paradigm across researchers (Bercovici et al., 2001; Cooper, 1994; Erculj, 2009). While some have approached the notion as generalists, conceiving of all aspects of organised life as culture, others have attempted to define culture more narrowly, separating it from other phenomena of social life such as climate or strategy (ibid.). I take the generalist view of culture because it aligns well with systems thinking, and agree with Stapley (1996) when he explains that unfortunately some people see culture as something an organisation *has*, in other words, something that is imported into an organization or created and manipulated by management. This ignores culture as systems of ideas where the actors play a central part in it's development. "Culture is something that an organization *is*: it emerges from social interactions, as the product of negotiated and shared symbols and meanings" (p. 12). Or put simply "culture is not just another piece of the puzzle, it is the puzzle" (Alvesson, 1993, p. 146).

One of the simplest definitions of culture is Deal and Kennedy's (2000) *"the way we do things"* (p. 4). Many others like Morgan (2006) take it a little further defining it as "the pattern of development reflected in a society's system of knowledge, ideology, values, laws, and day-to-day ritual" (p. 116), and Schein (2010) brings the notion depth explaining that culture is "both a 'here and now' dynamic phenomenon and a coercive background structure" (p. 3). In this, he means that at one level culture is constantly shaped by our behaviour and interactions with each other, but at the same time, culture also shapes us in return. "Culture implies stability and rigidity in the sense that how we are supposed to perceive, feel, and act ... has been taught to us by our various socialisation experiences and becomes prescribed as a way to maintain the social order" (ibid.).

This view of culture conceives of people as distinctly social animals who work together in an organised way in order to survive and thrive. Culture is the intrinsic social fabric through which organisation occurs, consciously and unconsciously, intentionally and unintentionally. Culture provides the code that allows human beings to predict behaviour, maintain relationships, and find meaning and purpose, it supplies us our language, which facilitates the meaning structure for living. Culture is ultimately the foundation of our social order (Schein, 2010).

How culture emerges

The emergence of culture may be seen through the lens of group psychology. The way culture forms "is identical to the process of group formation" (Schein, 2004, p. 87). This is because the very essence of group identity results in the patterns of shared assumptions that become a group's culture, and therefore "without a group there can be no culture" (p. 88). This is so true that Schein (2004) goes so far as to reference Bion's (1961) group relations theory, discussed in the previous chapter, in regard to the early stages of culture formation. He explains that at the early stages of culture formation people become preoccupied with themselves rather than with the problems facing the group. They operate "on the unconscious assumption of *dependency*—namely, that 'the leader knows what we are supposed to do' ... This group stage, with its associated feelings and moods is similar to what Bion described in his work as the *dependence assumption*" (p. 71).

This suggests that from a systems theory point of view, although not all systems are cultures, all cultures may indeed be viewed as complex systems, and so systems theory and cultural theory prove excellent siblings. However, unlike the therapeutic orientation seen in Bion's (1961) merger of systems thinking and psychoanalysis, cultural theory takes a more functional approach to understanding the phenomena of human groups.

From this functional perspective, culture evolves as a product of a human group's collective process of learning and problem solving in its effort to solve the universal problems of survival (Schultz, 1994). Schein (2004) explains that in order to do this, any group needs to address two fundamental problems:

1. The challenge of surviving in, and adapting to, the external environment, which he terms *external adaptation*.
2. The capacity of the group to work together, in a sufficiently cohesive and coordinated way, so as to maintain itself into the future, which he terms *internal integration*.

From an *internal integration* point of view, culture acts as "consensus-creating glue" (Schultz, 2004, p. 22) which holds the group together and helps to integrate it, and from an *external adaptation* point of view, culture acts to adapt the group to the demands of a changing and complex external world (Schein, 2004; ibid.).

These two evolutionary mechanisms were active in the earliest human tribes and continue today in twenty-first-century organisations. For example, early humans coped with a difficult external environment characterised by wild animals, inclement weather, and inconsistent availability of food, and, importantly, competition with other humans for resources. To address these challenges, early humans strategically worked together as a group in order to, for example, fight off danger-ous animals, build structures to manage the cold and rain and gather or hunt for food, and they did this competitively. These strategies for survival are forms of *external adaptation* and when taught to new mem-bers of the group become cultural phenomena. From a business per-spective, a competitor analysis that converts into a strategy to compete for market share is a form of *external adaptation* in exactly the same way. Furthermore, this same group of early humans needed to organise itself internally in order to survive. Group members would have divided up responsibilities so that, for example, some foraged for food whilst others hunted animals, or some specialised in making weapons whereas others built shelters. Importantly, early humans must have agreed to coordinate these processes in a way that maximised their survival and sustainability. In order to do so, they needed a shared meaning system and a common purpose. Such phenomena are mechanisms of *internal integration*, consensus-creating glue, and when shared across genera-tions in symbol, story, and ritual, form into tribal culture. Twenty-first-century organisational cultures use similiar integrative mechanisms to survive and thrive. For instance, divisional specialisations such as finance, marketing and IT, roles and responsibilities such as software engineer, market analyst and sales consultant and the management and remuneration systems associated with these are examples of mecha-nisms of *internal integration*. And similarly, a modern business coordi-nates and integrates using a shared meaning system and common sense of purpose, just like ancient tribes.

In this functional perspective of culture, all forms of group experience may be viewed as ways to cope with the challenge of *external adaptation* and *internal integration* encountered by the group. Key to appreciating this is an understanding of the way group decisions stem from deeply held, often unconscious, underlying assumptions about survival, and that these are considered sacred in that they underpin the script of life and death for the group. For this reason, cultural traditions and ways of doing things act as homeostatic mechanisms and are generally resistant to change.

Therefore, in understanding a culture, a great deal more needs to be appreciated than an organisational chart, business model, or set of policies. One must delve into the underlying assumptions about survival that underpin these more visible manifestations in order to achieve any meaningful access to the group's reality. In other words, culture manifests itself at the level of observable artefacts and shared espoused values, norms, and rules of behaviour, but "the essence of a group's culture is its pattern of shared, basic taken-for-granted assumptions" which lie beneath its visible aspects (Schein, 2010, p. 32). In analysing cultures, it is therefore critical to recognise that although artefacts are easy to observe, they are difficult to decipher, and that espoused beliefs and values often reflect rationalisations or aspirations as opposed to lived reality. Consequently, a coach must attune to the underlying assumptions beneath these and understand the learning process by which such basic assumptions evolve in order to appreciate the nature of the culture in question (ibid.). Schein (2010) represents these visible and less visible cultural layers as follows:

- *Basic underlying assumptions*—These are the less visible meaning structures of the group, and include deeper assumptions about reality and truth, time, space, human nature, human activity and human relationships.
- *Espoused beliefs and values*—These are the visible narratives that are proffered by the group about itself, and include statements about values, goals, mission, ethics, charters, rules, regulations, norms and stated practices. This level can be deceptive as it is commonly aspirational as opposed to lived, and may thus be subjected to rationalisations by members of the group.
- *Artefacts*—These are the tangible and often symbolic manifestations of the previous two levels and are reflected in language, rituals, behavioural patterns, dress, architecture, stories, myths and products.

For example, consider a company that holds the basic underlying assumption that in order to survive in its market its people need to be seen as individuals, openly express their opinions and challenge leaders without fear of negative repercussions. These assumptions originated from founders of the company having experienced repeated business success in the inception years when they allowed early staff members to offer their opinions and challenge ideas. It may not initially have been a conscious decision on the part of the founders to lead in this way, but rather a less conscious result of their character, ethnicity, or personal history. "Founders usually have a major impact on how the group initially defines and solves its external adaptation and internal integration problems. Because they had the original idea, they will typically have their own notion, based on their own cultural history and personality" (Schein, 2004, p. 227).

Now imagine that over time the founders become increasingly conscious of these shared assumptions and realise that they are causal to their success in the market, enabling them to be more creative and flexible than competitors. Imagine that a focused conversation between them ensues about how this made them successful, and they then decide to espouse these underlying assumptions within the broader company by instilling them in a set of beliefs and values to be taught to all new members. At the same time, they notice that this "way we do things" has worked best in an open office environment and so they develop policies that all staff, irrespective of level, must sit in open plan (an artefact of openness), and that people's titles will not appear on their business cards (an artefact of the non-hierarchical value). They also consciously begin to share stories about previous successes in the company achieved by respected leaders who followed these ideas. These become myths that are told colloquially and formally throughout the organisation (a further artefact). Eventually, the company begins to measure the behaviour of their people, qualitatively or quantitatively, against these cultural values, further embedding them. In this way, the organisation's culture evolves.

Organisational culture

Organisational culture is a relatively new notion with little reference in the literature until the 1980s when it blossomed and is now a basic concept in organisational theory (Stapley, 1996). Schein's 1985 definition remains relevant: "A pattern of shared basic assumptions that was learned by a group as it solved its problems of *internal adaptation* and *external integration*, that has worked well enough to be considered valid and, therefore, to be taught to new members as the correct way to perceive, think, and feel in relation to those problems" (Schein, 2004, p. 17). He draws on functionalist concepts of culture formation to underpin his definition by linking them to generational learning, offering the following two tables. The first, with reference to external adaptation, defines the "essential elements" of a "coping cycle that any system must be able to maintain in relation to it changing environment" (p. 88), and the second, with reference to internal integration, defines the essential elements that "enable a group to develop and maintain a set of internal relationships" (p. 111) that integrate it:

External Adaptation (p. 88):

1. *Mission and Strategy*—Obtaining a shared understanding of core mission, primary task, and manifest [overt] and latent [covert] functions.
2. *Goals*—Developing consensus on goals, as derived from the core mission.
3. *Means*—Developing consensus on the means to be used to attain the goals, such as the organisation structure, division of labour, reward system, and authority system.
4. *Measurement*—Developing consensus on the criteria to be used in measuring how well the group is doing in fulfilling its goals, such as the information and control system. This step also involves the cycle of obtaining information, getting that information to the right place within the organisation, and digesting it so that appropriate corrective action can be taken.
5. *Correction*—Developing consensus on the appropriate remedial or repair strategies to be used if goals are not being met.

Internal Integration (p. 112):

1. *Creating a common language and conceptual categories.* If members cannot communicate with and understand each other, a group is impossible by definition.
2. *Defining group boundaries and criteria for inclusion and exclusion.* The group must be able to define itself. Who is in and who is out, and by what criteria does one determine membership?

3. *Distributing power and status.* Every group must work out its pecking order, its criteria and rules for how members get, maintain and lose power. Consensus in this area is crucial to helping members manage feelings of anxiety and aggression.
4. *Developing norms of intimacy, friendship, and love.* Every group must work out its rules of the game for peer relationships, for relationships between the sexes, and for the manner in which openness and intimacy are to be handled in the context of managing the organisation's tasks.
5. *Defining and allocating rewards and punishments.* Every group must know what its heroic and sinful behaviours are and must achieve consensus on what is a reward and what is a punishment.
6. *Explaining the unexplainable—ideology and religion.* Every group, like every society, faces unexplainable events that must be given meaning so that members can respond to them and avoid the anxiety of dealing with the unexplainable and uncontrollable.

This functionalist conception of organisational culture underpins Deal and Kennedy's (2000) assertion that "every business—in fact every organisation—has a culture" (p. 4), and follows the notion of culture as a social fabric for surviving and thriving. This is because business is conceived as a social system that organises behaviour with the objective of succeeding in a competitive landscape. It should now be clear why organisational culture is something a business *is*, not something it *has*, and why it would be problematic to say "we can't think about our culture today because we have to think about doing business, we'll discuss our culture later when we have time". Thinking about "doing business" *is* thinking about culture, they are one and the same—the way you do business is your culture at every level from marketing to sales to operations and certainly to strategy.

This is not to say that organisational culture is always visible or easy to decipher. The visibility and strength of cultures vary extensively. Some cultures are more stable and ordered because of the length of time they have existed or because their value systems are highly conscious and communicated effectively. Organisational cultures vary in strength and stability depending on their age and emotional intensity (Schein, 2010). The degree to which members accept a shared set of values, and truly commit to them, impacts the level of consistency of behaviour throughout the organisation and is an indicator of cultural strength (Deal & Kennedy, 2000). Where organisational culture is weak, components or different departments within such an organisation tend to uphold different beliefs that do not necessarily align with the overall strategy of the company. This in turn can result in various areas of the business failing to work well together or even working at cross purposes, and has been linked to high staff turnover and low morale. In such a situation, the overall capacity of the organisation to survive and thrive is weakened (Brown, 1998). Strong organisational cultures tend to be high performing and more cohesive in that strategy is more aligned across business units, employees intrinsically motivated, institutional memory protected and talent more committed and loyal (Brown, 1998; Deal & Kennedy, 2000; Schein, 2010).

Leadership and organisational culture

In examining the relationship between culture and leadership, Schein (2004) maintains that these phenomena are two sides of the same coin as neither can be understood without the other. "If one wishes to distinguish leadership from management or administration, one can argue that leadership creates and changes cultures, while management and administration act within a culture" (Schein, 2004, pp. 10–11). From this perspective, leadership is seen as the act of influencing and shaping the behaviour and values of others thereby creating the conditions for new culture formation, whereas management is seen to be the activity that operationally sustains the existing system.

From this perspective, "leadership is originally the source of the beliefs and values that get a group moving in dealing with its internal and external problems" (p. 36). If what a leader proposes is viable, what once were only the leader's assumptions become shared assumptions. In this way, leadership responds to the human need for stability and meaning by providing character and identity definition for the group. Leadership is thus the function that inherently manages culture; in fact, understanding and working with organisational culture is the most central concern for a leader (Schein, 2010).

When culture becomes dysfunctional, leadership is the mechanism through which the group unlearns some of its problematic cultural assumptions and is able to become more adaptive and effective. Therefore a "central issue for leaders ... is to get at the deeper levels of a culture" (Schein, 2004, p. 37), to assess the functionality of the assumptions being made by the group and help them deal with the anxiety that is unleashed when those are challenged (ibid.). For this reason, when business coaches are working with business leaders, they are actually working with organisational culture, and thus an appreciation and understanding of its nature is essential.

At this point it might be useful to explore in depth the phenomenon of leadership. However, to do it justice would require a large detour from the primary narrative of this book as it is a very complex and multifaceted notion. The choice was made rather to maintain narrative focus and leave the concept of leadership here with the brief theoretical link made above. This is despite the acknowledgement that a thorough appreciation of the phenomenon is important for a business coach.

Attributes or typologies of organisational culture

Several theorists have attempted to analyse different cultures across contexts and geographies with the aim of deriving a set of meta-attributes or a typology of organisational culture. Some believe these to be helpful when approaching a new organisation as they are lenses through which to read this complex phenomenon, whereas others in the field see these as problematic (Bercovici, 2001). Critics of these typologies suggest they are overly simplistic and "have proved little more than interpretive intuitions" (p. 177). Supporters counter that they offer a framework through which to compare cultures, and that "simple 'typing' helps people become aware of their own culture and how it differs from others, making more immediate and accessible a complex and elusive concept" (ibid.).

From the critic's point of view, models such as these restrict rather than expand a coach's perspective for two reasons. First, they presuppose and prescribe the constraints for understanding the culture in view, as psychiatrist and cultural theorist Leon Eisenberg (1977) explains: "Models are ways of constructing reality, ways of imposing meaning on the chaos of the phenomenal world. And once in place, models act to generate their own verification by excluding phenomena outside the frame of reference the user employs" (p. 18). This means that in peering through a typology at unique cultural realities, one tends to see only in terms of the model's constraints, thereby excluding realities that do not fit with its prescribed dimensions. Second, typologies tend to reduce a culture into a small set of psychosocial dimensions that are rather simplistic and end up diminishing the rich depth and complexity of an organisation's culture.

Ultimately, coaches must find their own way of appreciating and understanding the culture they are working with. For some, cultural typologies may initially be useful until experience is acquired, then, over time, they simply inform a more open and receptive phenomenological approach. For others, these constructs are too simplistic and reductionist from the outset and should be avoided. Below is a summary of some of the more popular typologies for those business coaches who might find them useful.

Possibly the most famous set of meta-attributes of culture were offered by Geert Hofstede, Emeritus Professor at Maastricht University in the Netherlands, who surveyed thousands of IBM employees across seventy-two countries between 1967 and 1973, attempting to understand the cultural differences influencing behaviour across geographies. He later repeated the research outside of IBM and also included other regions. Hofstede initially found four (later identifying five) cultural dimensions, as follows (Hofstede, 1980, 2001; Hofstede et al., 2010):

1. *Power distance*—refers to the degree to which a culture expects there to be differentials in interpersonal power between managers and staff. In a culture with low power distance, it would feel appropriate to question your boss's decision on a task, whereas in a culture with high power distance, this would be unthinkable. Societies with low power distance scores tend to focus on equal rights and social equity for all people.

2. *Uncertainty avoidance*—refers to the degree to which a culture seeks to avoid uncertainty about the future through the utilisation of rational and non-rational mechanisms of adaptation. For example, many companies develop predictive IT systems, policies, and procedures, tracking and reporting methodologies, as well as advanced accounting techniques to plan for future market uncertainties. Organisations are also prone to using non-rational rituals for this purpose, such as charismatic speeches on the part of the CEO to inspire staff for a possible turbulent year ahead.

3. *Individualism vs. collectivism*—refers to the partiality of a culture towards a collectivist identity and focus versus an individualistic one. Collectivist cultures tend to have more of an emotional dependence of their members on the organisation, and if this is in equilibrium the

organisation will take responsibility for these members as a collective caretaker. On the other hand, in cases of extreme individualism the level of identification of the individual to the collective of the organisation is very low and can result in an "every man for themselves" type of environment. Hofstede maintains that capitalist market economies tend to foster individualism. However, it is possible for an environment to have both high levels of individualism as well as high levels of collectivism, such as would be the case where an individual maintains a sense of duty and allegiance to a particular group but simultaneously values his or her freedom to operate and capacity for personal authority.

4. *Masculinity vs. femininity*—refers to the degree of power equity in the gender relations and associated values and roles of a particular culture. Compare a company operating in countries where all women, regardless of age, are required to have a male guardian and cannot vote, to that of a company operating in Sweden where women and men share power and influence equally and operate in a culture that maintains that gender equity leads to a more just and democratic society (Swedish Institute, 2011).

5. *Long- vs. short-term orientation*—refers to the degree to which a culture delays gratification. Cultures with long-term orientations focus on the search for virtue, whereas those with short-term orientations focus on the search for absolute truth. Short-term orientation cultures tend to follow accepted norms, respect tradition, don't tend to save a lot for the future, and focus on achieving quick results. In cultures with a long-term orientation, individuals follow that truth depends on context, and therefore adapt traditions to changing conditions. They tend to save, invest long term, and persevere over long periods of time in order to achieve results.

In their research, Deal and Kennedy (2000) identified four types of organisational cultures, theorising that they are underpinned by two marketplace factors, namely the degree of risk associated with a company's key activities, and the speed at which companies learn whether their actions and strategies are successful.

1. *Tough-guy macho culture*: Here, the culture is orientated towards high levels of individualism, with a resultant high tolerance for risk and fast decision-making with quick feedback loops. This is an

"all-or-nothing" culture where the focus is on getting an enormous deal or event through the door. Examples are the entertainment industry, venture capitalism, or high-risk surgery (Morden, 2004, p. 166).

2. *Work-hard, play-hard culture*: Here, the culture is lower in risk tolerance but seeks high-speed learning and decision-making. An example of this would be seen in the restaurant industry (ibid.) or in an aggressive sales-based business where individuals get continuous feedback on how they are doing and the overall strategy is to maximise product sales through a pipeline. This results in certain individuals being seen as victors as they continuously achieve the highest number of sales, and causes intense competition between members.

3. *Process culture*: Here, risk and feedback are slower, such as is the case in large conglomerates with high levels of bureaucracy. The focus is on getting the procedural activities done in an accurate and efficient manner.

4. *Bet-the-company culture*: Here, decisions are high risk but the timeline to seeing the repercussions of a decision are very long. New technology or energy companies that are trying to develop breakthrough inventions are examples. Members often share a belief that what they are doing will eventually bring a great upside to be shared by all who have sacrificed and risked along the way.

There are several other examples of these rather simple cultural typologies, such as the four types offered by Charles Handy (1985):

1. *Power-based culture*—in which power is concentrated in the hands of a few key players.

2. *Role-based culture*—in which a person's power derives from their position.

3. *Task-based culture*—in which power derives from recognised expertise.

4. *Person-based culture*—in which individuals consider themselves superior to the organisation.

In summary, it is may be worth exploring simple typologies as an initial entry into appreciating and understanding organisational culture. However, eventually, the coach needs to develop his or her own "felt-sense" (Gendlin, 2007) so as to be open to the widest possible appreciation of the organisation's underlying assumptions. This ensures the coach is not constrained by a brief set of attributes or prescribed psychological dimensions, which may actually end up limiting or distorting the cultural reality of the organisation in view.

Coaching business culture

As discussed earlier, business exists firmly in the context of a marketplace with its associated culture, whereas coaching has theoretical origins in a different context, that of human sciences and in particular the field of psychology. "The coach–client relationship is often compared and contrasted with the counselling and psychotherapy relationships, with which it logically has common ground" (O'Brion & Palmer, 2010, p. 296). In fact, coaching is so heavily influenced by the practice of counselling and psychotherapy that a great deal of literature has emerged which tries to describe the difference, and indeed struggles to do so effectively (Bachkirova, 2010; Passmore et al., 2013). Given this conundrum, business coaches face the challenge of delivering their service in a cultural milieu, that of business, which is *other* to that from which they derive their primary theoretical foundation and method, that is, from the human sciences, particularly counselling and psychotherapy.

In his early paper "Aspects of Sociology of Business", one of America's leading sociologists and the fifty-eighth President of the American Sociological Association, the late Philip Hauser (1961), put it simply: "The objective of any science is to achieve understanding—that is, to achieve predictability and explanation in the field of phenomena in which it is interested. Business is not a science" (p. 167). Hauser suggested that the cultural drivers of science and business are fundamentally different.

More recently, in his book, *Global Problems and the Culture of Capitalism*, Robbins (2011) eloquently exposes the underlying assumptions that drive the culture of business. He explains that over the past six hundred years a distinctive culture emerged dominated by a belief in trade and commodity consumption as the source of well-being. "This culture flowered in Western Europe, reached fruition in the United States, and spread across the world, creating what is today academically referred to as the 'world system'. The most important idea that drives the world system is the notion of industrial and corporate capitalism" (p. xiii).

The spread of the capitalist world system has created its own particular pattern of social relations, worldview, food production and diet, patterns of health and disease and relationship with the environment (ibid.). As discussed earlier, every culture has its own artefacts and structure with associated beliefs and rituals that define for its members what is most important in life. "For the indigenous peoples of the American Plains, the key element of cultural life was the buffalo. For members of the culture of capitalism, the key element is money. Consumers want to spend as much money as they can, laborers want to earn as much as possible, and capitalists want to invest it so that it can return more" (p. 2).

Robbins (2011) furthers that the culture of capitalism can best be conceptualised "as sets of relations between capitalists, laborers and consumers, tied together by the pursuit of money, each depending on the other, yet each placing demands on, and often conflicting with, the others" (p. 3). Regulating these relationships is the nation-state which serves as a mediator, controls the creation and flow of money, and maintains the rules. "The prime directive of the culture of capitalism is that it must maintain economic growth. People must buy, produce, invest, and profit more this year than the last and more next year than this. Failure to maintain growth would threaten the economic, social, and political foundations and stability of our entire society" (p. 4).

In working with the culture of business, it is therefore critical to understand and appreciate the central importance that money plays, and the fact that in such a culture, all activity is designed towards economic growth. Business coaches need to shift from being dominated by the culture of science, particularly psychology, where the primary mission is *truth* and associated *health* (Lane & Corrie, 2006; Popper, 1963), and move towards the culture of business where *money* and all things associated with its growth, sit front and centre of every consideration (Robbins, 2011).

This is no small shift, and may require considerable psychological reflection and adjustment on the part of the coach. I have seen many business coaches struggle with what they perceive to be moral concerns, but which are actually underlying cultural assumptions of the human sciences, as they attempt to translate the purpose of their work from the influence of counselling to that of business. For example, a coach once sought supervision because she had difficulty working with a business that refused to acknowledge the need for "work–life balance". She judged the company as morally and ethically flawed, and questioned whether or not she should continue to provide services to them. I encouraged the coach to engage with leaders in the company with an open mind and calmly enquire into the *business* rationale for this ideology. She returned to supervision with a new appreciation as follows: "The CEO explained to me that the nature of work in his organ-isation required extensive periods of time away from home, work at night, and twenty-four-hour availability of key staff. Over many years, leaders in the organisation had learned through trial and error that indi-viduals who needed so-called 'work–life balance' inevitably failed to deliver and ruined both their own and the company's reputation in the process. He acknowledged that some staff suffered from burnout and health and family-related difficulties as a result. However, he explained that this kind of work was a choice, not a rule, not unlike being a soldier or a fireman, and that only people who chose this line of work with a conscious passion and hungry determination were desirable. Others were referred elsewhere to seek employment. He added that his com-pany financially rewards staff very well for this level of service and commitment, and that most employees are proud of what they do and thoroughly enjoy the intensity of the work and the personal satisfaction it affords them." This new level of understanding of the business at a cultural level left the coach, previously conflicted at a moral level, free from dissonance and able to work in alignment with the organisation's goals. Until this point, she had been sitting in judgement of the com-pany, having imported the cultural assumptions of psychology, particu-larly health psychology, into the context of business.

As discussed earlier, culture provides us with our language and meaning structures (Schein, 2010), which in turn form the way we think and perceive. In fact, cognitive research (Boroditsky, 2009, 2010) shows that language profoundly influences the way people see the world right down to the level of brain functioning. For example, Russian speakers, who have more words for light and dark blues, are better able to visually discriminate shades of blue. Some indigenous tribes say north, south, east and west, rather than left and right, and as a conse-quence have superior spatial orientation. The Piraha, whose language eschews number words in favour of terms like few and many, are not able to keep track of exact quantities. And in one study, Spanish and Japanese speakers couldn't remember the agents of accidental events as adeptly as English speakers could. Why? In Spanish and Japanese, the agent of causality is dropped: speakers say "the vase broke" when talking about an accident, rather than "John broke the vase". Lera Brododitsky (2009, 2010), professor of psychology at Stanford University and editor in chief of *Frontiers in Cultural Psychology*, asserts that these studies show that language is the answer to the question: Why do we think the way we do?

This explains why it is true that even those coaches whose formative influences are in business, and who later in their careers train as coaches, also import the cultural assumptions of human science into business coaching contexts. This cultural conversion occurs through the adoption of language, norms, and values, with their associated underlying meaning structures, in the process of learning to become a coach, and is a typical enculturation process as described earlier in this chapter. Ironically, I have found that some of the most "religious", individual-centric, and remedially orientated coaches began their careers in business and only later became coaches. This is not uncommon; many will be familiar with how easily people change their worldview and assumptions about reality soon after changing their group context (and hence language context). A common example is how once staunch workers' union members later in their career get promoted to management and turn out to be tough and unyielding managers.

As a result of this cultural disconnect between the field of coaching and the reality of business, many coaches continue to translate aspects of business culture using the underlying assumptions of human science, particularly those of counselling and psychotherapy. As explained, this tends to happen through the use of subtle, yet deceptively powerful, cultural language which is applied to workplace contexts. These language forms originate in the culture of human science, for example, psychoanalysis, counselling or medicine, and are applied unconsciously to the business context.

An example of how business culture is "translated" into psychoanalytic culture can be seen in the way authors steeped in psychology make theoretical links between the concepts of personality and organisational structure, that is, organisational structure is to a company what personality is to an individual (e.g., Auger & Arneberg, 1992; Stapley, 1996). "The board of directors, CEO, or manager can be compared to an individual's ego in that they are responsible for the long-range survival of the organisation, for managing turbulent environments, and for constantly posing quality issues. An organisation's hierarchy may be analogous to subpersonalities, and sometimes complexes of an individual" (Auger & Arneberg, 1992, p. 42). Although this conception may be useful and can be a valuable lens through which to view an organisation, it has a problematic cultural tendency when used blind to the culture of business. This is because it quickly, and unconsciously, imports psychopathological, remedial, or curative assumptions across into the workplace, which, as discussed earlier, are not always aligned to business culture. As an example, Auger and Arneberg (1992) take their analogy forward on the same page as follows:

> It is not uncommon for workers to project the Self onto the organi-
> zation or its leader ... this can be seen in the lives of people who
> seemingly 'marry' the organization or become workaholics ... In
> maturity the projections are taken back ... The leader may be seen
> as a 'good' or 'bad' father or mother ... In general, one must work
> through family issues before one is able to be a contributing mem-
> ber of an organization ... (pp. 42–44)

This is not to say that this analysis is incorrect, not in the least; I am of the opinion that what Auger and Arneberg describe is indeed often very accurate from a psychoanalytic point of view. But this is the point—from a psychoanalytic point of view, not from a business point of view. The theory works, but the cultural translation fails. A psychoanalytic perspective such as this is steeped in the cultural ideology of psychotherapy not business. In business, there are few contexts in which psychoanalytic language is deemed culturally appropriate; speaking about projecting your father or mother onto your boss as a good or bad object is a foreign language in business, even if psychologically accurate. More importantly, it carries with it the underlying assumptions of psychopathology, in other words, that such a relational state is a form of psychological illness or failure and needs to be healed. From a business culture point of view, whether or not one projects one's father or mother onto the organisation or leader is only relevant to the extent that doing so hampers business productivity. And it is worth pointing out that some people who project extreme positive fantasies onto their bosses or the organisation can be extraordinarily committed and productive as a result. So from a business point of view, that would not be seen as an illness, quite the contrary. Furthermore, it is not uncommon for those who withdraw projections from the organsational context to begin to see it in rather unaffected and dispassionate terms, and therefore reduce their levels of motivation and sense of belonging. This is despite the fact that such would be seen as a psychologically mature thing to do from a psychoanalytic perspective. And so, the narrative connection between psychoanalysis and economic prosperity is tenuous at best, and even if made initially, is difficult to sustain. This is because the central cultural object of psychoanalysis is psychological health and growth, and the central cultural object of business is economic health and growth, and these are not always aligned. As another example, think about some of the most successful business people you know of—is there an *automatic* psychological health and well-being associated with them? I dare say not. In most cases, these two cultural trajectories are tenuously linked, and in some cases they are mutually exclusive.

Again, this is not to say that working with psychoanalytic theory isn't valuable in the workplace; on the contrary, many excellent business coaches draw extensively from psychoanalysis, among many excellent psychological theories. It is also not to say that psychological health and workplace productivity are not linked, as it is clear that they often are. But rather, the point made here is at a cultural level, not a theoretical level, in order to illustrate the importance of appreciating the negative consequences that being unconscious of the underlying assumptions of human sciences might evoke in the context of business. Psychological theory is extremely useful and very relevant in working with business; as long as it is used in a culturally conscious way and in line with the primary driver for business (economic growth) not those of human science (health and associated wisdom). Put simply, any psychological insight that transforms an individual or organisation into being more *economically* prosperous is culturally aligned to business. However, not all psychologically orientated interventions can be linked to economic prosperity, and when these are applied to the workplace, occasionally, they can be seen as counterproductive or at odds with business culture.

From this cross-cultural perspective, it is therefore important for business coaches to be especially conscious of their use of certain terms and phrases that may trigger a cultural disconnect in the business environment. For example, in counselling and psychotherapy, a mainstay phrase is "How does that make you feel?" This question is used to elicit conscious awareness of affective states that inform the person's current reality. And in this sense, it is a powerful and important psychological question in any context, including the workplace. However, at a cultural level, in the business context, this question can have a different impact to the intention with which it was asked. This is because its cultural home is a counselling context, and most people are aware of this fact. In asking it in a business context, it can create immediate association to a therapy session. Many people may then consciously or unconsciously resist the question as a way of saying: "Hey, this is not therapy, we are here for business!" Business coaches need to be conscious of this type of cultural message sitting underneath their choice of language because it can undermine the purpose of their work, even when they are correctly focused from a theoretical point of view. How would people in business enquire into affective states given that affect is often avoided in the workplace? Perhaps the question: "Where does that leave you?" or "What's the feeling now?" might be better aligned. But even these can still trigger the same reaction. It is more important to be fully aware of the overall cultural dynamic playing out then to have a perfectly aligned language repertoire. This is because, first, such awareness keeps the coach *culturally attuned* to the needs of the client in the context of business, and second, the client will unconsciously read that the coach is aligned culturally because the coach is working with the underlying assumptions of business and not those of counselling. As discussed earlier, the deeper experience of culture occurs less consciously as it sits below the surface in the context's underlying assumptions, and in this sense is felt more so than seen.

Another important example of this form of cultural disconnect regards the practice of confidentiality in coaching. Business possesses a unique and distinct context and boundary system from that of medicine, particularly in the way it deals with agreements like confidentiality and feedback. In counselling or medical culture, the assumption is that the individual is primary and others in their environment are secondary as subjects. For example, if an individual consults a psychotherapist or doctor, he or she can assume the content of the discussion to be confidential. If third parties wish to know the outcome of the engagement, they would need the individual's permission, this is irrespective of who pays the bill for the service. This particular hierarchy of boundaries is based in the cultural ethics of science and medicine. However, business has its own set of ethics that stem from marketplace reality. Marketplace ethics are based in the principles of economics (Robbins, 2011). In business, confidentiality is a contractual obligation negotiated between parties, and importantly for coaches, should not automatically be assumed by service providers working in organisations. Also, in the negotiation of such boundaries, economic realities are seminal in determining who has access to information, and commonly the entity or individual paying for the service enjoys maximum ownership and access.

This is not to say that confidentiality is not possible or important between coach and individual client, on the contrary, it is critical, but rather that such boundaries need to be contracted very carefully because they are not assumed to be in place in business culture. Remember, in business coaching the organisation is also the client and is entitled to an equitable service and boundary consideration as is the individual being coached. This presents a significant challenge when it comes to ownership of information. Is the organisation entitled to know the content and outcome of the coaching sessions by virtue of its status as a dual client? Can the organisation share things with the coach that it feels are confidential and not to be shared with the individual being coached and vice versa? In the culture of business, these questions need to be asked and negotiated in each and every coaching engagement and the answers emerge as part of the tailored contract between the parties. The overarching question is an *axial* one:

> "What boundary structure would work best for **both** the individual **and** the business in this situation, at this time, in order to promote success for the organisation as a whole?"

To illustrate the importance of this, Greenfield and Hengen (2004) describe a business coaching case in which a coach shared the content of coaching conversations conducted with a CFO with the CEO of the company without his consent. This content included violently aggressive fantasies on the part of the CFO towards the CEO, which, only in small part, contributed to his axing. The CFO subsequently initiated a lawsuit for unfair dismissal and named the coach as a party in the action. Unfortunately, the coach had not contracted specifically about confidentiality at the outset of his coaching intervention. The court accepted the CFO's position that in the absence of a confidentiality agreement he could "reasonably expect a confidential relationship with the coach, even though no explicit guidelines existed" (p. 13). The company settled out of court and the coach's reputation was severely damaged.

In this case, the authors explain that the coach failed to "decide on confidentiality guidelines in advance" (p. 14) and in the absence of such the court fell in favour of the individual's rights over the rights of the company. Consider how differently the court might have ruled if it was a management consultant or HR consultant, as opposed to a coach, who shared the content of their consultations with the CFO with the CEO. This case is a startling illustration that the broad lack of differentiation between the practice of business coaching and that of counselling is so significant that courts see it as "reasonable" for a person to assume the confidentiality boundaries of counselling to be those of business coaching *unless otherwise specified and agreed upfront*.

In summary, the incredible wealth of research and understanding that the field of psychology brings to the table remains an essential part of business coaching practice, but to inform it, not to fundamentally culturally construct it—for that should be left to the world of business. Failure to do this tends to result in a cultural disconnect between coaching services and business, which in turn can limit its effectiveness and in some instances be counterproductive.

A word on creating a "coaching culture" in organisations

As explained in detail in Chapter One, business coaching is not so much a technique or skill as it is a relationship process inside of a systemic reality. This relationship process has been seen in broader "culture change" terms in the coming together of two distinct fields: coaching and business. To this end coaching is now fairly frequently positioned as a culture change intervention in that it can offer a new set of values and practices to the business world which, if adopted, result in behavioural change at a foundational level in business practice. Commonly, these focus on bringing to business certain values common to coaching culture and typical of human science such as "authentic individual action" (Clutterbuck & Megginson, 2005, p. 21). To this point, Sir John Whitmore, the coaching pioneer, recently wrote that coaching is a more advanced way of leading and managing others than instruction (in Passmore et al., 2013). He says: "Since a primary goal of coaching is to build self responsibility in others, it is in fact, an evolutionary need for humankind, for we have to move on beyond parental autocracy and hierarchy … Humanity needs to grow up and coaching will contribute to our evolutionary process" (p. xv).

The question is: "If we take the best of the underlying assumptions of coaching culture and merge these with those of business, what do we get?" Although there are exciting evolutionary possibilities for the society of business in this way of thinking, it also presents some cultural pitfalls. The idea that coaching brings to business a great evolutionary opportunity may have an Achilles heel in that an unintended consequence of this view positions the culture of business as lacking in some way and coaching as the bringer of the "light". Perhaps the curative underlying assumptions of coaching culture are being unconsciously applied to business at a broader culture level, that is, the fraternity of coaching will heal the human ills of business where coaching is the doctor and business is the patient with ailments. One might read the ailments to be that of "instruction, parental autocracy, and hierarchy". If this is even partly true, then the field of coaching needs to be careful otherwise it may be perceived to be missionary in form, holding almost religious beliefs that are cultural in nature and misaligned from the realities of business. Importantly, it also might give the impression that the field is somewhat blind to shortcomings in its own fraternity. When this happens, the world of business is construed as "needing" coaching because it lacks, is immature, or unconscious. The fact that coaching needs the world of business to survive more than the other way around, and that the coaching fraternity has its own forms of hierarchy, tricky power relations, and forms of coercive instruction is then forgotten, ignored, or just not understood.

A more mutually integrative consideration would be to look at both cultures as equally valuable to society in their own context and consider what a merging of the two might bring ... a third culture so to speak. At this stage, little seems to have been written in this regard, although Clutterbuck and Megginson (2012) provide an interesting point of entry into the debate with their work *Making Coaching Work: Creating a Coaching Culture*, as they begin:

> Coaching has come of age ... Coaches, with their emphasis on one-on-one relationships, are a bit like social teenagers. They can focus obsessively on a relationship and pay precious little attention to the wider society ... [Coaches] need to make a wider role in the world for [coaching], addressing questions of how it can contribute to organizational effectiveness. (p. 21)

CHAPTER THREE

The complexity of theory

Since the 1990s, an enormous range of theories has been used to support coaching as a service, mostly from the field of psychology. These include humanistic or person-centred theory, behaviourism, cognitive psychology, neuro-linguistic programming and psychodynamics through to narrative psychology, Gestalt theory, positive psychology, systems theory and more recently the field of neuroscience, and there are many others (Kahn, 2011; Page & Rock, 2009; Palmer & Whybrow, 2007; Passmore et al., 2013; Stout-Rostron, 2009).

This chapter considers the theoretical orientation that best suits the culture of business, and therefore business coaching practice. It does this by exposing and comparing the underlying theoretical basis for decision-making in business with that of human science. From this, the chapter shows how an integrative and eclectic theoretical orientation is most aligned with the world of work's decision-making culture. Finally, it offers the notion of the *modern scientist-practitioner* (Lane & Corrie, 2006) as a bridge to help coaches draw on *both* the objective power of science and the subjective freedom of business and remain aligned to marketplace reality.

Business culture and the underlying assumptions of science

Kwiatkowski and Winter (2006) assert that in order to function in the world of work one has to accept that this world is theoretically unique and distinct from that of science. They say that when offering services originating in a science like psychology, one draws from an "unavoidably personal model of science" (p. 158) that business clients may not recognise as legitimate. This is because the world of work is one in which "multiple views are held about how the world works and what is important, by multiple stakeholders, and traditional science is only one of those views" (p. 171).

The great sociologist Philip Hauser pointed out half a century ago: "People in business are required to make decisions irrespective of whether or not they have any knowledge derived from the methodology of science" (1961, p. 168), and therefore a businessperson "uses the best information at his disposal, information built up from his own experience and the experience of his colleagues, which often takes the form of following 'hunches'" (ibid.). In other words, business culture is partial to subjectivity more so than objectivity in its practice. More particularly, this subjectivity appears to be mediated by viability more so than validity in decision-making; in business, people are less focused on doing something because it has been statistically proven but rather act because it "makes sense", subjectively, and *feels* like it will work— Hauser's (1961) so-called "hunch". It's not that they ignore objective measures or statistics, they may well use these to inform decisions, but they do not require such to act. This way of being sits upon an underlying cultural assumption about survival in a fast and reflexive marketplace governed by instinctive forces where one is not afforded the leisure of time to prove something before responding. In business, the proverbial "early bird" really does catch the worm.

To illustrate this point, consider whether you would happily undergo dental work or ingest a particular pharmaceutical if your doctor said: "This should work, nobody has tried it before, but I've done my homework and it feels right, let's give it a go, open wide!" Yet, many business decisions are made like this, and business successes occur commonly in this way. As examples, when asked what method he uses to make stock decisions, an investment manager explained that investment decisions are ultimately made using a "best-guess strategy" (A. Bulkin, Financial

Mentors, personal communication, 22 July 2012). And a director of an advertising agency explained that their advertising campaigns "are developed in a way that is so unscientific that we specifically don't focus on the problem. In fact, if you focus too much on the problem, you aren't likely to find the answer. A creative solution usually just pops 'out of the blue' and you cannot usually even pin point where it came from, you just know when you have the solution, you just feel it. And yet we do have a very clear process that we follow, and we are clear on the brief, but you can't just add it up in an equation and get the answer" (B. Morris, Draftfcb Advertising, personal communication, 22 July 2012). In other examples, a senior banker explained that "sometimes you just look at a guy and you can see in his face that you should not deal with him even when the paperwork looks fine, you can feel it in your gut. Many times I have had that feeling it's ended up that that deal has gone sour down the line. So I have learned to listen to my gut even when the paperwork says something else and I try and teach the youngsters that they mustn't just look at a deal on paper. In business, there are things experience offers you that you cannot find in a book or a spreadsheet, you just know" (name and organisation withheld, personal communication, 19 July 2012). And an ex-director of a retail furniture chain explained: "When I started in the company I was a conservative accountant. My partner taught me to take a few risks, trust yourself and not be over-analytical. Because by the time you have analysed the situation fully the opportunity is often long gone, your competitor has snapped it up. That learning has stood me in good stead over many years in my career" (S. Sachs, personal communication, 23 September 2013). Finally, a wealth management executive had this to say: "The 'gut feel' that we get is often a throw-back to past experiences, our memories triggered by the fact that, whilst the current issue does not obviously match that of the past, the underlying nature rhymes. For instance, during a discussion around suitability of investment, those with business corporate memory tend to explain their decisions around a 'discomfort' not often apparent to a newcomer. It makes sense to delve deeper and not to brush 'gut feel' aside" (R. Goss, Investec Ltd, personal communication, 13 November 2013).

The above illustrates that the culture of business is indeed based in a "multiple view, multiple stakeholder" (Kwiatkowski & Winter, 2006) perspective, where subjectivity is inherent. In other words, personal opinions, "hunches", really count, especially when based in experience.

In this multi-theoretical context, there exists great subjective freedom as any input is welcome, no matter from where it comes, as long as it is focused on viability (what might work), not just validity (what has been proved). In such a culture, it seems logical that no one theory fits best, but rather an eclectic and integrative approach to theory is best suited.

Integrative and eclectic approaches to theory

Integrative and eclectic approaches encourage the use of diverse strategies without being restricted by theoretical differences, and practitioners use the most viable theoretical lens or intervention based on their experience and what makes most sense (Brooks-Harris, 2008; Norcross & Goldfried, 2005; Palmer & Woolfe, 1999). Passmore (2007), for example, offers an integrative approach inviting coaches to "work in an eclectic way, mixing tools and techniques from methodologies, but with a focus on the primary objective of executive coaching; enhancing performance in the workplace" (p. 76). An integrative approach to business coaching "allows for the strongest application of viability in any intervention, which from the context of business is particularly desirable" (Kahn, 2011, p. 195).

Although integration as a point of view has probably existed as long as philosophy itself, the first cohesive ideas on synthesising forms of counselling or psychotherapy appear in the literature in the 1930s, however these thoughts remained latent or were ignored altogether until the 1980s (Norcross, 2005). "Rivalry among theoretical orientations has a long and undistinguished history in psychotherapy, dating back to Freud. In the infancy of the field, therapy systems, like battling siblings, competed for attention and affection in a 'dogma eat dogma' environment" (p. 3). This was severe to the point that practitioners were mostly blind to alternative conceptualisations and potentially superior techniques if such did not originate directly from their particular school of thought. However, as the field of psychotherapy matured, notions of integration and eclecticism gained momentum, and the 1990s witnessed a general decline in ideological struggle in psychology (ibid.). Integrative theory then really gained traction because health-care practitioners, more so than academics, became dissatisfied with single-school approaches and started to look beyond school boundaries to see what could be learned—and specifically *how patients could benefit*—from approaches other than their own. "Improving the *efficacy, efficiency, and application* of psychotherapy is the *raison d'être* of integration" (Norcross & Goldfield, 2005, p. v).

From a business perspective, notions of *efficacy* (how well does it actually work?), *efficiency* (how taxing/expensive/onerous is it to do?), and *application* (how and where can it be used?) strongly resonate. In addition, integrative theory's clear focus on *how patients can benefit* (what is the value to the customer?), and its rejection of single-school approaches (many possible ways or options, no "sacred cows") further establishes it as culturally aligned to the context of business.

Although underpinned by similar principles, there is a distinction between integrative and eclectic approaches. Palmer and Woolfe (1999) explain that integrative refers to the integration of elements into one combined approach to theory and practice, whereas eclectic draws ad hoc from several approaches with a focus on a single case. Both these strategies are equally applicable to the business context depending on which seems more sensible to the coach and the client at the time given the nature of the business challenge and the respective inclination of the coach and client.

Norcross (2005) offers four useful points of entry for integrative and/ or eclectic practice:

1. *Common factors*:
   Here the strategy is to look for the common factors that underpin different approaches. Where similar ideas have been used successfully in many different theoretical offerings, the likelihood of their effectiveness is much higher. The downside of this pathway is a lowest common denominator effect and a resulting exclusion of unique aspects of singular theories which may be of great value.
2. *Technical eclecticism*:
   Here the strategy is to focus on searching for what has worked best for others in the past so as to offer the most effective service to the client based on prior ideas that have efficacy. This strategy allows for maximum flexibility across all possible theories without the requirement for a theoretically integrated offering. In other words, it doesn't matter if different aspects of the coach's approach to the same client do not theoretically link with each other, what matters is whether or not each aspect has a history of success in itself.

3. *Theoretical integration*:

    Here the strategy is to merge two or more approaches into a singular offering in the hope that the efficacy of the sum will be greater than any one of the parts. Many new theoretical approaches today are actually integrations of pre-existing theories. For example, in coaching, Chapman (2010) has taken David Kolb's learning theory and integrated it with Ken Wilber's Integral theory to produce an interesting model called Integrated Experiential Coaching.

4. *Assimilative integration*:

    Here the strategy is to deeply situate oneself in a single theoretical discipline but at the same time continuously assimilate ideas and practices from other philosophies and practices into that discipline. This allows the coach to mine the value that comes from mastery and depth of knowledge of a single theory but still glean the value of discoveries from other offerings.

Finally, these pathways are not mutually exclusive. In other words, a coach may draw from any or all of these in offering business the most viable service given the specific need or context presented.

The modern scientist-practitioner

In addition to drawing on an integrative and eclectic approach to theory in aligning to business, the concept of a *modern scientist-practitioner* (Lane & Corrie, 2006) is also very helpful for the business coach. This concept is useful because it ensures that the enormous value of science is not mistakenly abandoned when a coach aligns their theoretical orientation to the culture of business—one must not throw the proverbial baby out with the bathwater, for in the case of science the baby truly has some genius.

Lane and Corrie (2006) explain that the notion of a scientist-practitioner emerged in response to the inherent tensions between science and the actual practice of psychology where the discipline of science "proved insufficient to illuminate the muddled and murky realities of problems encountered in the 'real world'", and professional psychology practice found that in many ways it "developed largely independently of the research literature that was supposed to guide it" (pp. 1–2). And yet, practitioners have always acknowledged that "creativity which remains unfettered by the discipline of systematic evaluation will fall victim to individual whim and could, at worst, result in malpractice" (p. 3). The scientist-practitioner holds that *both* science *and* free practice need to coexist in "an approach to professional practice that encompasses rigour, science, artistry and ingenuity" (ibid.).

Historically, the extent to which psychology should, or could, be scientifically driven has its roots at the onset of the field. William James (1842–1910), a father of psychology in America and Wihelm Wundt (1832–1920), a father of psychology in Europe, argued in opposite directions—Wundt for the idea and James largely against it, favouring philosophical pragmatism instead (ibid., p. 10). Over the last century, the debate has swung like a pendulum with sensible points on both ends, ultimately arriving at the uncomfortable realisation that both notions are applicable and yet conflict with each other.

> One of the central difficulties in attempting to marry science and practice within a single model of practice, as noted previously by William James, is that scientists and practitioners have fundamentally different priorities. Whilst the scientist is arguably concerned with knowledge that is rigorous, objective and generalisable, the practitioner is more concerned with knowledge that is subjective, holistic and applicable to the individual. (p. 15)

This uncomfortable, yet necessary, interplay positions the scientist-practitioner model in a fairly tricky space where nuance and ambiguity are mainstays. "We can free ourselves from the notion that being a scientist-practitioner means working according to the dictates of any specific model or activity in favour of developing operational systems that enable us to organise and develop our skills in a systematic way" (p. 22), because "embedded within the scientist-practitioner model is a certain moral imperative to ensure optimum effectiveness. However, beyond this, we can assume little consensus definition, role, or function. At the current time, there seems to be more than one way of being a scientist-practitioner" (p. 20). The notion thus offers a fairly open way of working which is relatively free from constraints that may hamper its mission to deliver operationally viable services to the client that are ultimately effective. And importantly, it does not exclude anything from science that may be helpful in achieving that end. These ideas appear to resonate deeply with the culture of business (as discussed earlier), and perhaps this is understandable because in many respects psychology practice is indeed a form of business with a clear set of economic dynamics that drive its operations. As a result, we may well be able to import aspects of this conceptual journey for use in business coaching without fear of cultural blindness to the underlying assumptions of business practice.

Lane and Corrie (2006, p. 3) offer four themes as a framework for exploring what it means to be a modern scientist-practitioner that can be applied directly to business coaches:

1. The ability to think effectively. This encompasses the full range of practitioners' intellectual skills including reasoning, judging, decision-making and problem-solving, as well as understanding the implications of using theoretical and methodological frames of reference that have been drawn from diverse and sometimes conflicting traditions. [The resonance with integrative and eclectic approaches to theory relates here].
2. The ability to weave the information we gather into a story (or formulation) grounded in psychological concepts that has substantive implications for change.
3. The ability to act effectively. This refers to the ways in which we intervene, how we translate theoretical constructs into workable intervention strategies and how we design intervention plans according to the needs of the individual clients. We would include within this the ability to create, innovate and invent.
4. The ability to critique our work in systematic ways. This somewhat broad category encompasses any vehicle we use (officially or unofficially) to evaluate ourselves and our actions. Sources that support this may be as diverse as moments of private reflection, relevant reading, personal audits, use of supervision and choices about continuing professional development. For some it may also include a commitment to personal development in the form of coaching or personal therapy. Most significantly for scientist-practitioners, however, we would see this as commitment to the use of scientific enquiry to guide and evaluate their work.

It is important to underscore Lane and Corrie's (2006) assertion that the above skills are interconnected and interweave in a meaningful sense and that "without the capacity to be creative, practice can become formulaic, unrewarding and ultimately unresponsive to the needs of the client" (p. 3).

In summary, to theoretically align business coaching with the culture from which it derives its legitimacy and sanction, an integrative and eclectic theoretical orientation is suggested. This orientation aligns with the theoretical constructs that are embedded in the culture of business and, amongst other things, drive its decision-making process. Business process is inherently subjective. In other words, personal opinion, particularly when based in experience, really counts. And although statistical or scientific methodologies are embraced in business, these form one of many lenses that inform it, and may be rejected in favour of a "hunch" at any time. Thus, business culture focuses on viability more so than validity in its decision making process. The focus is thus on what works or makes sense to those in power rather than necessarily on what has been "proved" to be true. That is not to say that evidence-based decision-making is not required, but rather that such does not need to ultimately be *scientifically* valid. Instead, the argument needs to be convincing and persuasive. In this sense, the subjectivity of *who* presents the argument is as important as the objective argument itself. Therefore, in order to align with this theoretical culture, the notion of the scientist-practitioner is offered to coaches as a conceptual bridge between the theories of science and the practice of business. This orientation ensures that the enormous value of science is available to business coaches to use in their work without creating misalignment and disconnection with the theoretical culture of business.

CHAPTER FOUR

Introduction to the Coaching on the Axis framework

Coaching on the Axis (Kahn, 2011) is a systemic and integrative framework for business coaching that aligns the practice with marketplace reality and organisational culture. It is offered as an overarching approach that helps orientate coaches to the challenge of business coaching. Therefore, coaches may use whichever coaching models and techniques they like, as long as they are orientated within the *axial* framework.

This overarching approach positions coaching in a way that promotes success of an organisation as a whole, as opposed to just that of the individual being coached. It does this by systemically bringing personal, interpersonal, and organisational realities into an improved state of relationship through the coaching dialogue.

These relationships are articulated on an axis that stretches across two dimensions: *the environment* (incorporating the organisation) and *the individual*. At the centre of this axis sits *the coaching relationship*, which constitutes as the narrative bridge between the two and forms the third dimension. The notion of an *axis* is used as a relational metaphor to orientate the coach to their primary focus—relationship, thereby steering the process away from a remedial and individualistic orientation typical of counselling and psychotherapy.

The Coaching on the Axis approach works relationally by dialoging the narratives that unfold across the axis between the individual and the environment. This enables the coach to ensure that goals, insights and actions remain in integrity with business objectives as the individual coaching dialogue is continuously tested and aligned with the organisational reality. In so doing, the process works to generate a shared story, co-created by the individual and the organisation, based in a mutual sense of responsibility for the business, which promotes its success as a whole.

The Coaching on the Axis tree

The dimensions described above have been symbolically placed on the image of a tree to aid conceptualisation. This metaphor is used purely to assist the process of orientation. It is not necessary to adopt this metaphor in order to fully appreciate or understand the Coaching on the Axis approach, but it is hoped that its inclusion here will be helpful. For those that find the metaphor of no use, please feel free to discard it.

The Coaching on the Axis tree (Figure 3) illustrates the three dimensions of the approach alongside associated theory and sources of data in a single frame: the environment is reflected in the branches and leaves, the individual is reflected in the root system, and the coaching relationship is represented in the trunk which acts as the centre of the axis. The tree is used as a symbol to overlay the axis because it is a living system, just like an organisation, and is dependent on a set of complex relations between its parts and its external environment for growth, just like any business.

Chapter One offered a diagram (Figure 1) in which the notion of a coaching axis was first explained. This is overlaid in the Coaching on the Axis tree (Figure 3), where the notion of a "role" is situated inside the trunk of the tree and represents the interface (axis) between "organisation" (part of the environment) and "person" (individual).

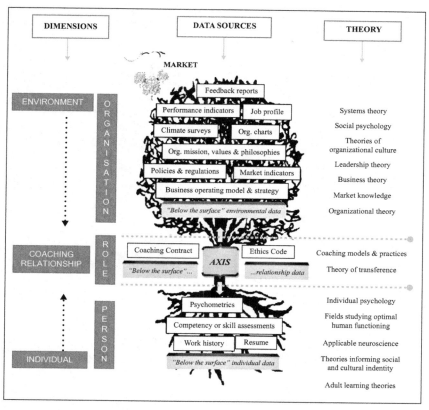

Figure 3. The "Coaching on the Axis Tree".

The remaining chapters of this book will repeatedly refer to the dimensions reflected in the Coaching on the Axis tree (Figure 3) as a way of assisting the reader to maintain an integrated sense of how this approach works as a whole.

CHAPTER FIVE

The environmental dimension

The environment reflects the systemic reality within which the individual being coached operates. This is characterised by the company's organisational culture which, as explained in Chapter Two, not only refers to its mission and values but includes phenomena such as its business model, strategy, structure, systems, history, rituals, myths and symbols, and importantly, the basic assumptions that underlie them. The environment also includes the market supra-system that mediates the company's survival. All these elements are seminal in appreciating the context within which the individual being coached is required to succeed.

In the visual metaphor of a tree (Figure 3), the environmental dimension is located in the leaves, branches and atmosphere. The physics of photosynthesis (Bidlack et al., 2003) is useful here in reflecting the chemistry between the individual and his or her environment. In the same way that the leaves of a tree convert light from the environment into chemical energy which nourishes the tree, facilitating its growth, individuals take up roles in an organisation to convert market energy into profit, facilitating economic growth. In this metaphor, the individual is not the leaf, the role is the leaf, and the individual is required to take up the role to facilitate interaction with the market. The various roles in a company are like different leaves, and the branches are like departments that channel energy through the system in an integrating way. Some organisations, as with some flora, have only a handful of leaves and branches that do this, whereas others have thousands that work together growing larger or smaller organisations. And as a tree depends on its position in relation to other plants competing for the same sunlight and environmental nutrients, so does an organisation compete with other organisations for market share.

Achieving an understanding of the market dynamics surrounding the individual's organisation is therefore a good starting point for coaches at the outset of a business coaching process. To achieve this, coaches can begin by simply asking the individual, his or her manager, or colleagues some of the following questions:

1. Please explain the market forces and metrics that mediate success for this organisation?
2. Who are your primary competitors, and can you share some history of this competition, including where you have won and lost business and why?
3. How does this department or team participate or contribute to the broader business?
4. What role do you play in the team in this regard?

The coach can then take this information and research the company and industry so as to become familiar with the business environment. Coaches who fail to undertake this exercise can miss critical behavioural cues that inform the coaching process. In my experience, many active coaches appear to understand fairly little about the business fundamentals that mediate their clients' success, and yet seem confident they can add great value despite working blind to the basic rules of the system.

Also, coaching training programmes, even those offered at excellent business schools, appear to offer comparatively little education about business and are heavily weighted in favour of studying individual psychology and its relationship with coaching practice. As mentioned in earlier chapters, this is likely due to the enormous influence of counselling on the field of coaching, but as should be clear by now, a very good understanding of the fundamentals of business are just as essential for a business coach.

The environmental dimension includes the individual client's role profile, required competencies and performance deliverables because although these may be thought to describe something about the individual they actually describe the role (the nature of the leaf)—an aspect of the environment. This is evident when one realises that role descriptions and competencies are in place prior to an individual arriving in an organisation and were assumed by his or her predecessor. They represent the most concrete expressions of the organisation's expectations of the individual and are cultural artefacts of the environment.

The physical ergonomics of the office are another aspect of the environment, for example the arrangement of the client's desk or office in relation to others in the organisation as well as the level of physical comfort or lack thereof that the office building provides. These factors have an influence on productivity and need to be considered, and importantly, they are artefacts of the culture of the company and therefore offer clues about the underlying assumptions that are at play. For example, covert hierarchies can sometimes be gleaned from where a person's parking bay is in relation to others and what floor their desk is on in the building relative to the executive floor. Many organisations reflect the power relations between departments and individuals through the affording of privileges, comforts, and conveniences, for example the walking distance between allocated parking bays and the entrance of the building or where in the canteen the person takes lunch. It can be valuable for the coach to carefully observe the client's physical environment.

Unfortunately, it is not uncommon to find a few coaches preferring to work at their own office, next to their favourite pot plant, clock, and bookshelf. This practice is a throwback to the influence of counselling on coaching practice discussed earlier, and sadly also appears to reflect a convenience factor for some coaches who prefer not to travel from venue to venue throughout their day.

Insights gleaned from visiting the organisation's physical environment can be very important and affect the nature of the coaching process. For example, I worked with an executive in a very large organisation and used the executive's office as a coaching space once a month. One day, upon arriving at his office, the executive proudly and spontaneously pointed to a new pot plant in the corner of the room. Curiously, I enquired as to the meaning of this, as there seemed to be nothing special about the plant, upon which he explained that he had been promoted and was now entitled to an extra pot plant. In this organisational culture, it was important to understand that privilege and status was reflected in a range of common artefacts, such as an extra pot plant. Subsequent to this experience, I was able to decipher several symbols in the building that revealed the company's underlying power and authority system, the "who's who", in a way previously hidden. In another example, upon entering the building and being handed a business card from a staff member, I noticed that her degrees had been removed from her business card. Enquiry into the meaning of this change revealed that the new CEO believed that a focus on education as opposed to delivery was a barrier to appreciating employee value. He had instructed the removal of educational indicators on all cards to reflect this new philosophy. This cultural change ended up re-scripting the narrative for success in the organisation, and indeed for the individual being coached, who was at that time planning to do another degree in order to promote his career prospects in the organisation and had not noticed the importance of this change.

To illustrate the importance of understanding the environment as the context for performance, the late Sumantra Goshal, past professor of strategy and management at London Business School, offered the following appreciation during a panel discussion at the World Economic Forum (Goshal, 2005, 2010):

> Now context, some manager called it "the smell of the place", is a hard thing to describe. Let me try to describe it from my personal experience. I teach at the London Business School and live in London and have done so for several years. Before that, I lived in France and taught at INSEAD at a place called Fontainebleau. But one look at me and the sound of my voice and anyone can tell that I do not come from any of these places. My hometown is Kolkata in India. That is where my parents lived. So every year, in July, I used to go to Kolkata for almost a month. Think about it: downtown Kolkata in July. The temperature is over 100°F with humidity of 98%. The reality was that I felt very tired during most of the vacation. Most of it I spent indoors and a lot of it simply in bed. As I said, I used to live in Fontainebleau. It is a pretty little town, 40 miles south of Paris. What makes it outstanding is that around it is the protected forest of Fontainebleau, which is one of the prettiest forests in all of Europe. You enter the forest in spring, with a firm desire to have a very leisurely walk and there is something about the smell of the air, about the trees, that will make you want to run, jog, jump up, catch a branch, to throw a stone, to do something. You will find that even though you entered the forest to have a leisurely walk, you are doing something else. Most large companies

end up creating 'Downtown Kolkata in Summer' inside themselves. What does 'Downtown Kolkata in Summer' look like in most large companies? I relate to this in the sense of the phrase, 'the smell of the place.' Try not to intellectualize it. We intellectualise a lot in management. The reality is that you walk into a sales office, factory, head office and in the first fifteen to twenty minutes, you will get a 'smell'. You will a get a smell in the quality of the hum. You will get a smell in the looks in people's eyes. You will get a smell in how they walk about. That is the smell I am talking about ... What is the smell when it is a part of a large organisation? Constraints! Top management is very wise, has lots of information, have good people. So, by products, by customers, by markets you create great strategies. You also work very hard—sixteen hours a day, eighteen hours a day. You take all the decisions, know exactly what needs to be done. But what does this mean for those working in the shop, in the office, sixteen levels below you? How does your hard work boil down for me, the lowly salesman? Constraints—that's what comes down to me. All the systems that top management create—human resource systems, manufacturing systems, planning systems, budgeting systems—each by itself is totally justified. However, collectively, what does it feel for me, sixteen levels below, down on the floor? That I have to comply. All those systems hang like a black cloud over me. So I start asking myself, why does my boss exist? Not just my boss, why does the entire management infrastructure exist? As far as I am concerned, they exist for one reason and one reason alone—to control me. To ensure that I do not do the wrong thing. The job becomes a contract. The budget is a personal contract, transfer prices are contracts, relationships between colleagues and departments and divisions are all contracts. That is the environment—constraint, compliance, control, contract—that is the smell of the place. And yet what is the behavior top management wants from me? You want me to take initiative. You want me to cooperate, voluntarily, with others around me. You want me to learn continuously and bring the benefits of that learning to my work, to my job, to the company, to its success. Where are we going to get those behaviours if this is the smell you create around me?

It is interesting to note that the Chinese, long ago, recognised this important systemic phenomena (*smell of the place*) in the ancient text of the *Sun Tzu* (also known as *The Art of War*), where it is offered in the concept of *Shih*—the fundamental expression of the world in terms of relationships. The *Sun Tzu* describes *Shih* in the metaphor of rocks rolling down a hill or over a cliff. When a rock is placed on an incline, its expected static nature changes through its relationship with its environment. Even square rocks will roll if the slope is steep enough. And so, the *Sun Tzu* explains that a wise general does not rely only on exceptionally brave troops (individual dimension), he relies on *Shih*—the relationship of his troops to the environment within which they are required to do battle (Denma Translation Group, 2001, p. 80):

> *One who uses Shih sets people to battle as if*
> *Rolling trees and rocks.*
> *As for the nature of trees and rocks—*
> *When still they are at rest.*
> *When agitated they move.*
> *When square they stop.*
> *When round they go.*
> *Thus the Shih of one skilled at setting people to*
> *battle is like rolling round rocks from a*
> *mountain one thousand jen high.*

The environment below and above the surface

The environmental context (*Sun Tzu's Shih* or Goshal's *smell of the place*) has both visible, above the surface, and less visible, below the surface, aspects. The notion of below and above the surface phenomena in psychological life was first used by Sigmund Freud a century ago when he drew on the image of an iceberg to reflect the conscious and unconscious mind of an individual (Freud, 1915e). More recently, the metaphor has been extended to incorporate the visible and less visible environmental realities that affect both individual and organisational functioning (Huffington et al., 2004; McLean, 2009). For example, an organisation's physical building and its branding may be said to be above the surface, but the effectiveness of team relationships are below the surface. Both phenomena impact an overall *smell of the place*, and need to be appreciated by coach and client if success is to be fostered through a coaching process.

Freud's conscious and unconscious attributes remain in the organisational iceberg in that an organisation may be said to be unconscious (unaware) of dynamics or patterns of relating which are "below the surface", and which impact its effectiveness. For example, a trend analysis report or a climate survey is an attempt to identify and raise phenomena above the surface from the unconscious of the organisation so that such may be fully appreciated, reflected upon, and inform conscious, above the surface, decision-making, and in so doing improve the organisational function.

Figure 4 depicts the organsational iceberg, illustrating the range of phenomena that exist below and above the surface. As can be seen, the

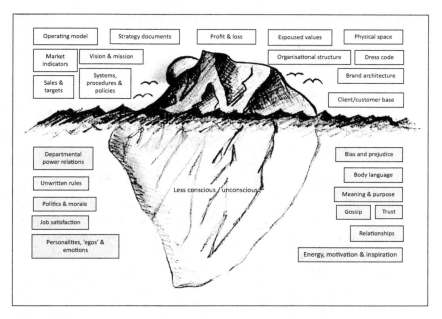

Figure 4. The organisational iceberg.

most commonly available or easily visible attributes of an organsation, such as its physical space, financials, and espoused values, appear above the waterline, whereas the less visible or available attributes, such as department power relations, levels of job satisfaction, trust, and morale, appear below the waterline and, metaphorically, account for the larger component of the iceberg's area. The iceberg, as a whole, represents the organsational culture.

The notion that organsational and individual life has a below and above the surface can be linked metaphorically to the Coaching on the Axis tree in that a tree has a visible exterior (above the surface) layer expressed in its bark, and a less visible interior level expressed in the core of the tree (below the surface). The bark may reflect one state of being which is very different from that which is occurring underneath. Trees carry their past experiences inside, reflected in their rings. Tree rings, otherwise known as growth rings or annual rings (Capon, 2005), reflect the experience of the tree over time, and the science of dendro-chronology (Baillie, 1995) analyses the patterns of these internal rings to determine, amongst other things, certain aspects of past ecologies experienced by the tree.

But perhaps Nobel Prize-winning writer Hermann Hesse (1984) put it best:

> When a tree is cut down and reveals its naked death-wound to the sun, one can read its whole history in the luminous, inscribed disk of its trunk: in the rings of its years, its scars, all the struggle, all the suffering, all the sickness, all the happiness and prosperity stand truly written, the narrow years and the luxurious years, the attacks withstood, the storms endured.

Uncovering the individual's relational system

An individual's relational system is core to the context, or *smell of the place*, within which they are required to operate and ultimately per-form, and it is commonly below the surface. To uncover it, the coach needs to explore the relationships in the client system (team or depart-ment) and related organisational politics. These below the surface set of interpersonal relations often underpin the organisational dynamics that support or disable an individual from succeeding.

The process of discovering a person's relational system begins with a study of the history of the area within which that person works. This provides important background colour to the emerging environmental view. Perhaps the business has been through a series of retrenchments, or perhaps the department was acquired from a competitor and most of the staff are new to the broader organisational culture. As this informa-tion emerges, it creates a systemic landscape upon which to place the organisation's narrative for the individual's success.

An important part of this enquiry, for instance, would be into how predecessors fared in the individual's role. For example, a study pub-lished in the *MIT Sloan Management Review* (Manzoni & Barsoux, 2009) revealed that a new manager's probability of success is often adversely affected by the reputation of his or her predecessor(s). They offer the example of a new recruit who was the fourth general manager for a business in three years. In that case, staff had lost faith by the time he arrived and were reluctant to re-engage for fear of yet another disap-pointment. "The new boss came in with a 'dead man walking' label already hanging over him" (p. 45). On the other end of the spectrum, the study exposed how incoming leaders suffer continuous comparison with much admired predecessors. "When the previous boss has cre-ated a strong collective view of what the ideal leader looks like, it's difficult for a new leader to match that image, regardless of the traits and abilities the newcomer brings to the role" (ibid.). Their research shows that discrepancies between the actual and ideal images of a leader strongly correlate with dissatisfaction with the current manager. "The circumstances surrounding the predecessor's departure also matter. The more unexpected the event, the more intense the employee emotional reaction. The new boss may have to contend with feelings of anger, grief, betrayal, or anxiety, especially among those who saw the outgoing leader as a mentor, friend, or coach" (ibid.). They found that such negative emotions leads staff to gather unfavourable "evidence" that tends to reflect badly on the new recruit, and that "even before the new boss arrives, team members tap their internal and external social networks for information" (ibid.).

To illustrate this from a coaching perspective, consider the experience of Derek who was recruited to lead a sales team in a software company that had a history of underperformance. Within a short time the team began to challenge Derek's leadership criticising him for being "too controlling". A coach was brought in by HR at the request of Derek's manager to "help him not be a control freak". Fortunately for Derek, the coach worked systemically and therefore did not accept HR's "diagnoses" at face value. Instead, he contracted with Derek to interview several of his colleagues and team members so as to better understand the environment within which Derek was required to succeed. Through this process, the coach discovered that Derek was the fourth team leader in as many years, and that each of his predecessors had received the same or similar feedback and subsequently been removed from the role or resigned. Furthermore, he learned that a long standing member of the team was an outspoken critic on each of these occasions and that she was a close friend of the wife of the CEO of the company. She was also an average performer and as a result was never considered for team leader. With this as the landscape, Derek and his coach were able to work with his "control issues" very differently than would have been the case had the coach failed to interrogate the relational field. As a result, Derek was able to expose options previously unavailable in his thinking. He managed to discuss the issue with his manager and CEO in a helpful way by bringing the history of the team into the conversation and sensitively raising the issue of the personal relationship between the CEO's wife and the team's loudest critic. The original goal of the coaching was then realigned as it became clear to all that the functionality of the team was not being hampered by the individual's "control issues". With renewed support from his manager and the backing of the CEO, Derek was able to introduce a more disciplined approach into the team which ultimately resulted in a role change for two members (including his loudest critic) and one year later Derek had delivered a dramatic increase in overall team sales and his "control issues" had "miraculously" disappeared.

Derek's story reveals that the way people, including the individual themselves, experience and describe the relational context and history of the environment, is critical to understanding the pathway for success. Therefore, coaches need to uncover the way the environmental system works and what the individual is "holding" for the system in their role as a result of their valence (as discussed in Chapter One). To achieve this, coaches can ask the following:

1. How do things work around here?
2. How does one get ahead?
3. Who is who, and who is ahead and behind?
4. What kind of things happen here that nobody would easily and openly admit?
5. What should one never and always do here?
6. What has happened in the history of this place that set the tone and direction?
7. What is the secret to success here?
8. How do decisions really get made?

These questions can be used to open a conversation with the individual early in the coaching engagement; however, they are just as useful when engaging any member of the organisation as part of the initial data-gathering process. Furthermore, they can be used continually to track changing dynamics and unlock deeper layers of environmental understanding as coaching progresses.

Environmental goals and expectations

Derek's story reveals how the environment articulates desired outcomes for an individual, often through their manager or HR. For Derek, the environmental goal was to "help him not be a control freak". However, this initial goal was suggested without proper interrogation of the systemic reality, and if taken at face value would have resulted in the failure of the coaching engagement. Good business coaches understand that part of the work is to help the environment as a client properly locate the most viable goal for the individual so as to promote success for the organisation as a whole. In Derek's story, as is often the case, this required a sensitive exploration of Derek's relational field which resulted in a significant reframing of the initial goal. This is an example of how a coach works in the axis between organisation and individual in scripting a mutually beneficial narrative for success. When this is done effectively, coaching can deliver significant business value.

Working with environmental goals and expectations in this way means it is important that coaches test the assumptions which underlie an organisation's initial expectations for a coaching process. This can be done by asking some of the following questions:

1. Please explain how the organisation came to this goal for the coaching.
2. What exactly has been happening that led to this request? Please give examples.
3. How does the organisation really know that this is the bottom of the issue or the crux of the challenge? What else could be at play?
4. Is this a common challenge that people experience in this team, department, company, industry? If so, how do others address it and what causes it?
5. Have others in this particular role succeeded previously? If so, how did they do it; if not, why not?
6. Why does the organisation believe that coaching is indicated here? Have other forms of intervention been considered?
7. To what extent is the organisation supporting the individual to succeed other than by requesting a coach? If there are other supports, how will the coaching work together with these in achieving success related to this particular goal? For example, is this person's leader working on this goal with them as well, and to what extent is this helping?

These questions are particularly useful in determining the systemic place that the coaching relationship will have in the organisational story. Often this type of enquiry will help the company reformulate a coaching goal if necessary, as was the case for Derek.

Asking these types of questions is also useful for uncovering situations where organisations request coaching for an individual to subvert responsibility for helping the person themselves. This sometimes occurs when a leader is failing to provide effective support for a person and coaching is proposed to compensate for that leader's shortcomings. Unfortunately this is a short term fix which eventually back-fires as in the end it de-authorises the leader or presents the coach as the leader's competition. In more sinister cases organisations have been known secretly to decide the individual is a failure and use coaching as a final support to preempt a performance management process that says: "We tried everything, even paid for coaching, and you still failed so it's time to part ways." In this case, it may be most helpful for a coach to push back on the request for coaching and suggest an alternative service. In the former case, it might be suggested that the individual's leader receive coaching instead, and in the latter the coach should resist participating in a predetermined performance-management process where the outcome is inevitable. This is one of the places where good ethical practice on the part of the coach is critical.

Environmental sources of data

Information is everywhere in an organisation. Data can be gleaned from small observations at the entrance of a company building to listening to conversations between staff in the elevator to reading documents on the company website. Important information is offered formally in a coaching brief and it can also emerge spontaneously in a chance conversation with a staff member. It is as much in what you are shown as what you are prevented from seeing; as much in what is said and done as it is in what is not said and done. As explained earlier, sources of data live both below and above the surface. Above the surface data sources are usually physical or factual in nature; below the surface data sources are usually non-physical and interpretive in nature.

For example, a strategy document is a hard data source, as is a business card, a dress code, a briefing document and a survey report. However, the energy levels of a team, commitment of an employee or sense of respect offered by a manager are commonly below the surface. Both levels reflect the extent to which a staff member or a department are valued by an organisation. Coach and client need to continually gather and explore both levels as a whole, looking for narratives that inform success for the individual.

For example, the following data might point to a team that is not highly valued in an organisation: Above the surface—the departmental strategy document does not prioritise or mention this particular team's tasks in its overall plan, the team was not invited to a departmental planning offsite and, when asked why, was told they are not required. Below the surface: when the coach asked several employees where in the building he could find this team they said they had never heard of it, and when he checked in at reception the receptionist was not sure who to alert that he had arrived as "it's been a while since anyone has needed to see someone from this team and I'm not sure who the secretary is there now." When asked how they felt about being in the organisation, team members said they felt "invisible." Information such as this can be very important as it is indicative of the culture, *the smell of the place* or the *shih*, within which the individual being coached is required to succeed. Consider how important it would be for a coach working with individuals in this team to understand and appreciate this context.

In each of the dimensions, a range of document-based, "above the surface", data sources can be gathered by the coach to inform the coaching process at its onset. For example, in the environmental dimension the following can be useful: company mission, vision and values, climate surveys, individual's role profile or job description, individual and team performance indicators and metrics, any feedback reports (especially 360, performance and leadership feedback), organisational charts including team structure and work flow, strategy documents especially competitor analysis, related market indicators, and relevant company policies. However, remember, these become meaningful only when seen in the context of the entire iceberg, and then worked through in the coaching dialogue. It is important not to see "above the surface" hard data in isolation, as on its own it tends to offer relatively little meaningful input. However, when it is seen together with data from below the surface, patterns and themes emerge that can be powerfully diagnostic. In fact, information from below the surface is often more revealing and rich than from above. Furthermore, gathering data is an ongoing activity rather than an event. A coach should be like an investigator observing and enquiring at every opportunity, continually expanding and deepening his or her sense of the environment throughout the coaching process. This is also important because the environment is never in a fixed state and its changing nature needs to be continuously tracked.

Feedback is not just data

It is particularly important in a coaching process to understand the way individuals being coached are perceived by others in their environment. This is specifically with regard to their performance and effectiveness as contributing members of a business. The extent to which their self-perception matches or departs from others' views, and the reasons for this, can be very valuable in informing the process

(Kets de Vries et al., 2007). Feedback of this nature provides key data that inform the direction coaching should take by pointing to the degree of alignment in individuals' relationships regarding their performance and capacity for insight. But this is not the only value it brings. Importantly, if done properly, it is an opportunity for the coach to promote success for the organisation as a whole by helping the system better articulate and understand its needs of the individual and vice versa. The results from facilitated feedback from others create insights about the way the individual being coached functions, as well as point to aspects of his or behaviour that need attention. "They can help redefine superior-subordinate relationships, setting the stage for a more open, network-orientated organisational culture. They can be used to create more effective executive teams" (p. 77).

As discussed earlier, the organisation and the individual are equally conceived as the client. It is therefore important for coaches to see all members of the organisation as clients as opposed to simply sources of data. This means that when coaches engage with others in an individual's relational field they are still in the role of a coach rather than a researcher. This is important as it infers a paradigm shift in that the nature of the dialogue with others in the organisation should also have the aim of promoting success for them as well, not just the individual. This is particularly true when the coach gathers feedback from others on behalf of an individual as part of a coaching process. This is an opportunity to support the entire organisation by helping individuals articulate, understand and refine their relational needs towards the individual being coached in a constructive and meaningful way, and vice versa. This means that asking for feedback is itself an intervention which acts to potentiate a positive change in the relationship.

The trouble with anonymous feedback

The practice of anonymous 360-degree or multi-rater feedback (Brutus et al., 1998; Scott, 2009) as a means of monitoring and regulating individual performance is commonplace in organisations today. Unfortunately, anonymity introduces a limiting and potentially destructive element into the feedback process that ultimately can prevent the process from potentiating the positive change it seeks to achieve.

Susan Scott (2009), in her bestselling book *Fierce Leadership*, puts it like this:

In what universe would anonymous feedback, anonymous anything, be considered best practice? No one I know wishes to be unremarkable, impersonal, faceless or unknown—and it would be difficult to argue that anonymity enriches relationships or strengthens connection with others. The fact is that anonymous feedback rarely creates real or lasting impetus for change, which is crazy because the whole idea is to encourage professional growth. (p. 29)

Commonly in anonymous 360-degree feedback between three and six colleagues provide perspective anonymously on an individual from all angles—hence the term "360-degree" (Antonioni, 1996). This is usually kept anonymous by virtue of an IT system that provides the interface for the written feedback against pre-constructed questions. Occasionally, an HR or OD consultant will be used as the agent for the feedback. What is most commonly missed in these processes is that for feedback to be truly meaningful it needs to be located in a context. As discussed in the early chapters of this book, systems thinking exposes how we are essentially relational beings and that what we know, and indeed who we are, is located in the context of our relationships. Feedback is inherently relational information. It asks us to let another person know what we believe about them. For this exercise to work, reviewers need to tap into their memory and experience of the way the person in question has impacted them through their relationship over time. Such information is therefore constituted through the systemic alchemy of the coming together of the parties and therefore expresses as much about the provider of the feedback as it does about the receiver. It is not objective information by any stretch of the imagination. On the contrary, it is inherently subjective. For this reason, one can sometimes find that particular feedback ends up telling us more about the person providing it then it does about the person to whom it is offered. Feedback is therefore significantly less valuable when taken out of the relational context from which it originates through "anonymous" sharing. This strips it of context and promotes a false objectivity as if the information is a fact about the other, when actually the information is a perception about the relationship between the provider and receiver of the feedback.

Furthermore, when a person does not know from which relationship the feedback comes they are unable to locate its full meaning. This is why people try to work out "who said this" when anonymous communication is provided to them. They are not necessarily being defensive, as some might like to believe, but rather are trying locate the relationship from which the communication emerges so as to truly understand its context. The corruption of meaning is further compounded because anonymous feedback is usually provided without examples in order to protect the identity of the reviewer. Again, without examples the real meaning of the feedback is difficult to work with as it exists in a vacuum, far from the lived experience of the receiver. Furthermore, in instances where the receiver does not fully understand the feedback, he or she is unable to query, clarify or enquire into its real meaning.

And if these issues were not enough to encourage open and personally owned feedback, consider the repercussions when anonymous negative feedback is provided to people working in a team where there is some tension between members. In such cases, individuals are likely to walk out the room from which they received the feedback and immediately begin a secret investigation into who said what, at times testing their hypotheses by "fishing" for information or reaction from their colleagues. And even when they have worked out who provided the feedback through deductive reasoning, they are prohibited from engaging the person about it as they are not supposed to know who said it. What happens is an under the surface "I know that you know that I know what you said, but I can't say and you can't say, so best we pretend accordingly". In the end, unhelpful, and often destructive, under the surface dynamics are introduced into the team. These dynamics ultimately serve to reduce team functioning by increasing anxiety that cannot be reality-tested and worked with openly and honestly. In such circumstances, team members can find themselves in a team culture characterised by secrecy and behind-closed-doors conversations where people are suspicious of each other and openness is avoided. This is not conducive to teamwork and undermines the business task in very destructive ways.

The above insights should be sufficient to dissuade any organisation from using anonymous feedback, so why do they still use it? Those in support might defend the practice by saying they expect their staff to be "mature" and work with identity-free feedback in a responsible and constructive way. Unfortunately, this is a rather naïve view of individual psychology and ignores the systemic complexity of team and organisational dynamics (as explored in Chapter One). Furthermore, if people are so mature why would they need to hide their identity in the first place, surely such maturity would underpin the courage to speak openly?

Perhaps a more rational defence in support of anonymity lies in the notion that people are likely to be more honest when their identity is protected because they need not fear the negative repercussions of their criticism. And indeed studies have shown that staff tend to reflect less positive feedback to a manager when they do so anonymously (Antonioni, 1996). But the question remains as to how valuable this feedback really is, as honest as it may be, given that it is provided in a relational vacuum, without specific behavioural examples and cannot be clarified or processed with the individual providing it. Furthermore the reviewer is not encouraged to think carefully about how to provide this feedback in the most constructive and balanced way because at face value there are few consequences to being blatantly critical. In this sense, reviewers needn't take responsibility for their own part or filter in holding their opinion and so what is deemed to be "perfect" honesty can sometimes be untested and unchallenged opinion. And then there will always be the odd individual who uses the feedback opportunity to attack the receiver as part of a personal agenda. Whilst these dynamics can play out in the psychology of the reviewer, on the other end the receiver is clearly aware that the feedback is anonymous and therefore, ironically, may allocate less veracity to it, believing that it comes with an agenda that cannot be subjected to challenge or contextual test, and, as explained, the receiver is occasionally correct. This is more likely to occur in the mind of the receiver when the feedback is negative and the receiver is feeling defensive, and once again this type of defence is impervious to challenge as not much in the way of example or context can be provided to shift it even when the feedback is actually entirely accurate.

What this all amounts to is that the anonymous "honesty" that is so prized ends up being compromised by the psychology that was invented to protect it. From this point of view, it is a lot more useful to work with whatever level of honesty is offered in an open way, even if it is only partially honest, than it is to work with "perfect" honesty, a fantasy in itself, that is offered anonymously. Furthermore, when the feedback is not anonymous the reviewer can carefully reflect as to how best to share the information in view of the relationship, and in so doing the feedback is more than just an offering about the receiver but also an opportunity to build the relationship on the part of the reviewer. It becomes about "us" more than just about "you", which is feedback that is more likely to be seriously considered by the receiver who might appreciate the courage and openness offered by the reviewer. In this case, the most important aspect of open feedback is the implicit invitation to engagement and dialogue that it offers. In other words, if I offer feedback to you without withholding my identity I am automatically opening the channel between us for dialogue. Not only don't we have to pretend that communication between us has not occurred (as with anonymous feedback), but I am expecting you to engage me and vice versa. The dialogue that ensues is an extremely valuable, possibly the most valuable, change opportunity for the receiver and the reviewer to transform and improve the effectiveness of their relationship. When this is done across a team, the clarity with which team members understand expectations and locate their pathway for success can be enormous. This is because it occurs not only on an individual level but at the relational level and team level as well, which means that the feedback is reality-tested, processed in the relational context, and aligned, and is, therefore, fundamentally systemic in nature.

Coaching using open feedback

From a business coaching point of view, it is, therefore, highly recommended that the coach use only open feedback. This is not only helpful because of the psychology described above but is also important with regard to the coaching relationship itself.

When a business coach gathers anonymous data for input into a coaching dialogue, a problematic dynamic between coach and client is created. The coach knows who said what but cannot tell the individual being coached. In such circumstances, a power relation plays out where the coach has valuable knowledge about the individual's environment that he or she withholds in order to protect others in the workplace. The person might wonder about what was really said to their coach by their colleagues and the extent to which the coach is screening or omitting feedback data. They also might wonder about the degree to which the coach was "influenced" by other team members and is now "judging" him or her but not revealing his or her opinion. Such dynamics negatively impact trust levels and can severely undermine the coaching process.

However, consider what happens when the coach gathers open feedback from the environment as input into the coaching process. In this case, business coaching becomes a conduit through which improved relationship for the client can occur. The coach is able to engage with others in the environment as a coach, not a researcher, assisting them to find the words to articulate their expectations and needs towards the individual client in the most constructive way. And that is not all, the coach is able to glean valuable environmental data for input into the coaching process through these interactions, which deepens the nature of the dialogue. This is especially the case when individuals make reference to colleagues, and the coach has direct personal experience of those concerned. And because all feedback from these relationships is gleaned openly, the coach does not have to censor or omit anything from the dialogue. In fact, the coach is now able to reality-test the client's interpretations of the feedback by offering perspective from their direct experience where necessary. Furthermore, the client is likely to trust the engagement more because nothing is withheld, and he or she is empowered by the process to engage colleagues and test or clarify information and assumptions.

Furthermore, this kind of open feedback directed into a coaching process tends to expose options for the client for needed engagement with colleagues that facilitates improved relational effectiveness. In fact, this approach in itself might form a significant part of the early coaching period. And, given that the feedback is open, there is no reason why the channel of communication with the coach should be closed for anyone in the environment. In fact, when further feedback for an individual is available, others might feel comfortable to offer it to the coach unsolicited for input into the coaching process at any time. These feedback channels can be invaluable when effectively utilised by a good business coach and truly meet the goal of "promoting success at all levels of the organisation by affecting the actions of those being coached" (Worldwide Association of Business Coaches, 2007).

However, there are some important guidelines for coaches concerning boundary management when using open feedback. Failure to do this might result in the backfiring of the whole process:

1. *Ensure contracting is done correctly.* This means that all the stakeholders, particularly the individual being coached, accept and understand the difference between open feedback and anonymous feedback,

and, importantly, buy in to the process before the coach embarks on any feedback.

2. *Maintain a completely open system.* Once feedback is open it cannot be closed. In other words, if some people are anonymous with their feedback and others are open, or if they are open about some of their feedback and not about other parts, a fundamental corruption occurs and the whole process can be counterproductive and destructive.

3. *Encourage direct communication as opposed to being an agent.* Wherever possible, encourage people to provide feedback directly rather than use you as an agent. Failure to do this may result in dependency on the coach for communication which is counterproductive. The coach should challenge defenses that inhibit open relating by consistently educating on the long term systemic value of openness.

Creating a relational map with the client

A useful exercise to do with individuals is to help them build a relational map of their environment. This captures in a single, web-like, image, the relational field that person is managing, and helps them appreciate the nature of each relationship in view of all the others. These maps are not necessarily strict and neat in nature or created with rules and scientific measures. Rather, they are imaginative illustrations that are part of a dialogue process for the purpose of raising awareness and igniting conversation.

The diagram in itself is not where the value lies, but rather the conversation that emerges in its creation. This exercise uses visual language to capture complex relational phenomena and, as explained earlier, these are somewhat invisible. Dan Roam (2009), in his book *The Back of the Napkin*, explains that picking up a pen and drawing out the pieces of a problem on a piece of paper is a powerful way to see hidden solutions because "visual thinking takes advantage of our innate ability to see—both with our eyes and with our mind's eye—in order to discover ideas that are otherwise *invisible* [and] develop those ideas quickly and intuitively" (p. 4). In this way, a relational map opens the way to seeing previously invisible patterns of relating and possibilities for improvement or even breakthrough.

For example, Figure 5 is a replication of a client's relational map, drawn by hand together with his coach, over a period of an hour and a half. Each scribble reflects a conversation point, an insight, or a question.

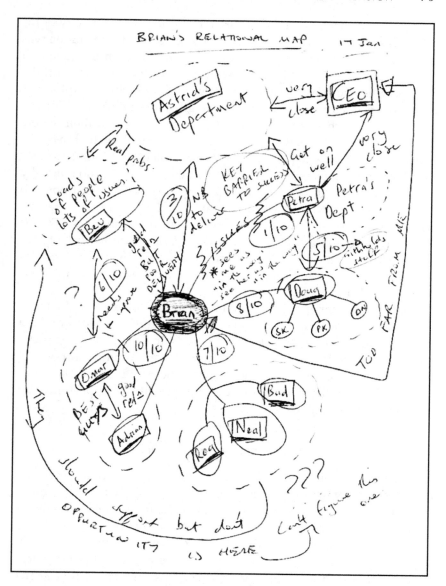

Figure 5. Example of a client's relational map.

In this map, Brian finds himself at the centre of a page filled with ten others he works with. The lines and arrows reflect the set of relations these ten people have with him and each other.

During the coaching dialogue, Brian chose to rate the quality of his relationship with each of these people on a scale of ten. Each rating was born from an exploration with his coach and was both intuitive and rational in its making. Where scores were low, Brian reflected on the cause of this and how he might be able to improve that relationship, and some actions were created accordingly. He also posed questions and located insights as he developed the map and noted them where relevant. For example, at the end of the exercise, he realised that "a blockage to success for my department could be unblocked if Reg, Neal, and Bud supported Bev's team a lot more". He realised that he did not really know why they withheld support, and he created an action point to enquire into this. When I asked him to "look back at the picture as a whole and notice whatever comes up", Brian noted that his CEO "is too far from [him]" in the picture. This gave rise to an important conversation of the effects of this distance for the optimal functioning of his department and himself, and Brian created another set of actions designed to bring his CEO closer.

These types of maps can be retained and new ones created later in the coaching process as needed. They are also useful when compared over time across a single coaching relationship. Coach and client can then reflect together on the relational field from a temporal point of view. This also demonstrates the growth trajectory that the client has enjoyed through the coaching process and presents the opportunity for further insight as a result thereof.

Environmental sources of theory

The theoretical frameworks that inform the environmental dimension describe the way human beings perceive and behave within their environment (system/group/company/market), and how the environment simultaneously drives their behaviour and perceptions.

As discussed in detail in Chapter Three, when drawing on theory to inform the way they work, an integrative and eclectic theoretical orientation is recommended for coaches. This orientation best aligns with the principle of viability typical of business culture. In addition, the notion of the modern scientist-practitioner (Lane & Corrie, 2006), specifically discussed in Chapter Three, is very useful in orientating a business coach to drawing on theory in a truly applied way. This keeps the coach closely connected with the realities and practicalities of business but still allows them to draw from any insights traditional science can bring.

Below are some good examples of both classic texts and recent literature that inform the environmental dimension for a business coach. Most of these were discussed briefly in earlier chapters; they are a good starting point from which to further explore this dimension:

- *Systems theory and social psychology*:
  Brunning (2006), Cavanagh (2006), Lencioni (2005), Lewin (1947a and 1947b), McRae & Short (2010), Senge (1990) and Stapley (1996 and 2006).

- *Organisational culture*:
  Deal & Kennedy (2000), Rosinski (2003) and Schein (2010).

- *Business models and business culture*:
  Chesbrough (2007), Collins (2001), Goshal & Bartlett (1997), Goshal & Westney (2005), Robbins (2011) and Sisodia et al. (2007).

- *Theories of leadership*:
  Covey (1989, 1992), Maxwell (1995) and Northouse (2010).

CHAPTER SIX

The individual dimension

The individual dimension refers to the personal psychology, competence, experience, and professional history the person being coached brings into relationship with their environment; their personal reality.

People bring their personality and psychosocial history to bear on much of what they do, often referring to this as their "mindset" or "personal make-up". And these are formed from the influences they have had throughout their life, both positive and negative. In the Coaching on the Axis tree (Figure 3), the roots represent the individual dimension because they reflect a person's roots in the sense of: "My roots tell you where I come from and describe the influences that made me who I am." Roots are also underground and therefore less visible, as is often the case with people and their roots—not obviously visible and sometimes requiring some sensitive digging for them to be exposed.

The individual below and above the surface

Just as there are both visible, above the surface, and less visible, below the surface, aspects in any environment, so is it the case with individuals. Peoples' resumes are useful visible, above the surface, stories about them as individuals. Naturally, peoples' competence and experience rooted in their career histories are primary to their ability to take up their role.

For example, consider the case of Stuart. His previous experience at Software Company A gave him skills and experience in a type of programming which he uses in his new role in Marketing Company B. But what about the less visible aspects of Stuart that he brings to this new role? How will these affect his ability to add value and succeed? These deeper, often hidden, aspects of Stuart's personality and history can mediate his success. For example, his personality type, authority and control needs, self-esteem, confidence, learning style and self-limiting beliefs play a powerful role in determining success and these are usually well hidden and mostly unconscious. What if Stuart has a deep need to work independently and tends to resist taking direction preferring to work alone. What if this need stems from a long history of disappointments with leaders that Stuart has had to contend with, and, as a result, he has deeply held beliefs that others are not to be trusted and he can only rely on himself for direction? And what if Marketing Company B has an organisational culture characterised by clear hierarchy, management controls, and collaborative work-based teams, where taking direction from managers and working in tandem with others are not only encouraged but expected? In such a context, the fact that Stuart has the programming skills necessary for the role may not be sufficient for him to be successful if he resists his manager's direction and avoids working with his colleagues. Nothing is 'wrong' with Stuart, he is not pathological in any way, he does not require remedial attention, however there is a problem in the relational interface between his individual makeup (his roots) and the organisational culture (branches and leaves). This relational problem is significant as it may result in a failure to achieve success for both Stuart and the business as a whole. The organisation may find that although Stuart knows what to do technically, he is difficult to work with because he resists the "way we do things." For example, he does not participate in team meetings, often not attending, and he complains that his team leader is micro-managing him. Whilst his team leader complains that he works without considering the implications of his actions on others in the team. Ultimately, this may result in Stuart and the organisation failing to form an effective relationship which, reduces productivity and may even threaten the success of the team.

From a business coaching point of view, what this means is that in order to promote success for the individual being coached, and for the organisation as a whole, it is critical that a coach access and understand the less visible aspects of the individual's story, and the way it interacts with that of the organisation.

Accessing the individual's story

A coach can begin to access the less visible aspects of an individual's story with a sensitive enquiry into his or her personal history. In order to do this, questions inviting an individual to articulate the story of who they are and from where they come may be used, for example:

1. Please tell me about yourself. Who are you really?
2. Where do you come from? What's your background?
3. Who has influenced you in life?
4. What experiences shaped you to become the person you are today?
5. How did you get into this role? What were the choices and influences that mediated your decision?

Just like a tree stands above the surface with roots below that influence it in ways unseen, so too a person carries roots below the surface which influences everything he or she does in unseen ways. Our roots live in the stories of our past, in the triumphs, failures and hurts we have endured, in the people we have known and the places we have been, in the schools we have attended, in the work we have done and all the learning we have garnered until now. All this history (his-story) is installed in our roots and is fundamental to the way we show up. We understand the present in terms of what we already know, and what we already know is a reflection of our past. As Chaim Potok put it in his novel *Davita's Harp*: "And, darling, everything has a past. Everything—a person, an object, a word, everything. If you don't know the past, you can't understand the present and plan properly for the future" (Potok, 1985, p. 10).

For example, Leigh, a smart middle manager in the distribution arm of a large FMCG business, was referred to coaching by her manager Mike. Mike explained that whenever he gave Leigh instructions, she challenged the thinking behind them "to the point of frustration". He accused her of "challenging for the sake of challenging" rather than for the purpose of understanding or improving the distribution processes. Leigh rejected this interpretation and explained that she "needed to know why she was required to do something before doing it" because she "was not a robot, but a thinking human being". This relational dynamic had deteriorated to the point that other members of the team complained that Leigh's need to challenge everything Mike said derailed the effectiveness of team meetings and was a constant irritation. Everyone acknowledged that Leigh was a clever and hard-working manager who delivered against expectations. She was regarded as someone who could see beyond the obvious and had several times solved bottlenecks in the distribution process with insightful solutions. Unfortunately, the continuous challenging from Leigh had got the point where both Mike and the team were so frustrated that they were prepared to lose her "if her difficult challenging behaviour didn't significantly reduce". In a briefing meeting with Leigh and her coach, Mike said he was happy to be challenged by Leigh, and that she had really good ideas and insightful questions; however, for every one of these, she had five comments or challenges which were poorly thought through, and she often came across as "nitpicking and introducing unnecessary noise for personal reasons unknown". Leigh offered some acknowledgement of her behaviour but believed it to be far less severe than was being suggested.

Leigh and her coach spent several sessions exploring her personal story. A breakthrough came when she explained that she had grown up in a family with two older brothers, now well-known attorneys in their father's firm, who "always knew everything", and a father that seemed only to value and acknowledge her when she "could contribute to the conversation by showing one of them up". When asked what "showing one of them up" meant, she explained that it meant "finding a hole in their argument". It emerged that the "roots" of Leigh's "difficult challenging behaviour" with her current manager were located in this personal story. Leigh interpreted the present in terms of the past by reading each interaction with Mike as requiring her to "find a hole in his argument" in order to feel valued and acknowledged. Coaching proceeded with a focus on reframing Leigh's story in a way that worked both for her and for the organisation. Eventually, she was able to see that her ability to "find a hole in any argument" was both her greatest strength and her greatest weakness. It was her strength when it was appropriately used to help the business. It was her weakness when it was inappropriately used to serve her need for acknowledgement, which ultimately backfired anyway. The real change in behaviour came when she was "able to move from automatic to manual", as she put it, so that she could choose to use her "challenging ways" when it served her and the business, but could "choose to be quiet when it didn't".

Leigh's story illustrates the importance of accessing an individual's roots as a means of unlocking the relational dynamic between the person and the organisation. However, relational dynamics are not always this simple to unlock. Many social and cultural phenomena entangle themselves with the effective functioning of workplace relationships in a way that is often difficult to ascertain or engage. This is often because they have roots that extend beyond the personal history of the individual into his or her community context and cultural history.

The roots of an individual's social and cultural identity

The term "roots" also reflects social and cultural identity in terms of an individual's community history such as their ethnicity, gender, mother-tongue, nationality, race, religion, sexual orientation, or any other cultural or community system that is important to them or has been formative in their psychological make-up. These often play a significant role in influencing the way someone views the world. Women, for example, may be said to experience reality differently from men; Americans may be said to have different social priorities from Africans; and a bohemian from California may have very different cultural expectations from a religious Christian from Texas. These social and cultural identities are formative and are part of the constructs that influence how an individual perceives and behaves in the workplace. Understanding them is not only an important part of appreciating a person, but also may prove to be a significant narrative in the relationship between the individual and the organisation. Coaches need to be "skilled at working across cultures between organisations and within organisations, as well as with individuals" (Kelley, 2007, p. 201).

The formative power of culture in influencing conceptions of reality may be so profound that individuals from one community may experience the same state of mind in radically different ways from those of another. For example, in South Africa, a white person hearing voices would commonly be deemed mad by their community, and be removed from society through admission to a psychiatric hospital, whereas a black person might in certain contexts be said to be receiving important messages from the ancestors and be admired and utilised as a shaman by his or her community (Hirst et al., 1996; Kahn & Kelly, 2001; Jones et al., 2003). This illustrates just how important appreciating and understanding social and cultural context can be. Kelley (2007) makes this point and explains that business leaders "must recognize and adapt to cultural complexities on many levels, and steer their organisations in a rapidly changing world. Doing this well can mean the difference between economic success and failure" (p. 200). She cites several troubled or failed mergers and acquisitions, such as Mittal's acquisition of Arcelor, UniCredit's acquisition of HypoVereinsbank, and the failed merger of KLM and Alitalia, as examples of where cultural misunderstandings and misconceptions created very negative business consequences.

Cultural and social identities may also have deeply rooted political and societal narratives that mask histories of injustice, suffering, and oppression. These can sit under the surface in profound ways and be very difficult to work with as they are complicated and evoke deep emotional reactions. Often, these reactions are not so much about the individuals in the organisation themselves but more about what they represent at a societal level. Examples of this are where national conflicts cascade into working relationships, such as for some Irish employees working for English companies in London who have personal history associated with the conflict between the IRA and the British government, or for a black employee working for a white boss in South Africa who previously was a political prisoner during Apartheid. To assume that such roots have no impact on the quality and effectiveness of business relationships is optimism to a fault. In most cases, people try to exclude this tricky systemic level from all conversation at work because it is riddled with psychosocial landmines. Nevertheless, these dynamics are present in every business, and a good coach needs to be ready to work at this level, especially when it undermines the effectiveness of the relationship between the individual and the organisation.

Gender is a common example. Women continue to struggle with disempowering social narratives that undermine their capacity to perform and ultimately reduce workplace productivity. As an example, Facebook COO Sheryl Sandberg recently published a valuable exploration of this narrative in her book *Lean In: Women, Work, and the Will to Lead* (2013), in which she argues that women are too passive as individuals in the workplace and need to assert themselves against society conditioning that influences them to defer to men, scale back their ambitions, and give up too early. She explains that success and likeability correlate positively for men and negatively for women. For example, when men are successful, they are liked by both men and women, but when women are successful, both genders tend to dislike them. She calls for modern culture to find "a robust image of female success that is first, not male, and second, not a white woman on the phone, holding a crying baby".

On the other hand, men have their own gender struggles, characterised by "scripts of primitive heroic mythology" (Kahn, 2002) where many struggle with "the immature expression of male aggression" (p. 531). Today, most men remain uncomfortable with emotional expression, and many are experiencing a crisis of meaning about what it is to "be a man" in the modern world. In response, the 1990s saw the emergence of a new psychology for men. Robert Bly's *Iron John* (1990), Sam Keen's *Fire in the Belly* (1991), and Bill Kauth's *A Circle of Men* (Kauth, 1992), amongst others, birthed the contemporary men's movement, such as *The Mankind Project* (Barton, 2000). These movements are an attempt "to reclaim that which has been lost for modern men toward a rebuilding of a new, more mature and more sacred, masculinity" (Kahn, 2002, p. 531). Bly (1990) writes: "It is clear to men that the images of adult manhood given by the popular culture are worn out; a man can no longer depend on them. By the time a man is thirty-five, he knows that the images of the right man, the tough man, the true man which he received in high school do not work in life. Such a man is open to new visions of what a man is or could be" (p. ix). Keen (1991) added: "Authentic manhood has always been defined by a vision of how we fit into the universe and by the willingness to undertake an appropriate task or vocation. Our modern rites of passage—war, work, and sex— impoverish and alienate men" (p. 7).

In this sense, both genders are embroiled in a complex social narrative that can, at times, significantly impact workplace contexts. It is therefore important for a coach to appreciate and understand these so as to be able to work at this level when required.

Race is another widespread example. There is much literature exploring the disabling experiences of black employees in dominantly white organisations (e.g., Batts, 1982, 1998, 2002; Kuttner & Spriggs, 2008; Muir, 2012; Rodgers, 2006). For example, Alleyne (2004) studied thirty black workers across the NHS in Britain and found repeated and consistent evidence that they experienced a subtle but pervasive silencing of their voices in the workplace. She writes: "The legacy of slavery and colonialism shapes black peoples' attachment patterns and relationships with white people ... leading them to feel that they are treated differently in relation to their white colleagues" (p. 8), and factors such as these consistently negatively affect esteem and work performance (p. 4).

Similarly, studies regarding gay and lesbian workers experiences also reveal social barriers impeding success in the workplace (e.g., Ludden, 2011; McNaught, 2010; Raeburn, 2004). Many gay and lesbian workers respond to this societal prejudice by choosing to hide their sexual orientation to avoid unfavourable consideration or social discomfort. This in turn has been found to impact work satisfaction and effectiveness negatively (ibid.).

Gender, race, and sexual orientation are well-researched examples of socio-cultural roots individuals bring to their roles that may impact workplace productivity. However, there are many other less visible forms of diversity that also significantly impact the relationship between an individual and the business context. Consider language, educational background, and age as examples. All these, and others, can negatively impact the capacity of a person to take up his or her role in a given environment. And for a specific individual, any may prove severe depending on personal make-up and environmental context. For example, many older people who are approaching a company's prescribed retirement age may experience a sense of being devalued; as if by virtue of their age they are no longer as competent or capable as they once were, when in fact the reverse might actually be the case. Or people with decades of extensive experience but who early in their careers did not acquire tertiary education can find themselves being covertly deauthorised in an organisation or may hold self-limiting beliefs about what they can or cannot do for the company.

Helping individuals manage power relations and rank

Valerie Batts (1982, 1998, 2002) explains that diversity issues such as those described above, and others, are caused by unconscious power relations between dominant and non-dominant groups within an organsiational context, and that these often underpin prejudicial behaviour. She offers a useful model exploring these dynamics in which she argues that the modern world is filled with less obvious forms of disparity between groups which are typically unconscious and, as a result, more difficult to identify and address. As a result, patterns of unintentional or unconscious prejudice emerge between people. In these situations, dominant group members remain blind to the advantage or privilege they enjoy by virtue of being in the dominant group (which she calls the non-target group) and entrench bias or disadvantage as a result. Correspondingly, non-dominant group members (which she calls the target group) suffer from negative or self-defeating behaviours having unconsciously internalised the prejudicial narrative.

For example, Sandra, a woman working in the logistics department of a courier company, came to coaching troubled by, as she put, "internal gender politics". She explained that it was becoming difficult for her to work because the four other women in her department "had issues". She said: "All the women here know that this is a male-dominated culture and that we have to demonstrate that we are as good as they are if we want to be taken seriously and get ahead. Problem is that I'm the only woman in the department that has chosen not to have children, and so the others feel that I have an unfair advantage because they all have kids." Sandra was being subjected to a range of social attacks from these women. For instance, she was not invited to their birthday lunches, was ignored, avoided, or shunned in social situations at work, and on several occasions these women had treated her with outright contempt during business meetings. It had got to the point where the week before our session she found herself in the bathroom in tears and was considering looking for another job. Her manager, Jeffrey, had contacted me in a bit of a panic as he rated Sandra as one of his best employees, and was desperate to retain her.

This situation is not that uncommon. The target group in this context, women, were playing out a form of internalised oppression (Batts, 1998, 2002) constellated as a result of the power dynamic between the genders. As Sandra eloquently explained, in this company culture, men hold the power and women need to "prove themselves" as equals. In such a context, pregnancy, maternity leave, and child-care means that women carry additional responsibilities, stresses, and personal taxation which men typically do not. As a result, the women in this department experienced a disadvantage in the workplace power game. Given that raising their discontent with those in power, men, could incur relational damage, where the men simply dismiss their objections in overt and covert ways, creating further workplace vulnerability for them as a group, the women, unconsciously, attack "one of their own", who happens to enjoy an advantage based in the oppressive narrative. Ironically, this advantage is one that she cares not to have, and is not so much an advantage as it is "not having a disadvantage".

It is important to understand that negative impacts such as these are often not raised with those in power by targets because their voices are silenced in the system. For example, it may be very hard for a woman in a boardroom full of men to raise the fact that she is not the only one who can take notes or pour tea. She could run the risk of being humiliated, belittled, or just plainly dismissed. Targets often run the risk of being dismissed, and for this reason choose to silence themselves.

As this story illustrates, power is an important phenomena for a good business coach to appreciate and understand. Arnold Mindell's (1995; 2000; 2002) process-orientated psychology or process work, may assist coaches in working with power relations. Mindell, originally a Jungian analyst, first developed his ideas applied to helping individuals, but later applied his theory to working with organisations. He offers the notion of *rank* (Mindell, 1995) to help understand power relations. *Rank* refers to the relative position of power that an individual has in relation to others. For example, in many workplace contexts, men outrank women. Or in English-speaking countries, first-language English speakers outrank second-language English speakers. Rank provides people with power and privilege. However, people have rank by virtue of context, which changes all the time, and so power and privilege change when the context changes. For example, if English speakers move to work in France, they automatically lose rank. This means that characteristics or preferences that are seen as mainstream in a context provide certain people, and not others, with rank in that context. Heterosexuality, for instance, is mainstream in terms of sexual orientation in most societies. Heterosexuals, for this reason, therefore dominate that context and enjoy more privilege and power by virtue of this rank.

Mindell's notion of *rank* relates well with Batt's concept of *target* and *non-target* groups, in that when people are without rank they automatically become targets. This is because people who have less power and privilege in a given context are vulnerable to being targeted for bias or discrimination, irrespective of whether such is intentional or not. Any difference may provide a person with rank, or deprive them of it, and in so doing position them as a target depending on the context. For example, the religion of Islam in Britain or the USA is not main stream. Muslims in these countries (as a context) are therefore automatically targets because they lack religious rank. Christians are non-targets in these countries. However, in Saudi Arabia or Iran, Muslims are non-targets, and Christians become targets.

Unfortunately, people are mostly unaware of the rank they enjoy and therefore of their power. It is easier to be aware of the power and privilege that we lack than it is to be aware of that which we enjoy, because people with rank commonly take it for granted. Men, for instance, are often unaware of how little they need to attend to their personal safety in comparison to women, and able-bodied people are often unaware of the privilege of their health until they lose it.

This lack of awareness of power and privilege on the part of the dominant group is one of the reasons why unconscious forms of prejudice and bias are often not corrected in organisations. For example, in Sandra's company she was once told the following by her manager, Jeffrey: "Sandra, you mustn't worry. I don't see you as a woman." When she enquired as to what he meant, he said: "I mean that I don't see gender, I just see delivery." Although Jeffrey's intention may have been positive, the resultant impact on Sandra, or any woman for that matter, was obviously negative. This deeply unconscious, however well intentioned, failure on the part of the dominant group member illustrates his profound lack of awareness of the power relations at play. Batts (1982, 2002) would describe this as a modern form of unconscious or unintentional prejudice—a modern 'ism'—called *denial of difference*. This is where non-target group members minimise or discount obvious differences between people as a way of masking or avoiding their discomfort with the power that difference affords them. In such a context, consider how difficult it was for Sandra, or any other woman in her situation, to respond to this statement by her manager in a way that would not damage the relationship between them. Sandra told me she just said: "Thanks", but inside she felt hurt and angry.

Mindell (1995) explains that even though people tend to be very aware of their disadvantage when they lack rank in a given context, they have little power, and hence have little chance of creating change in the system; in other words, they struggle to be "heard", and on occasions when they are heard, find themselves overtly or covertly dismissed by dominant group members time and time again. When people are not heard in a system, over time, they become more and more silenced and disempowered, and can become aggressive or radicalised. In certain cases, target groups can eventually go "underground", and form underground movements. These may be as small as informally coordinated "passage talk" in a large corporate or as big as well-organised terrorist movements.

Alternatively, targets that continually feel oppressed by virtue of lower rank may, over time, unconsciously internalise the disempowering messages they receive and begin to live up to them. In Sandra's case, the women in her department fell into this unconscious dynamic. Their feelings of hurt and anger at being disadvantaged in the workplace where diverted and came out as an attack towards their own gender. Batts (2002) would describe this as a form of internalised oppression called "missed or repressed significance", in which the members of a target group miss or repress the significance of what they are doing to their own group member as a result of the power issues at play between them and the dominant group. Another simple example of this would be a Jewish middle manager saying that he does not employ Jews because "they have a sense of entitlement", or a black businessman preferring to use white legal representation because "whites are more confident". In these cases, target group members are prejudicial or discriminatory towards their own group and completely miss or repress the significance of how these actions support the wider societal context in which they themselves are disadvantaged or prejudiced. And, of course, in all these cases, business effectiveness ultimately suffers as a result.

From a coaching point of view, in these types of situations, the object is to facilitate a process of recognising, that is, making the unconscious dynamic conscious, in order to create the option for a different behavioural choice for those in the system. This means helping the members of the organisation see how their social and cultural identity impacts on the organisational function, which allows for the creation of new cultural realities and possibilities.

In Sandra's case, the situation was resolved through a series of facilitated dialogues between her and the other woman in her department in which the dynamics explained above were named and discussed. This was not an easy process, and required considerable expertise to manage. In severe cases such as Sandra's, coaches who are not properly schooled in working with intense power relations of this kind should consider referring the case or bringing in an expert to assist them in the process. This is because failure to successfully facilitate this type of sensitive and potentially explosive process can have disastrous effects for both the individual and the organisation.

Kelley (2007) asserts that to be able to work well at this level, coaches need to "look for more rather than less complexity and be prepared to address the appropriate layers of cultural difference for the client" (p. 203). She argues that a coach is obliged to, at the very least, "know that he or she knows not, and to move toward knowing what he or she (and others) know' and then to accompany coaching clients as they travel along the same route" (ibid.).

Business coaching at the existential level

During coaching, people may find themselves exploring existential concerns—the search for meaning in existence (Blackburn, 2005). The philosophical works of Martin Heidegger (1962) and others such as Victor Frankl (1984) and Ernesto Spinelli (1989) inform this aspect of coaching work. These authors tackle the fabric of meaning that human beings create in the narrative of their lives. What does it mean to 'be' the person one is? Such considerations are 'deeply rooted' because they reach into the search for answers to the primordial questions: 'Who am I? Why do I exist?'

In business coaching, "the coach helps the client to articulate existential concerns such as freedom, purpose, choice and anxiety, and identify and replace limiting paradigms, thus leading to positive change" (Stout-Rostron, 2009, p. 234). This level of work can be important, especially when it influences the relationship between the individual and his or her organisation. What role does one's work play in the meaning-making narrative of one's life? Exploring individual meaning and purpose is a powerful entry into deeper layers of relating between a person, an organisation, and the underlying beliefs and meaning structures of the two.

Existential dialogues in business coaching can occur when an individual questions his or her own personal values and core beliefs in relation to those of the organisation, and can go so far as to touch on issues of morality, spirituality and faith. They also emerge when a coach prompts the client to examine why he or she holds particular views of the world. This often happens as part of the process of understanding what is happening in a business context around a particular choice or action.

For example, Bianca, a creative director in an advertising agency, held the belief that humans should not eat animals as "the practice of killing living beings is wrong." She appreciated that in the animal world many killed for survival, but maintained that human beings could survive without doing this and "the practice supported an ideology of aggression in the world." It was this ideology that she felt was problematic in that it underpinned many forms of suffering, both for people and the planet. As a result she was a strict vegetarian.

One day, during a coaching process focused on building Bianca's leadership abilities, she arrived at her session in a state of existential anxiety. She had been asked to lead a marketing campaign for a large fast food chicken chain. She explained that she was unable to work on this account because of her "values and beliefs." Unfortunately, the account featured as a major opportunity for her company who were thrilled to have won the work, and expected her to deliver her usual creative genius. "I just don't know what to do, I'm completely stuck?" she said in her coaching session. In this situation, the existential concerns of the individual were in conflict with those of the environment to the extent that the success of both, from a business point of view, was at stake. Furthermore, Bianca explained that as a leader in her organisation she felt it was her duty to take on this work and support the business she loved, and for which she felt a sense of loyalty and belonging. This further intensified her existential anxiety as her internal value system was in conflict with itself. On the one hand were her beliefs about a world free from harm to living beings, and on the other hand were values of loyalty and duty to her organisation and profession—both ran deep, both were extremely important to her.

The coaching dialogue that followed explored Bianca's deeply rooted beliefs about the nature of life itself. As mentioned, one of her belief systems was underpinned by the notion that for her to truly 'be herself' she could not participate in anything that supported being cruel to animals because "that is not what being a human being should be about. I need to know that my work, at least causes no harm, and wherever possible, fosters a better world." However, she also maintained an important and meaningful connection with her work in another way. This was about exercising her marketing talents through her agency with which she had a long history and personal connection. In this latter narrative, withdrawal from the account would mean disappointing her colleagues and creating a predicament for her agency. This challenged her existentially in terms of her loyalty and commitment to her craft—meaning structures which underpinned her sense of self and placed her role as a leader in her organisation in question in a way that troubled her deeply. Both existential narratives were very important to Bianca, and together, they formed the meaning structures for her "being in the world" (Heidegger, 1962). The challenge of the coaching dialogue was to find a way to reconcile and align these in a way that would work for both Bianca and her business.

The purpose of the coaching process here was to see if there was (and there may not have been) a way to authentically script a new meaning narrative that supported Bianca to work on the account without compromising her personal value system. If this was possible, success would be promoted for both her and the organisation.

It is important to see that because this is business coaching, and not counselling, the business objective of getting Bianca to work on the account significantly influenced the process. Not only was this not an ethical failure, it was an ethical requirement. If the coach had not influenced the process in this way, he or she would have been out of integrity with the organisation as a client because the coach would not have been working in its interests. At the same time, the coach must equally work in the individual client's interests. This means that in this kind of process, coaches need to be up-front with their intentions to seek a way to "make this work for both". They should also make it clear that they are committed to an outcome that supports the inner world of the individual just as much as the organisation's business objectives. In counselling, business objectives would be a second-level priority at best, and may not feature at all.

The first step with Bianca was to expose all the meaning narratives in the situation, and break them down into their essential meaning structures. Second, the coach brought these meaning structures into relationship with each other to see if there was a way to build a new narrative that incorporated all of them, authentically. The process looked like this:

a. Not killing animals: deeper meaning structure was to help the world transform into a place where humans helped each other and lived in harmony with all living things.

b. Loyalty and duty to her company and profession: deeper meaning structure was based in the notion of living in a world where people worked together, sharing and leveraged their skills as a community; where individual's needs were not more important than collective needs.

c. Leadership: deeper meaning structure based in the notion that she had a responsibility to model both of the above for others, and that this responsibility extended to a duty to protect and support the organisation she had participated in building.

Through several coaching sessions, Bianca explored the conversation between these meaning-making narratives in light of the challenge of working on the fast-food account. The purpose was to find a way to get them to all work together so that she could work on the account without feeling morally compromised. Bianca and her coach agreed that achieving such may not be possible, but that "it was sure worth a try for a win win".

Eventually, Bianca was indeed able to locate a script that pro- vided existential comfort to her for working on the fast-food chicken account. She had investigated the company in question in more detail between sessions and spent time with the CEO trying to understand the company's underlying value system. She discovered that it was very active in corporate social responsibility in Africa, leading the way with several impactful initiatives uplifting poor communities. They were also heavily involved in sponsoring the fight against malaria. She was moved by the passion of the CEO to make a difference for the con- tinent and experienced him to have many personal values kin to her own. These discoveries helped her reconcile her existential dilemma in that although her skills were going to be used to support the fast food world, they were also going to support significant and important initiatives to help people in need across the continent. Existentially, she found that the moral directive from the one somehow was enough to offset her deep discomfort with the other. She did wonder to what extent she was "kidding [herself]" and spent a session exploring that possibility too. But all things being equal, she got to a place where she "would rather work on the account than not, and that made the difference".

Bianca's existential triumph speaks to the father of existential analy- sis, Victor Frankl's, work. He references Nietzsche's *Twilight of the Idols*

(1889) in his classic *Man's Search for Meaning* (1984): "He who has a why to live for, can bear almost any how" (p. 126). From an existential perspective, business coaching can help people locate a "why" so as to positively engage with the business task at hand. This is because, as Frankl explains, ultimately, a human being should not ask what the meaning of his or her life is, but rather must recognise that it is he or she who is asked (ibid.). In this sense, we are empowered to make our own meaning rather than discover it hiding away inside us somewhere in the form of some absolute personal truth.

Not only does meaning allow us to "bear almost any how", but it goes much further. Martin Seligman (2004), a father of the field of positive psychology, talks about the power of a "meaningful life" (p. 260) where one uses one's signature strength in service to a world pregnant with meaning and filled with a sense of the sacred. Seligman suggests that those individuals who do this in their work are likely to experience a deep sense of well-being and as a result be considerably more productive and effective. This has been confirmed in research, for example, in a cross-sectional review of relevant studies, Lyubomirsky et al. (2005) report that the evidence repeatedly reveals that people high in subjective well-being are more likely to secure job interviews, be evaluated more positively by supervisors, show superior performance and productivity, and handle managerial jobs better. They are also less likely to show counter-productive workplace behaviour and are less vulnerable to burnout. This means that when an individual locates a purpose and meaning narrative that aligns well with the work that they do, not only is well-being fostered, but there are often significant corresponding benefits for the business in the form of increased productivity and effectiveness.

Individual goals and expectations

Although it is often the organisation's voice (even when expressed by the individual) that articulates expectations of coaching in the form of business expectations, the individual's personal goals and desires are equally important. And just as the coach needs to test assumptions underlying the origin of goals in the organisational context as discussed in Chapter Five under "Environmental goals", so too must the coach unpack assumptions underlying the individual's point of view. So, answers to questions such as: "What do you want to achieve personally in this coaching process?" need to be probed more deeply. In this regard, a coach might ask some of the following questions:

1. How will achieving this be important? What makes you think this is something you need?
2. What or who influenced you to set this as a goal?
3. To what extent is this goal what you want or what others want from you?
4. How does this goal fit in with what you want from your work and life?
5. Have you worked on this before? If so, how and where and what happened?
6. What else are you doing to achieve this? How will coaching align with that?
7. Who is supporting you? How can we align this coaching process with them?
8. How do you know that coaching is the modality you need to achieve this? Could other interventions like training, mentoring or workplace exposure be more suited?
9. Are there other related things that you need to work on? What are they?
10. To what extent do your personal goals align with the organisation's expectations of you? And how do you know this?

Sometimes, asking these questions can unlock fairly deep reflection for an individual. For example, Doug came to coaching with a clear sense of what he wanted from the process. "I am here to improve my leadership abilities as part of the leadership development journey I am on with the company." When his coach asked him what he wanted from the process *personally*, he seemed confused. "What do you mean? I want to be a better leader." The coach explained: "Yes, wanting to be a better leader is part of the organisational expectation of you in your role, and is therefore critically important for us to focus on. I was, however, also wondering about you as the unique person that is taking up this role, with your personal story that brought you to this point in your life. From that place, what is it that you would like from this coaching process for yourself?" Doug sat quietly for some time, clearly in a state of deep reflection. Finally he said: "You know, I've never really thought about it like that before. I mean I always just put myself aside in a way. I've kind of forgotten about what I really want for myself I guess. I just make what the company wants from me as what I want. Am I actually allowed to even go there in this process?" The coach replied: "I don't know, are you?" Doug again sat in quiet reflection. "Wow, I just realised how far away I have been from myself. You know, I've never really asked myself why I want to be a better leader for myself." The coach asked: "Okay. Why do you want to be a better leader for yourself?" More quiet. "You know when I was a boy I never really led anything. I was always following others. And it was okay, I guess. But I watched the other boys who led the group and I envied them. I mean why I couldn't be like that. Today I get to lead others at [company name] and I am one of those boys I envied. But the thing is ... [quiet] ... I not sure I am up to it ... And I really need to be up to it for myself. Do you get what I mean?" "Yes. It sounds like wanting to be a better leader is not just about meeting company expectations and facilitating career development for you. It sounds like wanting to be a better leader is something important for you inside, something that has been at play for you since you were a child." "Yes! Exactly!" Doug replied. "Jeez! I didn't even realise how important this was to me just until now ... OK ... where do we start?"

Individual sources of data

Important and relevant information about an individual is offered continually throughout a coaching process: in their bodies—the way they dress, the way they move, the way they look; in their voice—the way they speak, the words they choose, the tone they use; in their eye contact and handshake; in the way they make agreements about times and dates, the way they answer their phone and the messages they leave on yours; in the choice of car they drive, the family they have, the school their children attend, the friends and colleagues they enjoy; and in everything they do and say. A coach needs to attune to these because important data live in the nuances and signals an individual gives off all the time. For example, a person who never seems to answer their phone when the coach calls but interrupts coaching sessions to take personal calls might tell us something about where coaching fits in their priorities. That is powerful information and is unlikely to be found in a document or psychometric profile. Or a person who consistently shows up late to coaching, and waits until the last five minutes of the session to mention difficult events of the past week, may tell us something about the way he or she manages challenging experiences. Or, the fact that after a few months of coaching a person changes the way he or she dresses may tell us something about an internal psychological change.

In the same way that data can be gleaned from above and below the surface in the environmental dimension, so too in the individual dimension. And again, the same principles apply where surface data are often the least valuable, reflecting only the "tip of the iceberg". Nevertheless, hard individual data sources may prove useful, and coach and client can explore these as a whole, looking for narratives that help clarify what success might look like for the individual.

Examples of hard data sources that inform the coaching process in this dimension are documents reflecting an individual's work history (both prior and within the existing organisation), a résumé, and any psychometric profiles and associated assessments on hand. And as with the environmental dimension, these need to be seen, alongside data from below the surface, as a whole.

A caution on using psychometrics in business coaching

It is worth cautioning coaches on drawing too much on psychometrics that profile an individual against a set of norms. First, as discussed earlier, business coaching is a relational engagement based in dialogue as opposed to an objective evaluation of an individual. Psychometric assessments are just that—assessments. They offer a measurement of an individual compared to others in the world.

Profiling has a tendency to introduce several problematic psychosocial phenomena into the coaching process. If the coach is not careful he or she can easily become an agent of measurement and drive the coaching dialogue into a "How good or bad am I compared to my colleagues?" narrative. This moves the conversation away from a relational orientation into a remedial one characteristic of the culture of science, where a person is located on a normal distribution curve to determine to what extent they are normal or healthy. From a systems thinking point of view, psychometric assessments tend to be blind to the unique relational system the individual being measured exists within. In other words, the *shih* or *smell of the place* (as described in the previous chapter) is excluded from the picture. Psychometric assessments tend to focus on "elements of the intrapersonal system of the client [as opposed to interpersonal], such as ability, personality, self-concept, and/or aptitude" (Patton & McMahon, 2006, p. 155). Also, another problem is that part of the role of the coach becomes "to administer assessment instruments, interpret the results, and convey them to the client", which portrays "the role of the [coach] as one of an expert who would tell a client what to do" (ibid.).

As discussed in earlier chapters, in business coaching the focus is not about whether an individual is good or bad, healthy or sick, normal or abnormal. Rather, it is about the extent to which a particular individual in a particular organisational context creates relationship in a way that works for the business. In other words, the question should be: "Does it work for the business as a whole for you to show up in this way in your role in this context?" And not: "Are you better, healthier or cleverer, emotionally or cognitively, than your colleagues?"

Consider Winston Churchill: how would he have fared on a set of psychometric profiles? He is offered as one of the greatest leaders of the twenty-first century, and the most diversely gifted man in British politics (Best, 2003; Langworth, 2008). However, Churchill was also reported to be a very difficult and rather troubled individual, suffering from severe mood swings and rash decision-making, all made worse by alcohol dependence and lifestyle excesses (Andreasen, 2008; Best, 2003; Moran, 1966). How would he have shown up on a psychometric profile as compared to his colleagues of the time? It seems rather that Churchill's success was more about the particular context of war being a good relational fit for him at the time (Best, 2003; D'Este, 2008)—the *shih* was correct. This in contrast to him scoring the highest points on any hypothetical profile compared to colleagues of his day. All things being equal, one wonders if Churchill would have stood out at all had he been objectively assessed using current popular psychometric instruments.

In this view, assessment tools, if used poorly, can distract from the purpose of business coaching rather than assist. For this reason, coaches should be careful when employing them. To be clear, assessments can and do assist as data sources in business coaching process, but the way they are used needs to be very carefully considered. The following guidelines are therefore suggested:

1. An assessment is only valuable to the extent that it ignites an insightful dialogue that gives rise to awareness. The tool in itself is not valuable to coaching as a standalone.
2. Any assessment tool is limited by its design, constraints, theoretical model and the underlying cultural assumptions that influence it. It is

therefore *a* voice, not *the* voice, among many, and does not hold the primary wisdom or truth about the individual. The individual's own narrative about themselves is always to be regarded as primary by the coach; all other voices, including assessments, are simply others from the environment with which to form relationship.

3. Although all assessments are based in scales and mathematics, avoid assessments that lack descriptive narratives and just provide scores and graphs. These force the coach into the role of assessor; he or she becomes an interpreter of scores rather than coach. It's less problematic when the tool provides a narrative that coach and client, as thinking partners, can explore. The tool then becomes a voice from the environment that can be considered by the coaching dyad along with all the other environmental opinions, and is not elevated into a higher level of truth or meaning than, for example, a colleague's personal feedback.

4. From a coaching point of view, qualitative feedback from colleagues is to be regarded as potentially more powerful material than that gleaned from an assessment as it exists in the context of a real relationship and can therefore be processed more easily. Unfortunately, this is not possible with an assessment. For example, one can't ask an assessment report some key questions: "How do you know this about me?" "What behaviour of mine gives this impression; please give me a real example?" "What is the context for this feedback?" And finally, "From what point of view are you seeing me?"

5. Avoid introducing an assessment tool if you don't need to. There is usually more than enough feedback in an environment for the client to work with. However, should one, for whatever reason, wish to use an assessment, it is preferable to introduce it later in the coaching process rather than earlier. Early introduction of an assessment tool has formative influence on the nature of the relationship between coach and client (both individual and organisation), tending to position the coach as an "expert" and "agent of objectivity". This is counterproductive to the power relations that underpin the nature of healthy dialogue, which is better when there is a sense that all parties "do not know" and discover together. Introducing the tool later in the coaching process goes some way, but not the whole way, to counteracting this phenomenon, as a more equitable power relation will already

have been established prior to its introduction. It can then be more easily positioned as per point one and two.

Individual sources of theory

The theoretical frameworks that inform this dimension explain the way human beings perceive and behave as a function of their psychosocial history, personality and neurology. This is an enormous field, and below are a few classic examples as well as some current literature:

- *Individual psychology and relevant philosophy* such as psychodynamic psychology (Corsini & Wedding, 2008; Malan, 1995), humanistic psychology (Bridges, 2004; Schneider et al., 2001), behaviourism (Rachlin, 1991; Woollard, 2010), existentialism (Frankl, 1984; Schneider, 2008; Spinelli, 1989), narrative psychology (Sarbin, 1986; White, 2007), Jungian psychology (Hauke, 2005; Jung, 1965, 1996; Stevens, 1994), and integral theory (Wilber, 2000, 2006), to name but a few.
- *Fields studying optimal human functioning and related neuroscience* such as neuro-linguistic programming (Bandler, Grinder, & Stevens, 1979; Burn, 2005; Mathison & Tosey, 2010), positive psychology (Csikszentmihalyi, 1990; Peterson, 2006; Seligman, 2004), the brain and behaviour (Alexandrov & Martone, 2013; Page & Rock, 2009), and the related field of NeuroLeadership (Ringleb & Rock, 2009), as well as the whole field of emotional intelligence (Bar-On & Parker, 2000; Goleman, 2005).
- *Theories that help to understand social and cultural identity, and particularly those that address issues of diversity and power relations in the workplace.* For example, Arnold Mindell's process-orientated psychology (Mindell, 1995, 2000, 2002), Valerie Batt's work on modern "isms" (Batts, 1982, 1998, 2002), and any literature addressing the experiences of various target groups in the workplace, such as Sandberg (2013) on gender, Alleyne (2004) on race, and Raeburn (2004) on sexual orientation. It is worth noting that this level of theoretical input speaks as much to the environmental dimension as it does to the individual dimension. This is because, as discussed in this chapter, the relationship between an individual's social or cultural identity and the corresponding nature of the environment they find themselves in, mediates the degree of power they possess in that context.

- *Theories of personality* (Crowne, 2010; von Fanz & Hillman, 1991) including literature on commonly used personality assessments in the workplace such as the Myers-Briggs Type Indicator (Hirsh, 1985), the Insights® Discovery Profile (Benton et al., 2005), and assessments for the Big Five Factor model of personality (Costa & McCrae, 1992; McCrae & Costa, 1987).
- *Adult learning theory* (Kolb, 1984; Merriam et al., 2006) and related learning styles assessments (Kolb & Kolb, 2005).

CHAPTER SEVEN

The coaching relationship

The coaching relationship constitutes the centre of the coaching axis, and is its core. This dimension brings the individual and the environment into dialogue in a way that promotes alignment, integration, and improved performance. As Oliver (2010) explains: "A systemic orientation to coaching highlights the detail of coach/ client conversation as a core site of interest and as the place for analysis and the beginnings of change" (p. 108).

In the metaphor of the tree, the trunk, which connects the roots with the branches and leaves, symbolises the coaching relationship. This is used to reflect the idea of an "axis" where the continual focus is relationship between the parts—the individual (roots) and the environment (branches and leaves). A tree trunk channels nourishment in both directions, first, facilitating energy from photosynthesis in the leaves down to the roots and, second, channelling nourishment from the soil through the roots up into the branches and leaves (Evans, 2000). Similarly, the coaching relationship facilitates a conversation between the reality of the environment and the reality of the individual with the aim of potentiating a mutually constructed and shared reality that facilitates the success of both. And it does this through the coaching relationship. At one level, this is about the exchange and brokering of needs, but at a more profound level this is about creating a shared, inter-subjective, narrative that potentiates success holistically and systemically. In other words, the roots have their story and so do the branches and leaves, but the real story is the story of the tree as a whole which creates the realisation of potential for both, and in so doing the entire tree enjoys success. In this sense, it may be helpful to look at the trunk as being both part of the branches *and* the roots. The roots merge into the trunk, and the trunk merges with the branches. From the point of view of the coaching relationship, this reflects the notion that the organisation and the individual are not perfectly distinct; there is level at which the organisation is as much part of the individual as the individual is part of the organisation.

Working with purpose in the coaching relationship

Given that business coaching is born from the desire of both the environment and the individual to exist in an improved state of relationship, coaching goals may be seen as expressions of a call to relationship between the two. In this sense, a business coach works with the underlying purpose of the coaching engagement as the first opportunity to facilitate alignment and integration on the axis between the parties. This is because coaching goals often signal gaps or obstacles in their relationship. Coaching then involves practically taking the goals expressed in the environmental dimension and bringing them into conversation with those expressed in the individual dimension. This axial process facilitates alignment and integration between individual and organisational expectations and needs, capturing such in a common purpose that is both clear and mutually beneficial.

This is where the power of the "coaching axis" is often first observed to add real business value. This is because it acts to potentiate integration and alignment between an individual and their environment in a way that is difficult to see or achieve in the common course of business. It offers the opportunity for the individual and the organisation to co-script a mutually beneficial sense of purpose that emerges as a course of the dialogue across the coaching axis. To illustrate this, consider these three examples and the discussion that follows:

1. Wendy, a newly appointed executive, offered this to her new coach as a goal: "Since I've been promoted to executive, my manager

suggested that I need to move from a management mindset to more of a leadership mindset to be successful." Here the need is to shift something on the individual dimension, namely Wendy's *management mindset*, to meet an expectation on the environmental dimension, namely *leadership mindset*.

2. An OD consultant, Maria, expressed this to a coach: "Michael is emotionally very hard. He speaks without thinking about how others feel. Technically he is great, but when it comes to people his relationships are poor. In our culture, we believe in listening to others even when you disagree. Can you help with coaching?" Again, the environment calls for the individual to behave in alignment with certain *behavioural requirements* based in the organisation's culture, and looks to coaching to facilitate this alignment.

3. It might also be the case that an individual calls for the environment to shift according to his or her individual views. An example of this was when Frank, a new leader, arrived with a vision for his department: "These guys are behind the times. I need you to help me think through and implement *my new vision* for this department."

In all three of the above examples, something important is missing. That is a dialogue that processes the alignment of these goals between the individual and environmental dimensions.

In the first example around shifting to a leadership mindset, even though Wendy offered the goal, she shared it from the environment's perspective. Coaching questions to her were: "What are your personal thoughts about this goal? To what extent do you agree that this is something you need to do to achieve success?" These questions use the axis to interrogate the purpose of the coaching facilitating an authentic and meaningful exchange between dimensions. This is the trunk of the tree, exchanging energy from the leaves with nourishment from the roots in service to the overall success of the tree as a whole.

It turned out that Wendy privately didn't buy in to the idea that changing her mindset was necessary for success, and she had not shared this with her manager for fear that she would not be heard. The coaching dialogue's first step was to help Wendy focus on the nature of her relationship with her manager, and in view of that, how she might have the necessary conversation with him to achieve understanding and alignment. Wendy subsequently found the words and the courage to engage her manager. She discussed with him what she truly believed she needed to do to succeed in her new role. Both Wendy and her manager learned some things about each other and their environment in that dialogue which helped them better understand what was required for success. In Wendy's case, the purpose of her coaching was changed and mutually agreed as follows: "Help Wendy understand how she can build her relationships with three key stakeholders that control and influence the department in both subtle and overt ways." The notion of management and leadership mindsets disappeared from the coaching radar, and was replaced with a goal that was more clearly focused on what makes a difference in that business. Most importantly this was mutually agreed between the parties in the system. Furthermore, the by-product of the process was greater rapport, more trust and better understanding between Wendy and her manager. It's worth mentioning that at that point in the process her manager commented to the coach: "You already added so much value in getting us aligned and coaching hasn't even started yet." Well of course, it had.

In the second example, a range of behavioural criticisms had been levelled at Michael by the OD consultant, Maria. Coaching was sought to "help" him change accordingly. Some questions to Maria were: "Where does this feedback originate? Has it been shared with Michael, and how did he respond?" Here the coach is testing several axial concerns, first, the relational origin and context of the feedback underpinning the desired goal (as discussed in Chapter Five under the sections about feedback). Second, the extent to which the organisation has shared its discontent with the individual, and the history of that interaction as well as the quality of relationships between Michael and his environment are being gleaned.

Maria answered as follows: "Oh, Michael and I get on famously. I have had several discussions with him and he accepts that he has a behavioural problem. Even his manager agrees." But when the coach asked Michael about this he said: "Nobody has ever given me this feedback. The only thing that Maria in OD told me was that I should try and listen to others a bit more and not run ahead of everyone, and you will help me with that. My manager says that I am performing well, so I don't know what the big issue is." When the coach telephoned Michael's manager for direction he said: "I can't afford to lose Michael, he is technically my best guy. I do think that Michael could increase his EQ a bit, but please go easy on him. OD can be a little dramatic at times. Others in the team wish they could deliver like Michael does."

The axial work here required the facilitation of agreement between the individual and his organisation around the purpose of coaching. In Michael's case, the coach suggested facilitating a "coaching goal-setting" discussion between Michael, his manager, and OD. This axial dialogue not only ended up reformulating the coaching goal in a mutually aligned way, but raised a range of important insights for Michael's manager and Maria about the team dynamics in that area. Once these had been shared and discussed from all three perspectives, Michael's original coaching objectives seemed less severe in the context of the team's systemic story. This was because it emerged that he modelled some valuable behaviour around work ethic and emotional resilience that others in the team were lacking and which underpinned their lower levels of productivity. So, although the coaching did proceed with a focus on Michael's emotional intelligence and capacity to relate better with others in the team, several important things had changed from the initial goal-setting moment. First, Michael was on board with the process because he felt seen by both his manager and OD as a result of a more complete and balanced perspective achieved in the axial conversation. Second, although coaching was there to help him improve his ability to relate better with his colleagues, the direction of the coaching was more about how he should "not throw the baby out with the bath water" in the course of this learning. This meant that a part of his so-called "emotional hardness" was also valued as an asset to the business as it was acknowledged that there were others in the team who needed some of that emotional resilience to improve their business performance. It was just that he was always emotionally hard and he needed to see that some contexts required sensitivity. And third, for the organisation as a whole, Michael's manager and OD became more aligned about what was needed from a team point of view to increase productivity, and they designed a team intervention based on this new appreciation that came from that single conversation.

In the third example, the coaching relationship's purpose was originally conceived to help Frank, a new leader, realise his vision for the business. Here, the coaching axis appears to work in the other direction, seeking to attune the leader to his environment. However, conceptually, the axis always works bi-directionally, irrespective of the point of departure. Frank's coach explored the extent to which he had properly engaged, understood, and considered the existing vision of his department and its systemic history in the process of coming to imagine that they were "living in the past". He asked Frank the following: "What has given you the impression that they need to change in this way?" Frank's response centred more around anecdotal interactions with one or two of his direct reports concerning "the way they think". He was short on a more in-depth appreciation of these individuals' history in the company and, more importantly, had spent little time getting to know them as people. The coach wondered aloud about whether or not Frank was ready to "make a call" about how others were thinking in his business. This is an axial technique that invites the individual to consider the extent to which his or her assumptions are based in real relational or systemic appreciation, or perhaps he or she has jumped to conclusions prematurely. It also hints that relationship is probably lacking between Frank and his colleagues and that this is undesirable. Again, determining the purpose of the coaching is used here as an opportunity to increase alignment and understanding between the dimensions.

In Frank's case, he created some actions to test his "read on the environment" before committing to driving a new vision for the company, and of course, setting this as a goal for the coaching. In this sense, a new set of goals emerged initially, such as: spend some time with my direct reports getting to know them and building a sense of relationship and, during that process, learn about their history and perspective in the company, as well as be open to reformulating initial impressions that they "are living in the past".

In the following coaching session, Frank was a different man. He explained that he "had got this place completely wrong", and that "the guys [he] thought were living in the past were actually filled with institutional memory that was critical to not repeating mistakes". He reviewed his vision for the business in both process and content, deciding to rather "build a vision together with my team rather than creating one myself and asking them to implement it". The purpose of coaching was then reworked to focus on how Frank could approach this as a task in the months that followed.

This example again illustrates the power of the axis in working with coaching purpose not only as a means of shifting mindset, but also as a relationship-building process in itself. Consider how differently Frank's direct reports would have felt about him as a new leader had he taken the initial approach about implementing a vision to change "old ways of thinking". Compare that to how they must have felt about the collaborative approach he eventually decided to go with. And, even more importantly, consider the effect on the performance of the business between the former and the latter.

The three examples above illustrate that adopting an axial approach to working with the purpose of business coaching serves to "promote the success of the organisation as a whole by affecting the actions of those being coached" (WABC, 2007). Where coaches fail to work in this way, they tend to take direction for the coaching from only one of the dimensions. This means they sometimes end up blindly facilitating a process that is at odds with the business as a whole, and that may undermine the relationships in the system, negatively impacting performance. To appreciate this, consider the three examples above and think about the effect on the business and the individuals' relationships had coaching proceeded without aligning their respective goals. Coaches are particularly vulnerable to making this fundamental mistake when they hold an "individual-centric" approach to their work as result of the profound influence of the human sciences, especially counselling practices, on business coaching, as discussed in earlier chapters.

Goals are compasses not destinations

Because the reality of a marketplace is ever changing, the nature of a good business is flexible and responsive. This means that things change at an organisational level all the time and are rather unpredictable. Similarly, a person's life circumstances change and their inner worlds adjust accordingly in unpredictable ways. As a result it is important to see goals in a dynamic perspective when working as a business coach.

What this means is that goals that were set at the initiation of the coaching process must be continually revisited by the individual and with the organisation during the process. In this sense, a coaching goal should not be viewed like a fixed objective at the end of a project plan, but rather as a point of direction which guides the coaching dialogue in each conversation. So rather than seeing the goal as a destination for the ship, it is better to see the goal as the ship's compass in an eternal voyage that has no single destination and which changes depending on the weather encountered.

In view of this dynamic, the systemically agreed outcomes (between the dimensions) against which the coaching is to be measured, and which are central to the coaching relationship, change over the course of the coaching process. Therefore coaches need to continuously test and, where necessary, re-contract the purpose and/or goals of a coaching assignment as it progresses. Failure to do so may result in the fundamental integrity of the coaching axis becoming destabilised and success therefore compromised.

For example, remember Derek's story, described in Chapter Five under "Uncovering the individual's relational system", in which the original goal set for coaching was to "help him not be a control freak". Recall how once the relational system and history of the environment had been explored in terms of this purpose it emerged that control issues were not relevant to the case, and that in fact a very different trajectory needed to be followed to ensure a successful coaching intervention. This is a good example of how the purpose of coaching moves, and needs to be re-contracted on an as-needs and on-going basis. Similarly, in all three cases described earlier in this chapter, Wendy, Michael, and Frank subsequently reframed or, in Wendy's case, totally changed, the initial goals set for their coaching engagements.

Reflexive awareness—an axial imperative

Purpose and goals are not the only aspect of coaching that needs to be dialogued across the coaching axis. Indeed, the entire coaching journey needs to be continually processed across the coaching axis. This means that the level of alignment between insights and related actions from the individual's perspective and the requirements, expectations and cultural norms from the organisation's perspective need to be continually tested and reframed for agreement between the two. This is one of the imperatives of the Coaching on the Axis approach.

For example, a person may think that the solution to reducing work stress is to improve work-life balance by reducing working hours; however, the organisation may reject this as a solution. In considering this axial imperative, "it is useful to think in terms of reactive or reflexive patterns" (Oliver, 2010, p. 118). Huffington and Hieker (2006) offer the technique of circular and reflexive questioning as a means of achieving this in coaching practice. For example, a circular question might be: "If you reduce your hours how would this change impact the tasks and responsibilities of others, and to what extent will it set a precedent in the organisation?" And a reflexive question would be: "Let's imagine how your manager will feel when you ask her to reduce your hours, can we appreciate what that might bring up for her?" Or, "Can we imagine into the future a little and consider how you might feel going home early and leaving your colleagues at work, especially when the pressure is on?" This type of questioning creates an axial perspective empowering the individual to think systemically, and opens the way for a mutually beneficial outcome that serves both the individual and the organisation.

This means that insights achieved by individuals in coaching sessions are not necessarily viable unless they are also insights for the organisation. For example: An individual has an insight that he is thinking about his tasks in the wrong way but when he tests this with his manager, she rejects the insight and suggests that the obstacle lies not in the way he is thinking but rather in the way he is implementing. Without this systemic test across the coaching axis, the process may embark on a set of actions that lead to a cul-de-sac or worse; working against the organsational need.

The axis connects coaching with business reality

As discussed earlier, human science culture, specifically that of counselling practice, can influence coaches to adopt a curative and individual-centric approach to their work in which the primary objective is to improve the psychological health and general well-being of individuals. This is not always in alignment with the primary purpose of business coaching which is to improve business performance.

The work of a business coach is to focus on the degree to which an individual and the organisation work together in service to increasing business performance. In this perspective, the general health and well-being of an individual is not the primary focus, although it may be a secondary or adjunct one. In other words, this is not to say that improved health and well-being will not occur as a result of business coaching, on the contrary, it is likely that positive personal and interpersonal change will result as a course of a coaching intervention. But rather, that any health and well-being agenda must be specific and targeted towards the real purpose of business coaching which is to achieve meaningful business results. This can only be done where any individual transformation is properly linked with business expectations and firmly located in a business context. The improvement of a person's psychological or physical life cannot be an objective in itself because it is quite possible to have individual benefit from personal transformation through coaching which has little or no direct and meaningful connection with business results. Many coaches will attest to the fact a good deal of coaching dialogue can at times wander off into personal exploration that has a tenuous link, at best, to the business context at hand, but seems important to the individual in the moment.

Unfortunately, the notion that "anything that is good for the individual is good for the company" is problematic. This is because the idea that a more integrated and happy person will *always* make for a better employee is simply a rationalisation blind to the culture of business. Shareholders would never vote to support long-term spend on interventions that have such a flimsy narrative for a return on investment, and understandably so. As a CEO of a London listed resources business explained: "We are not here to do therapy!" (personal communication, name and organisation withheld, 18 August 2013). The suggestion here is that, although good coaching may be delivered where there is a win for the individual but none for the business, that is not business coaching. Business coaching is about business; otherwise it is unacceptable, possibly even unethical, for business to pay for coaching that is failing to deliver clear business outcomes and for which there is no obvious return on investment. This excludes situations where the individual is seeking life coaching, not business coaching, and hoping that the business will pay for this. This kind of request is probably best dealt with through another type of service other than business coaching, such as through an employee assistance programme, where business results are not the purpose, but rather the business pays for this as part of its health-care duty to its staff out of a prescribed budget.

The Coaching on the Axis' relational orientation ensures that the outcomes of business coaching are continuously linked to better business. It does this by focusing all aspects of the coaching dialogue on an individual's relationship with the business environment. The axial question foundational to the coaching relationship in this regard is:

> What do we need to work on to improve your relationship with this environment that improves business performance?

When the answer to this requires deep and meaningful personal transformation then business coaching is in integrity with its purpose to work towards this. However, the course of this personal transformation must at all times be firmly linked to clear and measurable business results, and most importantly, be agreed between the individual and the organisation sanctioning the service.

From this perspective, change and transformation may not always feature as a matter of course. The axial focus opens the door to occasional coaching outcomes that are not about change, but may be about acceptance of what is; letting go of the expectation of something different for both the individual and the environment and appreciating the value of what is already there. Or for that matter, the process could focus tactically on a set of simple actions or superficial behaviours, a process of decision-making or an organising of thoughts, none of which shift or transform the person psychologically in any profound way but do create impactful business results.

The axis helps avoid pathology-based orientations

The Coaching on the Axis's relational approach offers important methodological protection from pathology-based orientations.

Pathology-based coaching orientations occur in two ways:

1. where individuals are marked as bad, sick, or deviant and the coach is asked to "fix" them;
2. where organisations or systems are marked as sick or disturbed, and individuals use a coach as an agony aunt, complaints department, or ally in their fight against them.

Most coaches will attest to the frequency with which they are asked to assist organisations in dealing with a "difficult" individual. Coaching is especially sought in cases where the person is regarded as valuable to the company but nevertheless the cause of discontent or difficulty when it comes to their relations with others. And indeed, coaching is often an appropriate modality to use in such matters. Unfortunately, in these cases, there is a tendency for people to occasionally mark such an individual as pathological or psychosocially deviant in some way.

For example, it is not uncommon to hear something like this: "David is a particularly brilliant salesman. Probably one of our best. However, he is a real problem for the rest of the team. He is arrogant and lacks compassion, and he refuses to collaborate with others. Quite a few of the team say he is a narcissist. Personally, I think he has got some real psychological problems—bit of a 'head-case' if you'll excuse the expression. Have you ever heard of 'toxic' employees? Anyway, do you think you can help him change?" Coaches who fail to take a relational approach based in the culture of business may end up colluding with this type of 'pathologising' of an individual. Furthermore, the influence of counselling and psychotherapy on the practice of coaching can render some coaches more vulnerable to accepting curative or remedial invitations like this. In such cases, they would eagerly embark on a coaching intervention which would try to heal or transform David into a more digestible character for the likes of his team. And in the process, no doubt, such coaches would probably avoid sharing their 'diagnosis' with David, opting to couch it (pun intended) in more subtle or disguised language.

However, in adopting the Coaching on the Axis approach, one would address this coaching request in a very different manner. First, whether or not David suffers from narcissism, or any other psychopathology for that matter, or whether or not he is a "toxic (sic) employee" (Benoit, 2011), is not the focus. He may or may not be. The focus is rather the degree to which David and his organisation are able to find relationship that works for both. The response to this request is therefore to identify the relational disconnect between the individual and the environment without applying a psychopathological lens, and then work to improve that relationship. What that means is a response such as this: "It seems that you and others in the organisation are having difficulty relating with David, despite the fact that he achieves such high sales figures. The relationship with David must be pretty poor because it's got to the point where people are suggesting he suffers from some kind of mental illness. Can we perhaps move away from diagnosing him with something clinical at this stage and rather see if we can accurately describe examples of how he and the environment negatively interact at an interpersonal level. We can then sit with David and share this feedback with him. We will also be able to hear how he experiences the environment from his side. This process will lay the foundation for me as the coach to openly and honestly assist David and the team in finding a better way of relating that promotes success for both."

Naturally, there are many occasions in which the psychological health of a person may hamper his or her ability to work, however in such cases business coaching is not the modality to be used. Rather, referral to an appropriately trained mental health professional is required. If David wanted to address any psychopathology he may, or may not, be suffering from, he would receive more appropriate treatment from a psychologist or psychiatrist than a business coach. In fact, for a business coach to attempt to address real mental health problems would be unethical. Studies show that in Western countries almost twenty-five per cent of people experience a mental illness within any twelve-month period, about half the workforce manifests a diagnosable mental illness at some stage in their careers, and mental illness accounts for more days lost in the workplace than any other medical condition (Australian Bureau of Statistics, 2007; Center for Mental Health in the Workplace, 2013; National Institute of Mental Health, 2013). It is therefore likely that people and organisations will inadvertently seek business coaching to deal with mental health problems that should actually be referred to mental health care professionals who are properly trained and ethically contracted to attend to such. Indeed, it is very important for coaches to understand when to redirect requests for coaching that would be better suited to treatment from a mental health care practitioner. In David's case, this was not necessary, because once the coach established the axial approach described above, the nature of the difficulty was reframed. This led to a fruitful dialogue with David, and later between David and his colleagues, who were then able to share their behavioural expectations of each other in a way that had not previously occurred. The arrival of this missing conversation for the team fostered a better working environment for all, and David's supposed psychopathology disappeared from the narrative. In contrast, in another case, the same coach referred the client to a local clinical psychologist when asked to work with a different individual in the same organisation. This individual appeared to be suffering from significant mental health issues which disabled them from constructively participating in coaching dialogues and from being able to process or manage the dynamics of the organisation without becoming completely overwhelmed and distressed.

The converse of David's story may also play out. This occurs where the organisation is accused by the individual as being disturbed, sick, unethical, or immoral. For example, Eric, a middle-level manager in a large pharmaceutical corporation, shared this in his first coaching session: "This company is not transparent about decisions. Leaders work against you to promote themselves. Most of them are bullies and they support each other. This is a 'toxic company' (Sylvestre-Williams, 2012). There are some very disturbed things that go on in this place. People don't have integrity and lie all the time to cover things up. I have been a victim of this kind of abuse." Here the coach found that he was being coopted, consciously and unconsciously, into being an agony aunt or complaints department for Eric. He said that he felt that Eric was drawing him in "as an ally in the fight against the evil empire".

This is not to say that all organisations are healthy and safe places. Most of us are acutely aware of the sad list of unethical companies that have destroyed value and, along with it, many people's lives. From the fall of the Medici Bank in 1494, to the collapse of the South Sea Company in 1720, to the Great Depression of the 1930s, to the frauds of Enron in 2001, Worldcom in 2002, and HealthSouth in 2003, history has repeatedly demonstrated that organisations are as fallible and trustworthy as are human beings. And today, who can forget 15 September 2008, when the investment bank Lehman Brothers went bankrupt, the first major sign of what was to be known as the Global Financial Crisis. A crisis that threatened the systemic collapse of global financial systems and set in motion worldwide financial volatility and socio-political instability for years to come.

Nevertheless, coaches need to be particularly careful here. When people feel marginalised or excluded in an organisation, they are psychologically prone to experiencing that organisation as inherently bad in some way or form. Eric's story is similar to David's story in reverse. Just as members of David's team suggested he was mentally disturbed because they were aggravated with the ongoing interpersonal failures between David and themselves, so too is Eric jumping to "diagnose" his entire organisation as toxic and unethical because he feels frustrated and personally injured in his relationship with the company. Although there may well be occasions when a company is indeed crossing the line and full-blown whistle-blowing is required, these situations are actually very rare. This is especially true when compared to how frequently coaches are confronted with frustrated or hurt individuals who take it out on well-meaning organisations that are doing their best to manage difficult situations, and may simply have approached such in poorly considered ways. Furthermore, there are many situations in which the interpersonal relationship between manager and subordinate is strained or has broken down, and the subordinate, feeling helpless and unhappy, generalises this negative interpersonal context to the entire company.

Coaches that do not use the axial approach may find themselves unconsciously seduced into one or the other side of this irrational and often angry tension. What is important is that coaches, once again, focus their work at the centre of the axis by working relationally to avoid this. In cases where the organisation is pathologised by the individual being coached, such as with Eric, the response might look like this: "Eric, it sounds like you have been having a really hard time working here. I'm hearing that you have been disappointed with leaders, been excluded from decision-making and that your trust levels are extremely low. Can we be more specific about this? What exactly happened, when?" This invited Eric to reflect on specific examples which the coach exposed to questions that checked his assumptions and perceptions. Once this had occurred the coach enquired as to whether or not there were any areas in which Eric believed the company was doing good things or had good people. This question uncovered some positive in the organisation which further balanced his generalised negativity. This process of balancing perception about the organisation requires the coach to maintain and model an unconditional positive regard for both the individual and the organisation simultaneously by remembering that both are the client, and therefore that both deserve the same level of empathy and positive regard. From an axial perspective, at all times, coaches should offer reflections that give both the organisation and the individual the benefit of the doubt. This type of positive psychological brokering lays the foundation for improved relationship through modelling and through the provision of alternative, more constructive, possibilities of the intention of the other.

With this type of positive relational work by the coach, the coaching process is able to expose options for engagement that the individual might not have until then considered possible. In Eric's case, coaching questions exposed the option of an impartially facilitated discussion between Eric and his manager to reality-test his specific concerns—concerns that had grown devils horns in his mind over time to the extent that he had believed it impossible to raise such without him losing his job. The coach helped Eric plan his approach to the meeting with his manager through some role-playing and scenario planning which gave him the confidence he had lacked previously. Not only did this raise Eric's confidence, but the coaching process helped him find the most constructive way to articulate his concerns free from generalisations, leaps of assumption and related aggression. Fortunately, Eric's single discussion with his manager totally transformed his view that his company was "toxic", and the remainder of his coaching sessions focused largely on how he could have got himself into such a "bad head space" in the first place.

The coaching relationship below and above the surface

In the same way that the individual and environmental dimensions can be read for data that inform coaching process from both below and above the surface, so too is this the case for the coaching relationship.

Above the surface data for this dimension commonly constitutes, in the coaching contract, outlining boundaries, fees, timelines and expectations, the coaches' ethical code of practice, and any company policies or processes that affect the conduct of the coaching relationship. These are important and should be carefully considered. Some suggestions about how to build the coaching contract in an axial manner are offered at the end of this section, and there is also a piece on coaching ethics.

However, some of the most valuable data for this dimension can be gleaned from considering the less visible aspects of the coaching relationship. This level can act as a diagnostic indicator of the themes playing out between the individual and the environment. The below the surface focus here is on the quality of the coach–client relationship. This is often a matter of psychological "chemistry", and can be read in the interpersonal dynamics between coach and client. For example, in her third coaching session, Delia indicated that the reason she did not action commitments she made in her previous session was because she didn't really believe the insights that emerged and her coach had "seemed so convinced about them". The chemistry here appeared to be one in which Delia easily internalised her coach's interpretations at the expense of her own inner voice. This pattern turned out to be typical of Delia's way of relating with others in the workplace, and could be traced back through a series of relationships to childhood where her father would dominate the family with his assertiveness and intimidating intellectual ability. Delia's self-defeating pattern constellated quickly with her coach when he passionately and confidently offered interpretations in the previous session. She later realised that "it was like I was back at the dining room table as a teenager with my father".

Kemp (2008) suggests that the coach is "a central instrument in facilitating the relationship" (p. 33) and would describe the above example as "the coach's Achilles Heel" where the coach has "a tendency to overestimate the accuracy of his beliefs and opinions and to be more confident in these opinions then accurate" (p. 35). Awareness of this type of dynamic on the part of the coach can liberate insight for both parties as they explore what it means in terms of the coach and client's interpersonal patterns. It is important to remember that the coach experiences personal learning in each interaction as well, not just the individual being coached. In Delia's case, the coach and Delia were able to work with their interpersonal pattern in a way that allowed Delia to strengthen her inner voice in the face of confident others in her working environment. This only became possible after the pattern emerged between them, a pattern that had previously been invisible to both. Delia's coach also learned about himself in this experience, and became conscious of his problematic tendency to overpower his clients with his passion and tendency to over-confidently share his interpretations. It is here that one enters into the world of transference and counter-transference, where Delia and her coach may be seen to be in the midst of a powerful transference.

Transference and countertransference

Transference and countertransference are originally psychoanalytic terms that refer to the transfer of feelings, attitudes, and patterns of relating from a person or situation in the past on to a person or situation in the present (Hughes & Kerr, 2000; Racker, 2002). This transfer is unconscious, at least partly inappropriate to the present, and it reflects an aspect of the past relationship, not the entire relationship (Hughes & Kerr, 2000). Also, the person or situation "projected in the transference relationship may not be historically accurate, but is the current mental representation of a previously experienced relationship" (p. 59). Put plainly, transference is "the re-emergence of past relationships within present relationships" (de Haan, 2011, p. 190), or what the lay person might simply call "baggage".

Working with transference phenomena is an opportunity for self-understanding and personal development, as such provides a lens through which to understand how our previous relationships affect our current behaviour (de Haan, 2011). In coaching, transference offers "the promise of access to the 'shadow side' of our leadership aspirations, the aspects of ourselves and our past that propel us forward to take up certain roles and engage in certain relationships, but that are largely hidden from our own view, and barely accessible by reflection or introspection" (p. 190).

The concept was first developed by Sigmund Freud when he blamed it for certain failures in his treatment of his patient, Ida Bauer, who was suffering from Hysteria, referred to as the case of Dora (Freud, 1905e). He used the term "transference" when he recognised the arousal of feelings towards himself that related to her lover—which led to Dora's distressed and premature withdrawal from treatment (Hughes & Kerr, 2000). Freud had actually first observed the phenomenon in his previous collaboration with the physician Joseph Breuer, who became the object of intense affection from a patient, Bertha Pappenheim, referred to as the case of Anna O. Breuer was disturbed by the experience and reluctantly collaborated with Freud in their work *Studies on Hysteria* (Breuer & Freud, 1895d), which explores the case as an example of the way patients stray from professional feelings towards therapists, and the way therapists struggle with personal feelings about their patients.

Over the past century, the concepts of transference and counter-transference (the corresponding experience elicited in the therapist by the patient's transference) have enjoyed extensive investigation and application. Today, they are regarded as important phenomena in psychotherapy, counselling, organisational consulting, and coaching (e.g., De Haan, 2011; Kets de Vries, 1991; Malan, 1995; Obholzer & Roberts, 1994; Peltier, 2001). Transference has even been seen to extend across from the coach–client relationship into the coach–supervisor relationship. Harold Searles (1955) first observed this and termed it "parallel process", where transference occurs through the practitioner recreating the presenting problem and emotions of the coaching or therapeutic relationship within the supervisory relationship, and countertransference occurs when the supervisor responds to the practitioner in the same manner that the practitioner responded to his or her client. "Thus, the supervisory interaction replays, or is parallel with, the counselling [coaching] interaction" (Sumerel, 1994, p. 1). In fact, transference is not at all specific to a therapeutic or coaching context, but is a foundational phenomenon core to the human condition, as Freud himself maintained: "Transference is merely uncovered and isolated by analysis. It is a universal phenomenon of the human mind, it … dominates the whole of each person's relations to his human environment" (Freud 1925d, p. 42).

In the coaching field, many authors (e.g., Berglas, 2002; de Haan, 2011; Kahn, 2011; Palmer & Whybrow, 2007; Stober & Grant, 2006) have asserted the importance of the study of transference, both to become relationally more perceptive and to avoid very real dangers in business coaching. "Unnoticed or misperceived transference seems to lie at the root of mistakes and deterioration as reported in executive coaching relationships, such as misjudging the relationship, aggravating the status quo by collusion, the illusion of being all-powerful, or abuse of their power by coaches" (de Haan, 2011, p. 180).

To truly appreciate transference, it is worth reading some of Freud's original words on the subject:

> The patient is not satisfied with regarding the analyst in the light of reality as a helper and adviser who, moreover, is remunerated for the trouble he takes and who would himself be content with some such role as that of a guide on a difficult mountain climb. On the contrary, the patient sees in him the return, the reincarnation, of some important figure out of his childhood or past, and consequently transfers on to him feelings and reactions which undoubtedly applied to this prototype. This fact of transference soon proves to be a factor of undreamt-of importance, on the one hand an instrument of irreplaceable value and on the other hand a source of serious dangers. This transference is ambivalent: it comprises positive (affectionate) as well as negative (hostile) attitudes towards the analyst. (Freud, 1940a, p. 125)

> Another advantage of transference, too, is that in it the patient produces before us with plastic clarity an important part of his life-story, of which he would otherwise have probably given us only an insufficient account. He acts it before us, as it were, instead of reporting it to us. (p. 175)

Freud's concept of the *repetition compulsion* (Freud, 1914g) underpins transference at an intrapsychic level. The repetition compulsion occurs as a result of the mind's persistent and repeated attempts to resolve forgotten "unfinished business" from a past relationship. It does this by recreating the pattern of that relational difficulty in a current relationship in the unconscious hope of a different outcome. Unfortunately, it does this compulsively and unconsciously, as Freud explains:

> The patient does not remember anything of what he has forgotten and repressed, he acts it out, without, of course, knowing

that he is repeating it … For instance, the patient does not say that he remembers that he used to be defiant and critical toward his parents' authority; instead, he behaves in that way to the doctor. (Freud, 1914g, p. 150)

This instinctive psychological repetition is the fabric of a transference:

We soon perceive that the transference is itself only a piece of repetition, and that the repetition is a transference of the forgotten past not only on to the doctor but also on to all the other aspects of the current situation. We must be prepared to find, therefore, that the patient yields to the compulsion to repeat, which now replaces the impulsion to remember, not only in his personal attitude to his doctor but also in every other activity and relationship which may occupy his life at the time. (p. 151)

The concept of countertransference was first developed in Freud's *The Future Prospects of Psycho-Analytic Therapy* (1910d), where he described the phenomena as being the result of the patient's influence on the therapist's unconscious. Put simply, countertransference is the experience evoked in a practitioner as a response to a client's transference.

It is easier to identify thoughts, feelings, and behaviours that result from a countertransference when they are not congruent with one's personality and self-experience. Hughes and Kerr (2000) explain this in terms of a practitioner adopting "a projected role" on behalf of a client. "A projected role may be very different from any aspect of the recipient's personality and the recipient is able to recognise that this perception of his or her feelings or behaviour is a product of the patient's [or client's] mind" (p. 62). For example, if one is not commonly inclined to be curt or abrupt with clients but finds that one behaves in this manner repeatedly towards one particular client and this feels at odds with one's self-perception. Here, it is possible that the client is in a transference which replicates a prior relationship in which the other was rude or harsh. Or if one finds oneself repeatedly pulled into a sense of sympathy towards a client and it feels very "personal" rather than professional. Here, it is possible that there is a transference in which the prior relationship was characterised by overt "mothering".

However, it is not uncommon for a projected role in the countertransference to be congruent with an aspect of the coach's personality or personal history. In such cases, coaches may unconsciously accept and collude with the transference projection (Hughes & Kerr, 2000). A common example of this is where the transference is characterised by idealisation of the other. Here, clients unconsciously treat the coach as being very special, unique, or brilliant in some way, and coaches end up identifying with this idealisation as if it were a fact. In this way, countertransference can include unconscious reactions on the part of the coach that stem from his or her own past relationships and personal issues. This means that a countertransference left unchecked poses a danger to the coaching process and can go so far as to create ethical complications. It is therefore critical that coaches are able to distinguish between what their reactions to the client are telling them about the client, and what those reactions are telling them about their own neurosis and relational patterns (Malcolm, 1981). As Eric Berne (1972) explains: "Countertransference means that not only does the analyst play a role in the patient's script, but she plays a part in his" (p. 352). In other words, both receive script responses from each other, resulting in a chaotic situation which makes it impossible to proceed to the goal of the process (ibid.).

This means that it is important for coaches to become conscious of any countertransference reactions occurring in the coaching relationship as this will inoculate them against acting-out. Acting-out occurs where coaches unconsciously play out projected roles given to them by their clients or when they respond with anxiety or anger towards the client as a result of transference. Hughes and Kerr (2002) suggest that practitioners need to continually reflect on their own thoughts and feelings, and maintain a sound grasp of whether these deviate from good professional behaviour, in order to avoid acting-out. They suggest the following orientation as good practice (p. 63):

1. a questioning attitude towards one's own feelings and motives;
2. recognition that we all have "blind spots";
3. an understanding that practitioners are affected by clients [unconsciously];
4. an understanding that clients are affected by practitioners' behaviour [unconsciously];
5. recognition that practitioners often have strong feelings towards clients.

Once countertransference is made conscious, it opens up the possibility for insight into the client and can be a profound opportunity for transformation. This is because the coach can then offer transference interpretations to the client that provide insight and may even unblock previously entrenched dysfunctional ways of relating. From this point of view, transference and countertransference are seen as important mechanisms for awareness creation and transformation in coaching practice. De Haan (2011) explains that coaches can recognise the power of transference interpretations because when such are offered there is "the inescapable and often quite unhinging effect of feedback on here-and-now behaviour whilst it occurs. One senses an almost devastating power when such interpretations cut through a stuck situation just by bringing to someone's attention how they seem to initiate or respond here and now" (p. 185).

The following are some examples of acting-out in the countertransference commonly cited in the literature (Walsh, 2002) which I have adapted here with examples for business coaching:

1. *Needing clients to be dependent on coaching.* In this case, the coach may look to clients for fulfilment of this need by failing to support the client's own self-sustaining capacities in favour of the support the coach offers.

2. *Needing to be liked by clients.* This can be seen where a coach tries too hard to please a client, feels hurt by a client's criticisms, or has negative reactions to clients who are not emotionally forthcoming.

3. *Needing to demonstrate immediate effectiveness or be seen as the expert.* In the former, a coach may feel bored or irritated with a client who tends to make changes very slowly. In the latter a coach may devalue a client's thinking or ideas, for example, by countering a client's interpretation of a business dilemma in order to demonstrate his or her own business prowess.

4. *Needing to avoid forms of emotional expression* (such as anger or tears) *or certain topics* (such as abortion), and thus suppressing such in clients. For example, a coach who is uncomfortable discussing certain religious or moral topics may steer a client away from relevant existential discussions that are pertinent to the coaching process. Or a coach who is uncomfortable with tears may unintentionally suppress such in a sensitive client.

5. *Over-identifying with clients' problems or life situations.* Here, coaches may be blind to the part that clients play in sustaining their own problems or have trouble understanding a client's conflicts. For example, a coach who drinks alcohol may have trouble seeing that a client's alcohol abuse is problematic, particularly if the coach is in denial about his or her own level of use. Or a coach may project his or her own need to break away from organisational life and go it alone onto a client who is debating leaving his job. If the client does not do so, the coach may feel anger but be unaware of its source.

6. *Idealising, favouring, or obsessing over certain clients, based on strong positive feelings.* Many people possess strengths and talents about which a coach may be envious. For example, a coach who is a frustrated entrepreneur may be extremely impressed with the business accomplishments of a client. This might result in an idealisation that impedes the coach's ability to help the client achieve more basic goals. Or coaches may find themselves inclined to assist favoured clients with private activities that are unrelated to the coaching process (e.g., facilitating the purchase of a private vehicle). Or a coach may become preoccupied with a client because they are sexually attracted to them, resulting in excessive after-hours ruminations or unnecessary, inappropriate, or irrelevant forms of engagement that have no professional connection to the coaching process.

Creating an axial coaching contract

As discussed earlier, many cultural assumptions common to counsel-ling and psychotherapy tend to be unconsciously imported into busi-ness coaching practice. One of the areas in which this tends to occur is with contracting. In the former, patients are not commonly afforded the right to negotiate the boundaries of therapy. Most psychotherapists and counsellors work with fairly strict time frames and rules about how the process is to be conducted and patients are required to conform. For example, the fifty-minute therapy hour, conducted at the therapist's practice room once a week, for a prescribed fee with a twenty-four-hour cancellation clause. Also, no third parties are commonly permit-ted access to the process even if they are the ones paying (except in the case of children where parents have full access). In this sense, con-tracting is a one-way street, the therapist says: "This is how I work", and the patient either conforms or finds another service provider. This approach to contracting makes a lot of sense in therapy because it creates a powerful psychological container which acts to hold the healing process. However, in the culture of business, this approach is foreign.

Most providers to business are open to negotiation around boundaries and fees, and companies tend to expect such when they procure services in the free market. Also, remember, business coaching is not focused on healing; its focus is to improve business performance. And so the therapeutic container is far less relevant in business coaching because deep-dive healing processes are not on the table. If they are on the table, then business coaching is not the service to be procured, but rather referral to a suitably qualified health-care professional is in order. So what this means is that in business coaching practice, it is important to negotiate the boundaries and fees in each and every engagement so as to provide a tailored offering that fits the specific purpose of that particular business context and individual need. This is even more important when one considers organsational culture, as discussed in depth in Chapter Two. Every organisation has its own "way of doing things", and it is critical that the coach appreciate and understand this from the first moment of engagement. Remember, the organisation is just as much the client as is the individual being coached, and therefore, attuning to the organsational culture through the contracting process is as important as attuning to the individual's personality in the first session. Put simply, when contracting in business coaching practice, coaches need to attune to the organsational culture and unique individual needs of the client, and from there negotiate the most sensible set of boundaries and fees that are most likely to promote the success of the intervention.

In the end, a particular business coaching contract may indeed end up looking similar to a counselling contract, where the client attends sessions once a week in the coach's office for a set fee per session etc. However, it could just as soon resemble nothing of the sort where, for example, the coach spends three days a month shadowing an individual client in all her meetings and then spends three half day sessions over the next two months working through the observations with the individual and her manager in the office canteen. And maybe the whole process is paid for upfront in a single fee.

Furthermore, from an axial point of view, the creation of a coaching contract needs to incorporate systemic considerations and respect the duality of client in business coaching practice. This means that from conception, every aspect of the contractual negotiation must involve both the individual being coached and the organisation sanctioning the service, and, importantly, they need to agree. The following are some key points to aid the contracting process that coaches should keep in mind:

1. *Axially agreed purpose and goals*

   As discussed in detail earlier in this chapter, coaches need to ensure that the purpose of the coaching intervention, as well as any goals that are set, are always dialogued and aligned between the individual and organisation. This commitment should be articulated in the initial coaching contract. In addition, as discussed, the purpose and goals of coaching tend to change over time. It is therefore suggested that the coach educate the parties of this eventuality up front and that a clause be included in the coaching contracted that explains how re-contracting around purpose and goals will occur (the process of which needs to be negotiated).

2. *Axially agreed timelines*

   It is very difficult to know up front how long a coaching process needs to be to achieve its outcomes. At best, timeframes of this nature are simply educated guesses. However, it is not usually acceptable to most companies to leave a contract open-ended as budgets rarely allow for such. Also, individuals and managers often need a sense of containment, which time-line expectations provide. Therefore, it is suggested that coaches specify a time frame for the process based in a best guess of how long it is likely to take. However, it is important to educate the parties that this is a guess, not a guarantee, and explain the notion that "the map is not the territory" (Bateson, 1972). Consequently, it is worth contracting up-front as to the process that can be followed should an extension, or a premature termination, of the contract be required.

3. *Fees*

   In business culture, price is commonly open to negotiation. It is therefore suggested that coaches be open to negotiating their fees depending on the level of complexity of the coaching assignment in question and their level of experience. Other business considerations also need to be factored in: for example, supply and demand as well as affordability. Coaches might also want to consider what other coaches are charging around them in order to remain competitive.

4. *Boundary management on the axis*

As discussed in detail in Chapter Two under "Coaching business culture", business possesses a unique and distinct boundary system from that of science, particularly counselling and medicine where the individual enjoys primacy. It is therefore critical to negotiate the boundaries required in each and every business coaching contract. These boundaries need to consider the needs of *both* the individual and the organisation equally. Issues to be negotiated include access to information, confidentiality, feedback, and level of participation in the process, as well as the nature and format of reporting. Failure to negotiate and agree on such boundaries may result in people defaulting to assumptions which create ethical dilemmas, or worse, such as legal action, as in the example provided about confidentiality in Chapter Two. That case illustrated how in many situations, where boundaries are not negotiated with all parties up-front, individuals being coached tend to default to assuming the boundaries of counselling, whereas organisations tend to default to assuming the boundaries of a management-consulting process. This is because each of these fit the needs of the respective parties, but are not necessarily suited to achieving the specific outcomes of a particular coaching engagement in a particular context.

A point to keep in mind is that although mostly any type of boundary arrangement is possible in a business coaching context, there are some recommended boundaries that should be considered across most cases. First, as mentioned earlier, in counselling and psychotherapy practice, the highest level of confidentiality is maintained on behalf of the individual. This creates a powerful psychological container of trust between counsellor and patient, which potentiates the possibility of accessing deep layers of vulnerability at the heart of the issues that need healing. Although this profound level of containment is not necessarily required in most business coaching engagements, the lesson to learn from psychology is that a level of containment based in trust *is* necessary for people to feel safe enough to address issues that leave them feeling vulnerable. For this reason, it is recommended that business coaches advise the parties of this important insight during the boundary negotiation process at the outset of a business coaching intervention, and that such be calculated into considerations. Second, on the other end of the axis, there are occasions in which managers, being familiar with counselling themselves, in turn, obviate the need to know anything at all about what happens in the coaching of one of their direct reports. This is sometimes offered as a statement of support, something like: "I don't need to know anything at all about what happens with Joe's coaching journey. I trust Joe and the process completely. Just send me the bill." This is support that does not help. Instead it relegates the coaching process to a vacuum which prohibits a relational engagement with the organisation, and importantly, with the individual's direct manager. Such should in most cases be challenged, and a different boundary arrangement considered, one in which the individual's manager participates in the process in a way that makes sense given the culture and purpose of the particular engagement.

In general, the most helpful boundary position to hold for a business coach is one in which they avoid being seduced into becoming an *agent* or *go-between* for the individual or the organisation. This means that, wherever possible, in cases where the organisation needs to know something about the experience an individual is having in coaching it is best that they garner such directly from the individual themselves. Coaches can offer to facilitate the process of acquiring such, but should do their best to avoid providing feedback on the individual's behalf. The reverse is also the case. Where individuals wish to garner something about the organisation, and believe coaches may be able to provide such, coaches should instead explore options as to how the individual might achieve the outcome themselves. This boundary position on behalf of the coach underpins the notion that coaching is a relational intervention that seeks to improve the relationship between individuals and their environment in a mutually beneficial manner. If coaches become agents for the parties, they do just the opposite, and become a barrier between them, almost like being a messenger between two people in a marriage. Whereas coaches who challenge and support the parties in engaging directly act to build the relationship, which is ultimately the point of the process. This type of boundary awareness is important to explain to clients early in the contracting process. This is not only to ensure appropriate contracting between individual and organisation, but also because such awareness assists the parties in understanding the role the coach will play in the process.

Avoiding the position of being an agent can be difficult, especially when it comes to reporting. Many companies have a culture of reporting, requiring written feedback about the process. It is therefore important to negotiate the nature and purpose of reporting up-front with the organisation. Where possible, reports should be avoided, and the process itself should be appreciated at the level of dialogue and relationship. But if not, then it is recommended that reports headline the purpose of the coaching and then only outline logistics, that is, describe the frequency, dates, and times of contact, and especially the number and length of feedback events, and who was present at these. If a conclusion is required, then verbatim statements about the level of success of the intervention made by various stakeholders can be recorded as long as such is jointly preapproved by *all* parties. If pushed by the culture of the organisation, and challenges from the coach fall on deaf ears, then one might consider commenting on the quality of the engagement but not the content. However, these comments should be pre-approved by the individual being coached.

Evaluating success and wrapping up on the axis

In a global study of business coaching practices amongst 28,000 employ-ees in ten major industry sectors, Right Management (2009) found there to be "no robust proven methodology to measure impact" (p. 10) because "there is no algorithm or ROI calculation that can accommo-date the enormous number of variables that will influence the impact of a coaching program" (p. 4). They explain that it is not possible to accurately partition the impact an individual's behaviour has on busi-ness performance with the numerous and complex variables associated with it, such as the prevailing organsational culture, the person's own manager, the team's current and potential capability, market condi-tions and competitor action or inaction, all of which are operating at the same time. They argue that the only way to ensure a return on invest-ment is "to anchor your coaching activity in the context of your desired business outcomes and organisational capabilities", where individu-als "work with the coach to frame the objectives of coaching however, other stakeholders and systems should be factored into the process" (p. 10). They add that these stakeholder's include the individual's man-ager and representatives of key functions such as HR, "who share the responsibility of articulating the organisations strategic objectives with the coaching effort to ensure that the coaching and strategy agendas are properly aligned—in other words, that the organsational context is made relevant" (p. 10).

This study exposes two important realities in evaluating business coaching outcomes. First, quantitative measures, or "return on investment", need to be replaced with qualitative measures. In other words, the idea that some kind of financial equation, algorithm, or statistical metric can be used to indicate that success has been achieved should be abandoned in favour of a process where impact is qualitatively measured. And second, evaluation needs to occur across stakeholders, which include, at the very least, the individual and his or her manager, through a consideration of the degree to which the pre-set objectives for the intervention have been achieved. This approach contains aspects of an ROE methodology (Anderson, 2007), although perhaps less formulaic, where ROE is defined as "return on expectations" and refers to the amount of change, development, or improvement measured against original expectations. In ROE, an up-front agreement around expectations is made between stakeholders, these are qualified and focused to determine economic benefit, and then at the end of the process stakeholders are engaged to determine the degree to which these have been achieved.

This approach to evaluation fits fairly well with an axial framework to business coaching but requires some adjustment. First, it is preferable that it is an *inter-subjective* process; an open discussion between stakeholders facilitated to the point of alignment. Remember, in an axial approach, these parties participate in a purpose and goal setting process at the onset of a coaching engagement, and, importantly, the coach would have facilitated continual testing and aligning of progress across the axis throughout the process. In this way, inter-subjective evaluation has already been at play from the start, where each party has been offering his or her own subjective point of view. These views have been continually dialogued into a shared story—an inter-subjective narrative—of what shared success looks like for both the individual and the organisation. Second, measurement against expectations is not the only consideration. Given that the map is not the territory, as discussed earlier, there are likely to have been a range of unexpected benefits of the process which need to be acknowledged as well. And these benefits would not only have been for the individual being coached but may well have been enjoyed by others, and the organisation as a whole, during the process. So these need to be included in any evaluation conducted.

Following on from the same intersubjective philosophy that underpins evaluation as described above, first prize in terms of wrapping up a coaching process from an axial perspective would be if the coach facilitated a closing dialogue with all the parties in a single session. The object of this dialogue would be to discuss and ultimately align perspectives across the axis on the coaching journey in retrospect; what was achieved, as well as what challenges the road ahead may still present and how these are to be handled. This process also produces content for any finalised qualitative assessment of coaching impact, should that be required, in which all parties offer preapproval, together, of what is to be recorded. Once this is concluded, it is recommended that a one-on-one termination session between individual and coach be conducted. This allows for a more personal and private conclusion that honours the journey the two have travelled together in a more sacred way.

Coaching ethics on the axis

To a degree, coaching appears to enjoy a fairly well developed base in ethics for such a young field. This appears to be a result of the influence of psychology on coaching practice. The field of psychology has been grappling with ethical considerations for decades, for example, the American Psychological Association's Committee on Scientific and Professional Ethics has been handling ethical complaints since 1938 and has since then revised its ethical code of practice many times (Pope & Vetter, 1992). Most coaching associations and groups maintain an ethical code and have done so from inception, and today there is a steadily growing body of literature specifically focused on coaching ethics (e.g., Lowman, 2013; Passmore & Mortimer, 2011). A cursory screening of the ethical codes of practice for coaches reveals they are unsurprisingly similar, and in several aspects identical, to those of psychologists. This is not a bad thing; quite the contrary, what a blessing to have such a strong ethical base as a launching pad for a new field. Most others have had to build theirs from scratch, and as someone once said: "A wise person learns from their mistakes, but a very wise person learns from others mistakes." Coaching is very wise. But as discussed earlier, the culture of psychology and the culture of business are not the same. As a result, the ethics of psychology practice and the ethics of business practice will not be identical, although they are likely to be in tune in terms of universal principles.

The following section focuses on specific aspects of ethical practice when viewed through the lens of the Coaching on the Axis framework. It does not cover the full ethical landscape that a good business coach needs to traverse. In that regard, the reader is referred to the following texts, as a start: Corey et al. (2011), Lowman (2013), and Passmore & Mortimer (2011) for a broader explication of commonly accepted ethical practices in coaching. Below are some key ethical points to consider that specifically apply to the delivery of coaching services in the context of business culture and in light of the notion of a duality of client:

1. *Ethics for multiple clients*:
   A seminal tenet of this book is that in business coaching there are always two clients—the individual and the organisation. And, as explained, both are equally the client and both deserve equitable consideration throughout the coaching process. From an ethical point of view, this means that it is unethical for coaches to bias towards either the individual or the organisation in the delivery of their services. For example, Chapter Six explored the case of Bianca, who faced existential questions about whether or not to work on a fast-food chicken company account given her beliefs about cruelty to animals. In this case, the coach explained that the objective was to find a way that *would* allow her to work on the account by authentically re-examining, and hopefully thereby accommodating, her personal beliefs in such a decision. Not only was this not an ethical failure, but on the contrary, it was an ethical requirement. If the coach had not influenced the process in this way, he would have been out of integrity with the organisation as a client; he would not have been working in its interests. At the same time, the coach needed to equally work in Bianca's interests, which meant ensuring that the process was not ultimately causing her to compromise her personal values and beliefs. This ethical balancing act is very different from the ethics of individual psychotherapy, counselling, or medical practice in which the individual's concerns and needs are prioritised over others with whom they are in relationship.
   Unfortunately, historically, the development of ethical practices for psychologists has not focused on addressing the ethics of services that involve multiple clients (Fisher, 2009; Pope & Vetter, 1992). Fisher (2009) points out that the APA Ethics Code recommends that psychologists *specify* only one individual or entity as the client. "This

single-client recommendation sometimes appears even when the Ethical Standard itself implies the plural. For example, in therapy cases involving multiple clients [such as with couples counselling or family therapy] who are related to each other, Ethical Standard 10.02 requires psychologists to ask: 'Which of the individuals are patients or clients?'" (p. 2). In other words, practice ethics for psychologists concentrate on issues facing the delivery of *individual* psychological assessment and psychotherapy. This is probably because these are the core modalities that account for the vast majority of psychologists' services offered in the market today. However, the fact that psychology is statutorily regulated as a 'health profession' in most countries fundamentally entrenches its relatively narrow ethical focus to exclude applications of the field outside of that context (Strawbridge, 2010).

As a result, in this particular aspect of ethical practice (i.e., multiple clients), business coaching can draw relatively little from the ethics of psychologists and would probably glean more from those of family therapists and couples counsellors, who also manage multiple clients. For example, the American Association for Marriage and Family Therapy's Code of Ethics (2012) explains that "the client in a therapeutic relationship may be more than one person" (p. 4). And point 1.3 of their code prescribes that: "Marriage and family therapists, upon agreeing to provide services to a person or entity at the request of a third party, clarify, to the extent feasible and at the outset of the service, the nature of the relationship with each party and the limits of confidentiality" (p. 3). The alignment of business coaching with family and couples counselling is also made easier because, as Corey et al. (2011) explain, "much of the practice of couples and family therapy rests on the foundation of systems theory" (p. 449). This theoretical position is a match with that of business coaching. For example, family and couples therapists "need to be sure that the status of one partner or family member does not improve at the expense of the other partner or family member" (p. 455). Corey et al (2011) further explain that to manage this ethically, "therapists can respond to ethical dilemmas over conflicting interests of multiple individuals by identifying the couple or family system rather than a single individual as the client" (ibid.). In other words, in working with couples, family therapists see the relationship as the client, as opposed to either the wife or the husband, and in family therapy, the family is seen as the client as opposed to any one member over another. In this way, the ethics of the process are guided by the notion that counsellors act in the best interests of all the parties by focusing and prioritising that which would help the marriage or the family at all times. This wisdom suggests that for ethical purposes it may be helpful to view *the relationship* between organisation and individual in business coaching practice as the client, as opposed to *either* the organisation *or* the individual. In this way, both are appreciated as clients, equitably, in that their common interests are prioritised by virtue of the fact that both are invested in the relationship.

This relational focus for ethical decision-making fits perfectly with the Coaching on the Axis framework which holds that the purpose of business coaching is the promotion of success of both individual and organisation through the improvement of their relationship. This means that by focusing on the relational axis, the coach is naturally guided to work more ethically in that such ensures that coaching process is continually focused on the mutual interests of all parties. It also supports the notion that business coaching needs to always have a meaningful business focus to be ethical. In other words, by working on the axial relationship as a priority, the broader business needs are always included in the coaching dialogue and hence kept ethical. So, for example, when business coaching dialogue steers heavily towards an individual's personal life, a coach that works with the coaching axis will be asking the question: "How does this exploration relate to the business context, our coaching objectives and your relationship with the organisation?" This is then not just a reflexive or strategic question, but also an ethical one.

2. *Confidentiality*

As discussed in Chapter Two, under "Coaching business culture", the boundaries of confidentiality in business culture are very different to that of individual psychotherapy or counselling practice for two reasons:

First, in the latter it is axiomatic to assume that the individual receiving treatment enjoys primacy as the client. Hence, ownership of information resides with those receiving treatment, irrespective of whether or not they pay for the service. Also, confidentiality is assumed to be in place and is rarely a negotiated process. Whereas, in business, confidentiality is never assumed, and ownership of information is generally linked to financial ownership i.e. those who pay usually own related information.

Second, as discussed in point 1, the challenge of managing the ethics of multiple clients equitably, further increases the complexity of addressing confidentiality. This is not the case in common counselling practice, where a single individual is identified as the client in the same way that a person becomes a medical patient when seeing a doctor.

From an ethical standpoint, this means that when coaches work with confidentiality in business coaching they need to ensure that:

a. They negotiate boundaries with all parties, and re-negotiate such if and when circumstances change. Family therapists and couple counsellors have this ethic entrenched in their practice. For example, the American Association for Marriage and Family Therapy's Code of Ethics (2012) prescribes that confidentiality be negotiated with all parties up front in light of the recognition that in their work there is always more than one client.

b. They never bias in favour of either the individual or the organsation, but rather, define the boundary arrangement in a way that makes the most sense to all parties, agreeably, given the objectives of the unique intervention, the organsational culture and the psychology of the individual being coached. This practice resonates with the concept of *viability*, as discussed in Chapter Three, and is therefore theoretically aligned with the culture of business.

3. *Other contractual obligations*

a. *Changing the purpose or major goal along the way*: As discussed earlier in this chapter under "Goals are compasses not destinations", coaching process can unfold in fairly unpredictable ways, and so the purpose and goals of the work change over time. Nevertheless, it is unethical to proceed in new directions without renegotiating the new purpose and objectives with all the parties. This is because it might transpire that the new direction may not be agreeable to all.

b. *Termination*: There may be a tendency for coaches to unnecessarily push for an extension of a coaching contract following the achievement of preset objectives or beyond the scope of the purpose of the work. This can be motivated by an unconscious reluctance on the part of the coach to terminate a meaningful relationship and/or garner further income from the client. Given the positive rapport that is often established in a coaching relationship, clients (both organisation and individual), tend to be vulnerable to coaches' arguments for extensions, particularly following initial success. Coaches need to consider this vulnerability and avoid arguing for extensions of their contracts when such are not really necessary and fall more into the category of "nice to have". This also applies to situations where objectives have been reached earlier than estimated in the initial contract. In such cases, coaches need to terminate their contract prematurely if needed, and avoid the temptation to simply carry on "because budget has been allocated anyway, and there is always more we can do".

c. *Accepting unreasonable or misguided requests*: Coaches have an ethical responsibility to push back on clients who make unreasonable requests. A common example of an unreasonable request is one in which the timeframe requested to achieve objectives is too short to be viable but budgetary constraints allow only for so much coaching work. Coaches also need to educate clients on misguided requests. A common misguided request is where clients seek coaching to address issues or manage challenges which are more appropriately dealt with by another type of service provider other than a coach, for example, a management consultant, trainer, or psychologist.

A word on supervision

Managing these ethical landmines and many others, as well as the many complexities associated with the interpersonal process of the coaching relationship, can be a formidable task for a business coach. There are times when a coach may become bewildered and confused, finding it difficult to sustain a systemic perspective and balance on the axial tightrope constellated in the ethics of a duality of client. Issues of transference can be tricky to manage without external support, and the continuous need for coaches to be aware of the role they play personally in their coaching processes is a tall order. From all of this, coaching supervision (Hawkins & Schwenk, 2010; Moyes, 2009) offers a reflective and helpful refuge and thinking space.

In addition to the common criteria that are important in the selection of a supervisor, for example experience and reputation, it is recommended that the following knowledge and experience (in no particular order) be considered when choosing a supervisor for business coaching:

1. a systemic orientation with an appreciation of organisational theory and the notion of a duality of client in business coaching practice;
2. a functional understanding of organisational culture;
3. a background in working in, or consulting to, organisations with sound business knowledge;
4. a comprehensive theoretical base in individual psychology.

Theory informing the coaching relationship

The theory that informs this dimension comes from literature that specifically explores coaching practice and the coaching relationship above and below the surface. Examples are coaching journals such as *The International Coaching Psychology Review*, as well as coaching and relevant consulting texts such as Flaherty (2005), O'Neill (2007), Palmer and Whybrow (2007), Peltier (2001), Stout-Rostron (2009), Schein (1999, 2009), Stober and Grant (2006), and, of course, this book. Also, literature that specifically informs interpersonal process, the phenomena of transference, ethical practice, and supervision (e.g., Lowman, 2013; Palmer & McDowall, 2010; Passmore & Mortimer, 2011; Racker, 2002) are relevant.

CHAPTER EIGHT

Coaching on the Axis: technique

The Coaching on the Axis approach does not strictly prescribe one particular model or set of techniques for its implementation. It is rather an overarching approach or framework that helps orientate coaches to the challenge of business coaching. It is therefore possible to use this approach as a general framework, and to use many different coaching techniques and models in its application.

For instance, perhaps a coach is partial to using structured sequential questioning typical of the popular GROW (Whitmore, 2009) or ACHIEVE (Dembkowski et al., 2006) models of coaching. Or maybe he or she prefers employing reflective interpretations typical of psychodynamic psychotherapy (Malan, 1995), or anchoring and reframing techniques from NLP (Bandler & Grinder, 1983), or reality-testing methods from cognitive therapy (Beck, 1979) or role-playing from Gestalt therapy (Woldt & Toman, 2005). All of these, and many others, can be applied in the Coaching on the Axis approach.

The following chapter offers only some of many possible techniques and practices that a coach may use within the Coaching on the Axis approach. In most cases, a coach works best with a set of techniques he or she has trained in, refined, and personalised over many years. In this chapter, coaches may simply find some useful methodologies for integration into their existing technical repertoire, or be inspired to pursue new practices.

The practice suggested below integrates several techniques in a narrative methodology. Using an informal and open conversational style, the coach works with the stories of both the individual and the environment, bringing them into conversation with each other. Through this dialogical process themes emerge which elicit awareness and prompt action. This conversational, story-based, and thematic technique resists reductionist temptations and helps to hold the necessary complexity required in business coaching practice. Furthermore, the notion of story facilitates exploration in both conscious and unconscious ways as it is imaginative and realistic, and allows for real depth and feeling.

Although this technique was developed and refined by the author (Kahn, 2011) over many years, it is by no means original. It has been influenced by, and draws heavily from, many sources, not the least of which come from methods used in insight-orientated psychotherapy (Scaturo, 2010), Jungian archetypal psychology (Hillman, 1989; Jung, 1996) and central practices in counselling and psychotherapy (Corey, 1996).

The story of imagination

What is the language of our mind? Is it English or Chinese? In what language do infants think? What is the language of our dreams? The answer: imagination (Brooke, 1993; Hillman, 1983; Jung, 1996; Romanyshyn, 1989). As Shakespeare put it in *The Tempest* (Act 4, scene 1): "We are such stuff as dreams are made on."

Avens (1982) and Brooke (1993) explain that imagination *is* reality. It is only through imagination that we access the depths of the psyche. "Astrum in homine, coeleste sive supracoeleste corpus—Imagination is the star in man, the celestial or supercelestial body" (Avens, 1982, p. 43). It is imagination that mediates our lived connection to our world. Knowing that an oak tree is made of atoms and molecules does not bring that tree into our experience. We have to imagine that oak tree, as it stands above the rough ground in the dawning light by the lake, for it to take form in our minds. Robert Romanyshyn (1989) uses the example of a kiss to illustrate this well by presenting the artist Alex Grey's *The Kiss*—a painting, showing the neuroanatomical features of a man and woman kissing, and saying the following: "It is a strange perspective, for while it is certainly true that a kiss is such an event [i.e., a neurochemical event], it is also equally certain that I neither know of nor care about such things when I kiss another. No one ever kisses another in this fashion" (p. 104), for whoever kisses with such an attitude will, indeed, never wholly kiss you. In order to allow something to be born into our psyche, it must enter through "the world of the image, the *mundis imaginalis*: a world that is as ontologically real as the world of the senses and that of the intellect" (Corbin, 1972, p. 72).

James Hillman, the first director of studies at the C. G. Jung Institute in Zurich in the 1960s, adapted Jung's ideas in a field called archetypal psychology (Hillman, 1997). A great portion of Hillman's thought focuses on the language of the psyche as revealed in images and story. He suggests that story, in the form of tales, myths, fantasies, symbols, and dreams, is the mind's vehicle for creating "imaginative possibility" (Hillman, 1975, p. x). In this sense, our mind is a great story-telling poet, speaking in images and tales, as it makes sense of the chaos of the phenomenal world.

Clients use their stories in different ways. "Some tell stories as entertainments to while, or wile, away the hour, others are reporters, others are prosecuting attorneys building a plaint. Occasionally, a tale becomes wholly metaphorical in which every aspect of what-I-saw-yesterday ... all refer as well to figures within the [client's] psyche and their interplay" (Hillman, 1983, pp. 14–15). Hillman further explains that "entering one's interior story takes a courage similar to starting a novel. We have to engage with persons whose autonomy may radically alter, even dominate, our thoughts and feelings, neither ordering these persons about, nor yielding to them full sway" (p. 55). In this sense, client and coach are "drawn together like threads into a *mythos*, a plot" (ibid.).

Story as formulation

In mainstream counselling and psychotherapy, the use of a formulation is considered standard practice as a means of generating "an explanatory account of the concerns with which a client is presenting", and this technique is "one of the most important activities that those using psychological approaches undertake as part of their work" (Corrie & Lane, 2010, p. xxxi).

In clinical psychology, for example, formulation is defined "as a hypothesis about a person's difficulties, which links theory with practice and guides the intervention" (British Psychological Society, 2011, p. 2). It is considered "both an event and a process", which "summarises and integrates a broad range of biopsychosocial causal factors", and "is based on personal meaning and constructed collaboratively with service users and teams" (ibid.). Put in more broadly applicable terms, a formulation is a meaningful and theoretically informed story about a client that captures his or her issues, and in doing so, offers clarity regarding their current situation and indicates possible ways forward.

However, the construction of a formulation is by no means simple, it is complex because "the task is not simply a matter of eliciting meaning from the mass of information gathered", but requires "the judicious application of theoretical and empirical knowledge, and also an ability to construct a meaningful narrative and design a way forward" (Corrie & Lane, 2010, p. xxxii). A story of this kind "requires an investigative procedure, devised from nomothetic knowledge and principles of enquiry, with a personal story that speaks to the distinctiveness of the client's life" (ibid.). There is no single correct way to go about constructing a story-based formulation, nor any single correct story for any individual case.

Corrie and Lane (2010) explain that a story-based formulation is co-scripted in the narrative between the client and coach. In other words, it is written together in an emergent fashion as the coaching dialogue proceeds over time. As client issues are explored, insights generated are threaded together in an overarching and integrating narrative, informed by theory and experience. This narrative provides a meaningful lens through which to understand the clients' history and exposes transformative or instructive options (Corrie & Lane, 2010).

The uniqueness of the client's narrative begins with the distinction between a 'story' and 'a tale'. A story is a compilation of a number of tales integrated into a central theme, whereas a tale is a single explanatory account (ibid.). In this sense, story-based formulation may be said to work thematically, where themes are extracted from tales emerging in the coaching dialogue, and then scripted together to form an ever-emerging story of the client which acts as a formulation.

When imagination and story are seen through the discipline of formulation, story as formulation emerges as a powerful technique in business coaching practice. These stories frame the narrative for success (Cohen, 2009), and in this sense, business coaches are facilitators of the courageous co-scripting of clients' stories for the purpose of promoting their mutual potential.

Working thematically

The process of working with the client's story begins at first contact. As soon as a coach engages, he or she can begin to track themes. From the first conversation these emerge, most commonly in the form of tales about the individual and the environment. These narratives express issues to be addressed, expectations or goals, relevant experiences, and history.

The following example of Jacob is a fairly simple illustration of a series of tales captured as themes and then translated into a story that acts as a provisional formulation:

A. Jacob's tales:

1. Jacob's HR consultant: "Jacob needs to shift his mindset from manager to leader because he has always been good at telling people what to do, but now, in his new role, he has to influence them rather than tell them. If he fails to make this shift, he will not be able to deliver in this role because people will work around him and not support his strategy." This is a tale about Jacob as a leader and the requirements of the role, and the theme is "influence with a leadership mindset".

2. Jacob: "I just seem to give people the wrong impression when I speak to them; they fail to understand me, often thinking that I mean something else of which they disapprove. Please can you help me get people to understand what I'm trying to say?" This is a tale about Jacob's interpersonal skills, and the theme could be "get my meaning".

3. Jacob: "In this place, people just don't tell you what they really think. I've seen how they don't give you feedback when you miss something, and they just watch you burn." This is a tale about the level and quality of feedback the individual experiences which colours his relational landscape; the theme could be "watch you burn".

4. Jacob's manager: "This area of the business is under market pressure to perform since we lost our biggest account to our competitor last month. We need to put some points on the board now, not later." This is an environmental tale about competition and related delivery

expectations that impact the organsational climate; the theme could be "performance pressure".

5. Jacob's colleague: "Our culture is unforgiving. There is not much room to fail; Jacob needs to deliver without excuses." This is a tale about the organsational culture; the theme could be "no second chances".

6. Jacob: "I don't believe that I'm fully backed in my role; I suspect that my manager is not convinced I will succeed." Jacob is sharing a tale about the degree of support in his role; the theme might be "doubting support".

7. Jacob: "To tell you the truth, I'm not feeling that strong right now. I'm not sure I'll pull this off." Here, Jacob provides a tale about his inner world; the theme might be "in search of confidence".

As is evident in the above examples, environmental tales are captured in a thematic way, as are individual tales that speak to the inner world of the person. In addition, it is important to notice that coaching goals are seen as tales in themselves, and therefore also captured thematically. This is because goals are also stories. They tell the tale about the desired future state. Goals are always in play; they are key stories that guide the process.

B. Jacob's themes:
Environmental themes:

1. influence with a leadership mindset (initial goal)
2. performance pressure
3. no second chances
4. watch you burn

Individual themes:

5. get my meaning (initial goal)
6. in search of confidence
7. doubting support

C. Jacob's provisional story as a formulation:
In his new role, Jacob needs to shift from his naturally directive leadership style to one in which he influences and collaborates with others towards a shared strategy that everyone buys into. Both Jacob

and others in the organisation see this as a real challenge for him, and Jacob himself is not feeling very confident he can succeed. This is because, first, he is unsure of the level of support he has from his manager and, second, he has a history of struggling to get others to understand what he means when he communicates his business ideas. Environmentally, the pressure is on for this area of the business, having lost a major account recently, and, in any event, the organsational culture is not very forgiving. As a result, there is a sense that Jacob will not be given a second chance if he initially fails to deliver. This just intensifies the pressure and challenges Jacob's confidence that much more. And if that is not enough, Jacob worries that delivery will be made that much harder because he believes those around him might not provide the honest feedback he will need to guide his progress in the task.

Story as iterative and emergent learning

After the initial development of a provisional story as a formulation, tales continue to spontaneously emerge, and the thematic picture gradually increases in complexity and may change significantly. This emergence happens as part of the iterative process inherent in a coaching dialogue, which includes sensitive and repeated interrogation of all the available data, both above and below the surface. Throughout this process the coach continuously offers his or her appreciation of the emerging themes to the individual being coached and others, where relevant, in the environment. This includes testing assumptions, clarifying, summarising, and reframing. For example, Jacob's doubt about being supported, as well as his sense that others would "watch him burn", changed when, as a result of the coaching process, he tested these in reality. This reality-testing was iterative, that is, it happened across and between several coaching sessions. The process, in turn, boosted his confidence which enabled him to communicate his ideas more effectively, and ultimately he succeeded in building a strategy for the area that his colleagues supported.

As one can see from Jacob's story, core to this iterative process is the practice of articulating the individual's "internal model of the organisation" (Roberts & Jarrett, 2006, p. 21) or what Armstrong (2005) calls the "organisation in the mind". Here the individual learns to become aware of, and reflect on, his or her emotional experience of the organisation as crucial data in itself, where "the assumption is that whatever the client brings is at some level an echo or reflection of the organization" (Roberts & Jarrett, 2006, p. 21). So Jacob's organisation at the outset of coaching was indeed really one in which people watch you burn and don't provide support. And this organisation changed during the course of the coaching process into one that backed him and was honest with its feedback. In this view, there is no such thing as the organisation's story separate from that which occurs in the individual's mind. People hold the organisation's story in their own unique way from their own point of reference; it's a bit like a hologram. From this perspective, there can be no single objective organsitional story, and each individual's "organsation in the mind" is one of many true reflections of the organisation's story as a whole.

This means that coaches need to always "be alert to the organisationally determined dynamic in the client's material, whether the conversation is about a critical experience at work, a new strategy or project, or an anecdote apparently unrelated to the client's work preoccupations" (Roberts & Jarrett, 2006, p. 21). In this process, the coach continually looks for points of alignment and misalignment in the narratives of the environment and the individual, and reflects these back to the parties. At the same time, clients repeatedly gain deeper understanding of their organisation as a system, and an enhanced capacity for using the full range of their experience as a resource for understanding their own and other's behaviour. Coach and client "together develop working hypotheses [stories] about what is going on, which the client then tests out in the workplace" (ibid.). This iterative process evolves as the client moves back and forth between the organisation and the coaching sessions: the learning in each setting informs and feeds into learning in the other. As deeper aspects of the person's experience are uncovered, insights emerge, often spontaneously, on the part of the client and the coach. These insights are captured, reflected, tested in the environment, occasionally reframed and then integrated into the clients' evolving story. "Over several such cycles, the client also 'learns how to learn' in this new way—the process becomes internalized" (ibid.).

Let's use the story of Sandy to illustrate this iterative process rather simply. Sandy realised that she was limiting herself by assuming her colleagues would not accept her authority in her new role. This insight emerged when her coach noticed this assumption in a tale she shared during one of her coaching sessions. He questioned how she really knew that "nobody will listen to her" when she had not actually tested that assumption in reality. This question uncovered a previously hidden distortion in her belief system, which spontaneously liberated the insight. Once this insight emerged, the coach looked to embed it into action—real, preferably measurable, behaviour. In Sandy's case, the coach asked: "Now that you have the insight that your own self-limiting beliefs around power have been in the way of your feelings of authorisation in your role, how will you *act* differently?" Sandy was then able to describe very specific examples of how she would behave differently in certain workplace contexts. The coach then challenged Sandy to experiment with this change in her environment. In a subsequent session, once Sandy had tried out this new way of being, the coach worked to integrate her new insight and behaviour into her overall story.

In a single coaching session, many actions might be captured or none for that matter, depending on the number of insights that emerge. Also, some insights are not related to obvious behavioural change, for example, realising the impact of a past negative experience on self-image. In such an insight, the action is intrapsychic and the transformation is immediate, though not obviously visible in behavioural terms.

Never-ending stories

In a coaching process, no single point is ever reached where one can say: "There are no more themes, no more insights, nothing to work on … we can declare victory and end coaching." Mostly, it feels like we are forever in the middle of one story or another, and even when one of these seems to be ending, like the last day of our current job, we are simultaneously in the middle or the start of some others. Perplexingly, all these stories seem to be inherently entangled in some overarching narrative that is forever just beyond our grasp. In this sense, coaching stories have no real end, they are *never ending stories*.

However, most of us are accustomed to stories having an end. The stories we were told in childhood always had one, and mostly they read: "They lived happily ever after, THE END." This is despite the fact that in life, endings of this sort are extremely rare, if they ever occur at all. So if coaching works with story, and the real stories of peoples' lives seem to have no end, what does the end of a coaching story look like? This is an important question. It speaks to the coach's ability to locate an appropriate and ethical point of termination, without which coaching process can continue interminably. Ending a coaching journey is therefore a very conscious act that commonly requires a balanced assessment of "where things are" in the relationship between the individual and the business. Ethically, business coaching interventions need to remain in integrity with their contracted purpose and goals. When such are *sufficiently* achieved, coaching should be terminated or, where appropriate, a new contract agreed based in a set of new outcomes. The litmus test is therefore to ask: "Is there sufficient alignment between the environment and the individual against the backdrop of the prescribed purpose and goals of the process?" If the answer is *largely* in the affirmative, then coaching is probably nearing its end and a termination process should probably begin. However, this is a question that sits "above the surface", what is the question about ending the process that speaks to the level below the surface?

To answer this, allow me to draw on a story, *The Neverending Story* (Eichinger et al., 1984), a movie from the 1980s based on the German fantasy novel by Michael Ende. The story centres on a boy, Bastian, who is fearful and lacks confidence as a result of being neglected by his father and being bullied by other children. Whilst running from some of them, Bastian hides in an antique book store where he finds a book called *The Neverending Story*. Whist hiding, he reads it and finds himself magically part of it. The book takes place in Fantasia, where a force called the Nothing has made Fantasia's Empress ill and threatened the land. She sends a boy, Atreyu, to find a cure for her. Atreyu is a brave young warrior of Bastian's age. In the course of his quest, Atreyu discovers that Fantasia is a representation of the dreams and fantasies of the real world and that the Nothing is an effect of the denial of dreams and aspirations that make anything possible for human beings. He learns that to save Fantasia a real human child must give the Empress a new name and then re-build Fantasia with his imagination. Atreyu returns with Bastian to the Ivory Tower, where the Empress lives. But Bastian is limited by his lack of confidence and fear, and he hesitates …

EMPRESS: He doesn't realise that he's already a part of the Neverending Story.

ATREYU: The Neverending Story, what's that?

EMPRESS: Just as he is sharing all your adventures, others are sharing his. They were with him when he hid from the boys in the bookstore.

BASTIAN: But that's impossible!

EMPRESS: They were with him when he took the book with the Auryn symbol on the cover, in which he's reading his own story right now.

BASTIAN: I can't believe it, they can't be talking about me.

ATREYU: What will happen if he doesn't appear?!

EMPRESS: Then our world will disappear, and so will I.

ATREYU: How can he let that happen?!

EMPRESS: He doesn't understand that he's the one who has the power to stop it. He simply can't imagine that one little boy could be that important.

BASTIAN: Is it really me?

ATREYU: Maybe he doesn't know what he has to do!

BASTIAN: What do I have to do?!

EMPRESS: He has to give me a new name. He's already chosen it, he just has to call it out.

BASTIAN: It's only a story, it's not real. It's only a story.

EMPRESS: Bastian, why don't you do what you dream, Bastian?

BASTIAN: But I can't! I have to keep my feet on the ground!

EMPRESS: Call my name! Bastian, please! Save us!

BASTIAN: All right, I'll do it. I'll save you. I will do what I dream!

BASTIAN: MOONCHILD!

Pause … silence …

BASTIAN: Why is it so dark?

EMPRESS: In the beginning it is always dark.

A small light appears

BASTIAN: What is that?

EMPRESS: One grain of sand. It is all that remains of my vast empire.

BASTIAN: Fantasia has totally disappeared?

EMPRESS: Yes.

BASTIAN: Then everything has been in vain.

EMPRESS: No, it hasn't. Fantasia can arise in you. In your dreams and wishes Bastian.

BASTIAN: How?

EMPRESS: Open your hand.

She puts the grain into his hand ...

EMPRESS: What are you going to wish for?
BASTIAN: I don't know.
EMPRESS: Then there will be no Fantasia any more.
BASTIAN: How many wishes do I get?
EMPRESS: As many as you want. And the more wishes you make, the more magnificent Fantasia will become.
BASTIAN: Really?
EMPRESS: Try it!

Bastian realises, in truth, that our stories never do end, but actually begin again and again in every moment, limited only by the extent of our imagination to create new future possibilities.

And so, the question that sits below the surface about the end of a coaching journey speaks to the level of self-realisation and autonomy in the client; the necessary awareness, capability, and confidence to continue the journey independent of a coach. Simply put, when the client is fully and confidently able to say: "Thank you coach, I'm relatively OK to take it from here on my own", then coaching is at an end because Bastian has all he needs to write the next chapter on his own.

CHAPTER NINE

Case study

The first meeting

Des, a newly appointed executive in a multinational company, engaged my services as a business coach based on a referral from another client. Des contacted me directly and said she needed coaching to help her "step up" in her new senior executive role.

In our first meeting, she explained that she needed to move from her preferred task-based, managerial mindset into more of a relationship-orientated, leadership mindset. She said that an ability to influence and empower, as opposed to direct and control, was necessary to achieve the kinds of business outcomes she was now tasked with.

Although these goals were initially articulated as *individual* development outcomes, they were actually *environmental requirements* for her role. Des explained that her manager, the CEO, and her job description made it clear that "leadership through influence" was a role requirement, and she added: "My boss emphasised that success in such would be an important consideration come bonus time."

When I asked her what she *personally* thought about this challenge [individual dimension], she said: "I'm not good at this politics stuff … it's a load of bollocks most of the time … maybe because I just think people should do their work and stop playing games … But I do see that people need leadership … know what I mean?" This response revealed Des's ambivalent, and somewhat hostile, perspective on the environmental objectives for her coaching journey. I reflected such to her and she agreed by saying: "Yip … Guess you got your work cut out for you then!"

My initial impression of Des was a focused, articulate, and determined individual. As she shared more, I noticed a softer inside peeping through, but it was quickly defended away. Her posture and physical manner were forward-moving, upright, with opening motions indicating confidence and receptivity. She moved easily and spontaneously, indicating freedom from significant anxiety and comfort with the context and her personal power. I made a note: "Tough and confident but not hard."

Her tonality, pace, and speech indicated an obvious partiality to a masculine culture (no nonsense, matter of fact, and direct, with sharp eye contact), and I wondered already at this stage about her relationship with woman and the feminine in herself. I made another note: "What about the feminine?"

She described her company as delivery-orientated, results-focused, and committed to maintaining its status as the international leader in the industry. She said the company "only employs the best" and "expects staff to score winning runs". I noted: "No second best". Des shared a sincere appreciation for such a culture and a deep desire to "put points on the board". I noted: "We only love winners".

As we chatted in this initial meeting, I asked myself a series of questions to determine if coaching was the right service for this brief, and if so, whether I was the right coach?

1. *Is business coaching the appropriate service here?*
   Business coaching is indeed commonly used to address mindset change, particularly when it involves development of leadership competencies as required in a complex business environment (Stout-Rostron, 2009). In such a case, training, although useful, would not be sufficiently tailored and responsive. Management consulting would be inappropriate as a "solution on a silver plate" was not required, and counselling wouldn't be right as the focus was not one of health or wellness. Mentoring might be helpful, but not necessarily more so than coaching. I was also aware that the company had made

use of business coaches with some success before, and that the HR department supported the modality. So coaching looked like a good fit at this early stage.

2. *Is there good chemistry between the client and I?*
   This question is an early axial tap for the quality of the coach–client interpersonal relationship. I noticed that Des and I established rapport easily and quickly. The conversation flowed both ways without struggle. Her body signals increasingly indicated openness to the dialogue and an initial level of trust and safety that was promising. I felt an eagerness and interest to engage further.

3. *What is the individual expecting? Do they understand coaching process?*
   Des had received coaching before in her previous role. A brief discussion about that experience revealed that her understanding of coaching process was sound. She recognised the difference between coaching and other modalities and expressed this as "therapists love, consultants answer, trainers teach, and coaches ask the important questions". I enjoyed the simplicity of her statement and noted a further theme here around her remarkable ability to understand quickly and make complex things simple.

Contracting

Des explained that she ran her own budget, and her manager had already agreed to sign off for a coach. She would not need any triangulation in reporting on progress. She would let her manager know herself how the coaching was going. Curiously, she insisted that HR was to have no involvement in the process. She agreed that her colleagues, manager, and subordinates could participate in a feedback process in an open and honest way (as described in Chapter Five). In terms of confidentiality, she insisted that no reporting was required and that HR was not to be informed of anything without her permission. However, she was comfortable for me to discuss her progress with her manager independently if he wanted this, as long as I subsequently shared the content of these discussions with her and did not censor or "sweet talk" the issues. I noted: "No sweet talk" as a theme. When I enquired as to why HR was not to be involved, she said: "Not necessary, they won't add value." There was a strong emotional content to this response, and I sensed that it would not be a good idea to push this point further right then. I noted: "What's with HR?"

We then discussed contractual issues such as rates, logistics, cancellation procedures, and a six-month initial timeframe renewable for a further six months. Our meetings would average twice per month for approximately two hours at a time, with availability on email and telephone as needed. I agreed to prepare a proposal and send this to her for approval.

Gathering data from the dimensions

We began our coaching process by turning our attention to gathering data from the environmental dimension. Des nominated her boss, two colleagues and two direct reports for me to interview in an open and honest 360 feedback process that focused on her leadership. From the individual dimension, Des and I spent two sessions in which I took a comprehensive personal and work history over two hours. I also perused a range of company documents she provided which included her divisional strategy, company mission and values, Des's performance scorecard and her job description. In our fifth session, I administered an Insights Discovery Personality Profile (Insights® Learning and Development, 2005) to assess Des's personality style, at her request.

Our early sessions focused on exploring all the data sources as a whole, looking for emerging themes. The task was a collaborative one in which together, coach and client, acted as archaeologists, excavating Des's individual roots and environmental branches.

The following themes and insights emerged in early sessions:

1. *Individual dimension*
   Des's personal history was populated with repeated and consistent threats to her social and emotional survival. Nothing had come easy. This had resulted in high levels of independence and a need for total control of her environment. She carried the following beliefs: "God helps those who help themselves", and "in this world, there is only one person who looks after No. 1, and that is No.1". She admitted that she secretly believed that if she could not take care of herself one day, "nobody will give a damn", and she would "probably die in a gutter somewhere" (she laughed). I did not laugh; instead, I reflected how hard it must be for her inside to carry this sense of the world. For the first time, she revealed just how vulnerable she was underneath all her armour by nodding and her eyes welled up

as she bit her lip. There was a silence that followed here that shifted our rapport to a new level.

Her work history was truly impressive. Success after success based on solid delivery and target-breaking achievements; twenty-five-hour days and an absolute, unbridled determination and focus. It was obvious why she had made senior executive at the age of thirty-eight. I noted: "She is a machine".

Throughout her career, all her roles were strongly operational in nature. She had little experience with influencing. She had always been focused on control and directives. As she explained: "there was always a clear task and deadline to meet, and come hell or high water, I was gonna meet it with time to spare!" For this, she had been rewarded by the environment with promotions and bonuses for over thirteen years.

Her personality was strongly so-called "Type A" (Friedman, 1996): ambitious, organised, and status-conscious, but also sensitive, truthful, and impatient (McLeod, 2011). Type A personalities like to help others and tend to take on more than they can handle. They are proactive, push deadlines, and despise delays and ambivalence (ibid.). This view was supported by her Insights Discovery Profile (Insights® Learning & Development, 2005). Des had high scores in the extraverted thinking range and very strong judging functions. In Insights® terms, she was ninety-two per cent Fiery Red with only six per cent Earth Green. This meant that she expected people to "be brief, be bright and be gone!", and she had little or no patience for non-task-based dialogue and was unlikely to "show how much she cares" even when she did.

2. *Environmental dimension*

Feedback from her colleagues was fairly aligned in opinion. They all expressed a degree of respect for Des based on her solid history of delivery and "no-nonsense" straight-talking approach. However, there were varying degrees of concern about her ability to "lead from influence" as opposed to "control and direct". Some called her autocratic. Others described her as tough, honest, and fair. Idiosyncratic responses included that she failed to understand the importance of "certain relationships" in the system and that this would end up being her downfall as an executive if she was not careful.

The culture of the company was characterised by an aggressive focus on delivery in a partial meritocracy. Hierarchy was in place only so much as it served delivery. Long work hours were expected and admired and the place had a reputation for being "unforgiving", "hard", but "fair". Generous bonus based remuneration for performers were the order of the day. I characterised the underlying cultural motto as "perform, perform ... and then we will love ... but stop performing and the love is gone", and several staff, including Des, confirmed it as accurate. We explored the company culture and discovered it changes at executive level. What was previously a delivery-orientated focus now changed to a relationship-orientated focus. Hierarchy existed in terms of "who you were in with" and whether or not you had the CEO's ear. Also, deliverables on several counts were rather subjective and the "softer" skills of people management and leadership were seen as more important than whether you hit a particular number or not. Here the common feeling seemed to be that "politicians rule". Once again, on this theme, Des had an acute reaction: "Screw that!" she said. "I am not playing politics. Firstly, I am crap at it and secondly its bulls..t!" It was clear that she was deeply at odds with something here.

Interpretation of Des's scorecard suggested leadership skills and emotional intelligence to be important as well as stakeholder management. When I juxtaposed this with the above point about politics Des recognised the challenge and said: "I've got a lot of inner work to do to deliver on this baby!" and pointed to her performance scorecard.

We also spent some time creating Des's relational map at this stage (as described in Chapter Five). We gleaned many insights from it as we explored each of her key workplace relationships and the connections between and across them. I made sure that each point of conversation was linked back to the task deliverables her department was responsible for by continually asking questions like: "And how does that aspect of this relationship impact the task?" and "If this relationship was improved in whatever way, how would that improve the business?" But perhaps the most important insight occurred once she stepped back and looked at the image as a whole. She said the following: "I've never really looked at my work in this way before. I always just visualised the tasks. But here (pointing to the relational image) is the first time I can actually *see* what everyone means about relationships being important. But hell, it's a mine field!"

Des's journey in themes

Over time, Des brought her daily experiences to our sessions. Each was unpacked thematically and explored in terms of other themes. An integrative thematic picture slowly took shape and grew richer as sessions progressed. Several of the most important themes are summarised below:

1. *HR Jane*

    Des came to one session in an aggressive mood expressing a need to "vent" her frustration with the HR director, Jane. "She is just a typical bleeding heart female who knows as much about delivery as I know about brain surgery!" Further probing revealed that Jane had confronted Des on her "harsh tone and shortness" in addressing Jane's HR team members after they had (in Des's view) failed to deliver on a talent project Des had commissioned some months earlier. When Des rejected Jane's critical feedback on her style, Jane raised several other circumstances where she had observed Des in this manner and asked Des if she was "in denial about her inability to appreciate how others feel." Des promptly told Jane that the only denial that was happening was the one where the company denied just how dysfunctional the human resources department was. It now became fairly clear why Des had initially instructed that her coaching was to have nothing to do with HR whatsoever.

    We decided to use the session to explore Des's relationship with Jane, who, as you may recall, she had consciously excluded from the initial feedback process. In this process I asked her to imagine, in an appreciative and reflexive way, how Jane's mind worked and what it must be like to be Jane. We also looked at whether there was anything at all about Jane's feedback, even if only in a tiny part, that might be true and worth exploring.

    Several insights emerged. She recognised that Jane in many respects represented all the things that Des was not. She was "into people more than tasks, feelings more than ideas, and she speaks softly and tentatively." Des was particularly activated about the fact that Jane wore bright summer dresses to work. Des further explained that Jane was seen to be "a good listener and a poor driver of people", and that she came from a happy family, best education, married money, and was a mother of three, whereas Des was divorced, had no children, and was self-made.

An important insight emerged for Des when I proposed that Jane could be a valuable psychological barometer for Des in achieving her goals. The very things that hooked Des about Jane were the same themes that she was challenged with as a leader, and for which coaching had been sought. Ironically, her rejection of Jane was a rejection of the outcomes both her and the environment had set as behavioural deliverables. This was not an easy session for Des. She moved between moments of outright resistance to the conversation and emotional expression, and I had to carefully challenge her to stay with the process and trust. But eventually, the lights came on and the action she decided to take out of this session was profound. She said: "I am gonna go to Jane and apologise. I am gonna tell her that I am short on what she is long, and I am gonna ask her to support me."

This was powerful not only for the reversal in perception, in which she owned her part, but on a deeper level. For Des to ask for support was something that went against her every fibre. She was fiercely independent, and this shift was so big that I was taken aback. I realised that Des's emotional competence was stronger than I had previously predicted, and I shared this with her. She smiled and told me that most men underestimated her. At this point, I remembered an important theme that had been there from the start: "the feminine".

2. *The feminine and dresses*

Des had commented that it irritated her when woman wore light short dresses to work in summer. We explored this as "the summer dress theme" and discovered a deep value system challenge. She judged that "woman use their sexuality to get ahead and it's unethical and pathetic and work is not a place for fairies and flowers". We then explored her sense that men underestimate her, and she explained that this happens because men are used to women not delivering and being short on certain competencies, and that she was as good as any man, if not better, since she was a woman.

It seemed to me at the time that Des carried an ambivalent relationship with the feminine; at one level she rejected it and at another saw it as her edge over men. I reflected this to her and a great debate ensued. As a man I suddenly found myself in a strong transference in that moment as it felt like Des was experiencing me as the "other", a representative of all the men in her life. My own countertransference was activated, and I found myself getting entangled in the conversation with my own personal views. Eventually, I became conscious and took a step back to separate my coaching role from my personal process. The session was uncomfortable and it felt like rapport had been injured in some way. I took the experience to a supervisor that week for some reflection. The supervision session helped me recognise the transference more acutely and allowed me to focus on serving Des and not myself in this particular dialogue, and thankfully so, as it emerged repeatedly in subsequent sessions.

Over time, it became clearer for Des that there was a strong link between her capacity to listen, show care, and tune into others' feelings (as capacities she was seeking to acquire as a goal in the coaching) and her ambivalent relationship with the sense of the feminine in herself and the world. This struck her one session when we did a scan of her friends and realised that her best friends had always been men. It also made sense to her when she connected her divorce into the theme and recalled that her husband had accused her of "being the man". She also made the connection to the fact that she had no interest in having children, something other women had challenged her on repeatedly.

As actions around this theme Des began to 'play' with the feminine in her workplace context. For example, she decided to wear makeup to work and even tried a dress on one day "just to see how it feels". She reported that people complemented her on how she looked and that it made her feel "uncomfortable but nice". She found it curious that during this coaching experiment she found she was "less harsh with people" and wondered if it was the dress. I interpreted that the makeup and the dress were simply expressions of a psychological shift inside her, a shift that welcomed rather than rejected the feminine. She laughed and said: "Nonsense! It's the dress. Sometimes life is simple and you just make it complicated." But her body language and smile indicated she had accepted the interpretation, and I just smiled back. Rapport was deeper now than it had ever been.

3. *Simplification as a strength and Achilles heel*
   Des explained that one of the other directors, John, had picked her out about cutting him short when he spoke in meetings. In a subsequent discussion with Henry, another person whom she respected and who attended the same meeting, he explained that Des "can't

cope with ambiguity" and "tended to deconstruct everything into simplifications which were often unhelpful and sometimes ignored the complexity of the situation". Des was perplexed by this feedback because she always had felt that her ability to "cut through the bulls..t and makes things simple" was her greatest strength.

In exploring this feedback, we separated out the usefulness of her ability to simplify "noise" and get down to the bottom of things quickly from the kind of behaviour being pointed out by John and Henry. The former was a useful competence that did not need to change; the latter could be a problem. I asked Des to think about the difference between the two. At first, she was unable to see any difference at all, but after more reflection she realised that the latter had something to do with "the grey". She said: "I guess when an issue doesn't lend itself to a bottom line of black or white and actually leaves me sitting in the grey, I find it hard to handle." I wondered aloud if this might mean she has difficulty managing ambiguity and she agreed. It appeared her tendency to simplify things was at one level very helpful, when simplification was required, and at another level very unhelpful, when complexity and comfort with ambiguity was required. In the latter, her tendency to simplify acted as a defence against sitting with ambiguity because to do so meant that she was in "the grey" and therefore not fully in control.

Des found this session very helpful and the insight shifted her belief system. At an action level, she decided to mentally track each time she fell into this behaviour and remind herself to "sit in the grey ... and just hold." She would make a note of each of these occasions in her coaching diary.

We subsequently were able to link this theme into the emerging thematic story by suggesting that cutting through the noise to the bottom line was a truly masculine competence and being able to 'hold' ambiguity is a truly feminine competence. We also had an interesting conversation at this point about the brain, and discussed left and right brain functioning, but for purposes of this case illustration it is not necessary to explicate that further here.

4. *Politics*

It was a fairly common thing in the early sessions for Des to describe how "sick and tired" she was of having to play politics. She kept finding herself on the short end of various "political" relationships because, as she explained, she "spoke so straight without calculating if this one or that one was going to be put out".

One day, she arrived at a session in a rare state of fluster, explaining that she had been picked out "once again" for doing something without "including the right people" in the decision-making process. The "right people" in her estimation were "the wrong people" in terms of execution, but her CEO had picked her out nevertheless, explaining that it wasn't up to her to decide who she worked with and "if she couldn't play nicely with the other children, she would have to reconsider if this was the right playground for her". In this session, Des admitted that she had taken "a hit". The CEO had been particularly annoyed with her deliberate exclusion of two other executives in a project he had personally commissioned. She realised it was important that she come to understand and really face up to her choices in this dynamic, as they were clearly at odds with her coaching objectives and, more importantly, putting her "at odds with the big boss who wasn't the type to offer second warnings".

We spent several sessions exploring the theme of "politics", moving between separating out different meanings that she was attributing to the phenomenon and reality-testing her perceptions and judgements. We delved deeply, at an existential level, into her value system and ideas of ethics. The dialogue unearthed several early experiences of "politics" in her teenage years at school that wounded her deeply (particularly relating to other girls). Over a period of time, Des began to reframe her distaste for the phenomenon as she found insight after insight through our dialogue. Some key insights were that she had "thrown the baby out with the bathwater" in seeing the entire phenomenon as bad due to the wounds she had experienced at school.

She began to see that "good politics" was really about managing relationships, collaboration, and community, which are good for business, and that "bad politics" was about manipulation, intrigue, and off-task behaviour, which was bad for business. This separation into good and bad politics was helpful in shifting her appreciation for relationship management—a key goal in the coaching. She realised that she could still attack or ignore "bad politics" but she could embrace "good politics" and maintain her personal value system. What she really needed was the ability to tell the difference. We renamed "good politics"—relationship management.

We once again threaded this theme into the overarching thematic picture. Working well with relationships (good politics) and leading in a way that encourages collaborative work culture might be said to be feminine in vision, whereas driving passionately for targets in a task-based, single-minded fashion might be said to be masculine in vision. Whether theoretically valid or not, this thread was viable for Des and constellated a powerful guiding dialectic that she used to manage her development in the work environment.

In a subsequent mid-course feedback session with the CEO, Des and I spent a good forty-five minutes discussing this particular theme with him. He was thoughtful and supportive, and I was struck by the degree to which he was prepared to spend time on the matter. His relational sponsorship of Des was becoming increasingly clear and powerfully motivated her to continue to challenge herself and grow in the coaching process.

Conclusion

Throughout the coaching process, Des would return to sessions and we would reflect on how she was shifting around the overarching goals. We continued to meet together with her CEO every few months, and she shared what she was learning with him. Their relationship grew increasingly meaningful, and after a while his appreciation for her became obvious.

Des's relationship with Jane, the HR director, blossomed into a kind of unusual friendship which in turn moved Jane to support Des in recognising "good politics" when it was important. More importantly, Jane brokered some critical issues that Des needed to resolve with two of her colleagues, and after that things seemed to really gain positive momentum.

After a year of coaching, Des was not free from critical feedback, there were one or two executives who maintained a fairly negative view of her leadership style. However, a 360-review showed significant positive change in the way she was experienced by her sub-ordinates and an overall moderate improvement from her colleagues, and she now included Jane in the feedback process. Her CEO was the most positive in his feedback, and he told me that he believed the coaching had been instrumental for Des. He said that he had initially been worried as to whether or not she "would make it" but was now confident that she "will be fine". Of course I told Des, and she just beamed.

REFERENCES

Alexandrov, A. V., & Martone, M. (Eds). (2013). *Brain and Behavior.* New Jersey: Wiley Periodicals.

Allen, P., Maguire, S., & McKelvey, B. (2011). *The SAGE Handbook of Complexity and Management.* London: SAGE Publications.

Alleyne, A. (2004). Black identity and workplace oppression. *Counselling and Psychotherapy Research, 4(1)*: 4–8.

Alvesson, M. (1993). *Cultural Perspectives on Organisations.* Cambridge: Cambridge University Press.

American Association of Marriage and Family Therapy (AAMFT) (2012). *AAMFT Code of Ethics.* Alexandria, VA: AAMFT.

American Management Association (AMA) (2008). *Coaching: A Global Study of Successful Practices: Current Trends and Future Possibilities: 2008–2013.* New York: AMA.

Anderson, V. (2007). *The Value of Learning: From Return on Investment to Return on Expectation.* London: CIPD.

Andreasen, N. C. (2008). The relationship between creativity and mood disorders. *Dialogues in Clinical Neuroscience, 10(2)*: 251–255.

Antonioni, D. (1996). Designing an effective 360-degree appraisal feedback process. *Organizational Dynamics, 25*: 24–38.

Armstrong, P. (2005). *Organisation in the Mind.* London: Karnac.

Auger, R., & Arneberg, P. (1992). Analytical psychology and organizational development at work (pp. 38–52). In: M. Stein & J. Holliwitz, *Psyche at Work*. Wilmette, IL: Chiron.

Australian Bureau of Statistics (2007). *National Survey of Mental Health and Well-Being: Summary of Results*. Catalogue No. 4326.0. Canberra, ACT: Australian Bureau of Statistics.

Avens, R. (1982). *Imaginal Body*. Washington, DC: University Press of America.

Bachkirova, T. (2010). Role of coaching psychology in defining boundaries between counseling and coaching. In: S. Palmer & A. Whybrow, *Handbook of Coaching Psychology* (pp. 351–366). London: Routledge.

Baillie, M. G. L. (1995). *A Slice through Time: Dendrochronology and Precision Dating*. London: Batsford.

Bandler, R., & Grinder, J. (1983). *Reframing: Neurolinguistic Programming and the Transformation of Meaning*. Moab, UT: Real People Press.

Bandler, R., Grinder, J., & Stevens, J. (Ed.) (1979). *Frogs into Princes: Neuro-Linguistic Programming*. Moab, UT: Real People Press.

Bar-On, R., & Parker, J. D. A. (Eds.) (2000). *The Handbook of Emotional Intelligence: Theory, Development, Assessment, and Application at Home, School and in the Workplace*. San Francisco, CA: Jossey-Bass.

Barton, E. R. (Ed.) (2000). *Mythopoetic Perspective of Men's Healing Work: An Anthology for Therapists and Others*. Westport, CO: Bergin and Garvey.

Bateson, G. (1972). *Steps to an Ecology of Mind: Collected Essays in Anthropology, Psychiatry, Evolution, and Epistemology*. Chicago: University of Chicago Press.

Batts, V. A. (1982). Modern racism: a TA perspective. *Transactional Analysis Journal, 12(3)*: 207–209.

Batts, V. A. (1998). Modern racism: new melody for the same old tunes. *EDS Occasional Papers*, No. 2. Cambridge, MA: Episcopal Divinity School.

Batts, V. A. (2002). Is reconciliation possible? Lessons from combating "modern racism". In: I. T. Douglas (Ed.), *Waging Reconciliation: God's Mission in a Time of Globalization and Crisis*. New York: Church.

Beck, A. T. (1979). *Cognitive Therapy of Depression*. New York: Guilford Press.

Becvar, D. S., & Becvar, R. J. (1998). *Family Therapy: A Systemic Integration*. Massachusetts: Allyn and Bacon.

Benoit, S. (2011). *Toxic Employees: Great Companies Resolve This Problem, You Can Too!* Falmouth, MA: BCS Publishing.

Benton, S., Schurink, C., & Desson, S. (2005). *An Executive Summary of the Development, Validity and Reliability of the English Version 3.0 of the Insights Discovery Evaluator*. University of Westminster's Business Psychology Centre.

Bercovici, D., Grandy, G., & Mills, A. J. (2001). Organizational culture as a framework for organizational analysis: renewed fad or enduring heuristic? *Proceedings of the Atlanta School of Business Annual Conference*, Halifax, 15–17 November: 170–180.

Berglas, S. (2002). The very real dangers of executive coaching. *Harvard Business Review, 80(6)*: 86–92.

Berne, E. (1972). *What Do You Say after You Say Hello?* New York: Grove Press.

Bertalanffy, L. von (1962). General System Theory—a critical review, *General Systems, 7*: 1–20.

Bertalanffy, L. von (1968). *General Systems Theory: Foundations, Development, Applications*. New York: George Braziller.

Best, G. (2003). *Churchill: A Study in Greatness*. Oxford: Oxford University Press.

Bidlack, J. E., Stern, K. R., & Jansky, S. (2003). *Introductory Plant Biology*. New York: McGraw-Hill.

Bion, W. R. (1961). *Experiences in Groups*. London: Tavistock.

Blackburn, S. (2005). *Oxford Dictionary of Philosophy*. Oxford: Oxford University Press.

Bly, R. (1990). *Iron John*. New York: Addison-Wesley.

Boroditsky, L. (2009). How does our language shape the way we think? In: M. Brockman (Ed.), *What's Next? Dispatches on the Future of Science*. New York: Vintage Press.

Boroditsky, L. (2010). Lost in translation. *Wall Street Journal*. 24 July.

Bowen, M. (1978). *Family Therapy in Clinical Practice*. New York: J. Aronson.

Breuer, J., & Freud, S. (1895d). *Studies on Hysteria. Standard Edition of the Complete Psychological Works of Sigmund Freud, 2*.

Bridges, W. (2004). *Transitions: Making Sense of Life's Changes*. New York: De Capo Press.

British Psychological Society (2011). *Good Practice Guidelines on the Use of Psychological Formulation*. Leicester: British Psychological Society.

Brock, V. G. (2008). *Grounded Theory of the Roots and Emergence of Coaching*. Unpublished doctoral dissertation, International University of Professional Studies.

Brooke, R. (1993). *Jung and Phenomenology*. London: Routledge.

Brooks-Harris, J. E. (2008). *Integrative Multitheoretical Psychotherapy*. Boston: Houghton-Mifflin.

Brown, A. (1998). *Organisational Culture*. London: Pitman.

Brunning, H. (2006). *Executive Coaching: Systems-Psychodynamic Perspective*. London: Karnac.

Brutus, S., Fleenor, J. W., & London, M. (1998). Does 360-degree feedback work in different industries?: a between-industry comparison of the reliability and validity of multi-source performance ratings. *Journal of Management Development, 17(3)*: 177–190.

Burn, G. (2005). *NLP Pocketbook*. London: Management Pocketbooks.

Capon, B. (2005). *Botany for Gardeners* (2nd edn.). Portland: Timber.

Cavanagh, M. (2006). Coaching from a systemic perspective: a complex adaptive conversation. In: D. R. Strober & A. M. Grant (Eds.), *Evidence-Based Coaching Handbook*. New Jersey: John Wiley.

Center for Mental Health in the Workplace (2013). *Why Mental Health in the Workplace Matters*. Downloaded from http://www.workplacestrategiesf ormentalhealth.com/display.asp?l1=2&d=2 on 21 September 2013.

Chapman, L. (2010). *Integrated Experiential Coaching*. London: Karnac.

Chartered Institute of Personnel and Development (CIPD) (2011). *Learning and Development: Annual Survey Report 2011*. London: CIPD.

Chartered Institute of Personnel and Development (CIPD) (2012). *Coaching and Mentoring Fact Sheet*. Downloaded from http://www.cipd.co.uk/hr-resources/factsheets/coaching-mentoring.aspx#link_0 on 3 July 2013.

Chesbrough, H. W. (2007). *Open Business Models: How to Thrive in the New Innovation Landscape*. Boston: Harvard Business Press.

Cilliers, F. (2005). Executive coaching experiences: a systems psychody-namic perspective. *South African Journal of Industrial Psychology, 31(3)*: 23–30.

Cilliers, F., & Terblanche, L. (2010). The systems psychodynamic leadership coaching experiences of nursing managers. *Journal of Interdisciplinary Health Sciences, 15(1)*: 1–9.

Clutterbuck, D., & Megginson, D. (2005). *Making Coaching Work: Creating a Coaching Culture*. London: CIPD.

Cohen, J. (2009). *The Astonishing Power of Story*. Raleigh: Lulu Press.

Collins, J. (2001). *Good to Great*. London: Random House.

Cooper, A. E. (1994). *BPR and Organisational Change*. Masters dissertation, Henley Management College, Oxon, England.

Corbin, H. (1972). Mundis Imaginalis or the imaginary and the imaginal. *Spring*: 1–19.

Corey, G. (1996). *Theory and Practice of Counseling and Psychotherapy* (5th edn.). London: Brooks/Cole.

Corey, G., Corey, M. S., & Callanan, P. (2011). *Issues and Ethics in the Helping Professions*. Belmont: Brooks/Cole.

Corrie, S., & Lane, D. A. (2010). *Constructing and Telling Stories*. London: Karnac.

Corsini, R. J., & Wedding, D. (2008). *Current Psychotherapies* (8th edn.). Belmont, CA: Thomson Brooks/Cole.

Costa, P. T., Jr, & McCrae, R. R. (1992). *Revised NEO Personality Inventory (NEO-PI-R) and NEO Five-Factor Inventory (NEO-FFI) Manual*. Odessa, FL: Psychological Assessment Resources.

Covey, S. (1989). *The Seven Habits of Highly Effective People*. New York: Free Press.

Covey, S. (1992). *Principle-Centred Leadership*. Sydney: Simon & Schuster.

Crowne, D. P. (2010). *Personality Theory*. New York: Oxford University Press.

Csikszentmihalyi, M. (1990). *Flow: The Psychology of Optimal Experience*. New York: Harper & Row.

Cytrynbaum, S., & Noumair, A. (2004). Group dynamics, organizational irrationality, and social complexity. *Group Relations Reader 3*. Jupiter: A. K. Rice.

Deal, T. E., & Kennedy, A. A. (2000). *Corporate Cultures*. New York: Basic Books.

De Haan, E. (2008). *Relational Coaching: Journeys Towards Mastering One-to-One Learning*. Chichester: Wiley.

De Haan, E. (2011). Back to basics: how the discovery of transference is relevant for coaches and consultants today. *International Coaching Psychology Review, 6(2)*: 180–193.

D'Este, C. (2008). *Warlord: A Life of Winston Churchill at War, 1874–1945*. New York: Harper.

Dembkowski, S., Eldridge, F., & Hunter, I. (2006). *The Seven Steps of Effective Executive Coaching*. London: Thorogood.

Denma Translation Group (2001). *The Art of War: Translation, Essays and Commentaries by the Denma Translation Group/Sun Tzu*. Boston: Shambhala.

Eichinger, B., & Geissler, D. (Producers), and Petersen, W. (Director) (1984). *The Neverending Story*. West Germany: Neue Constantin Films.

Eisenberg, L. (1977). Disease and illness: distinctions between professional and popular ideas of sickness. *Culture, Medicine and Psychiatry, 1*: 9–23.

Erculj, J. (2009). Organisational culture as organisational identity—between the public and the private. *Organizacija, 42(3)*: 69–76.

Evans, E. (2000). *Tree Anatomy*. NC State University, downloaded 9 July 2013 from http://www.ces.ncsu.edu/depts/hort/consumer/factsheets/trees-new/text/tree_anatomy.html.

Fisher, M. A. (2009). Replacing "who is the client?" with a different ethical question. *Professional Psychology: Research and Practice, 40(1)*: 1–7.

Flaherty, J. (2005). *Coaching: Evoking Excellence in Others* (2nd edn.). Boston: Butterworth-Heinmann.

Fraher, A. L. (2004). Systems psychodynamics: the formative years (1895–1967). *Organisational and Social Dynamics, 4(2)*: 19–39.

Frankl, V. (1984). *Man's Search for Meaning*. New York: Washington Square Press.

Freud, S. (1905e). Fragments of an analysis of a case of hysteria. *Standard Edition of the Complete Psychological Works of Sigmund Freud, 7*. London: Hogarth.

Freud, S. (1910d). The future prospects of psychoanalytic therapy. *Standard Edition of the Complete Psychological Works of Sigmund Freud, 11*. London: Hogarth.

Freud, S. (1914g). Remembering, repeating and working-through. *Standard Edition of the Complete Psychological Works of Sigmund Freud, 12*. London: Hogarth.

Freud, S. (1915e). The unconscious. *Standard Edition of the Complete Psychological Works of Sigmund Freud, 14*. London: Hogarth.

Freud, S. (1925d). An autobiographical study. *Standard Edition of the Complete Psychological works of Sigmund Freud, 20*. London: Hogarth.

Freud S. (1940a). An outline of psychoanalysis. *Standard Edition of the Complete Psychological Works of Sigmund Freud, 23*. London: Hogarth.

Friedman, M. (1996). *Type A Behavior: Its Diagnosis and Treatment*. New York: Plenum Press.

Gendlin, E. (2007). *Focusing*. New York: Bantam Books.

Gold, J., Thorpe, R., & Mumford, A. (2010). *Leadership and Management Development* (5th edn.). London: Chartered Institute of Personnel and Development.

Goleman, D. (2005). *Emotional Intelligence*. London: Bantam Books.

Goshal, S. (2005). *Want success? Change the smell of your workplace!* Rediff.com downloaded 21 March 2013 from http://www.rediff.com/money/2005/mar/10bspec.htm.

Goshal, S. (2010). *The smell of the place*. Video of talk delivered at the world economic forum in 2004. Downloaded from You-tube http://www.youtube.com/watch?v=UUddgE8rI0E on 21 March 2013.

Goshal, S., & Bartlett, C. A. (1997). *The Individualized Corporation: A Fundamentally New Approach to Management*. New York: Harper Business.

Goshal, S., & Westney, D. E. (2005). *Organization Theory and the Multinational Corporation*. New York: Palgrove Macmillan.

Green, Z. G., & Molenkamp, R. J. (2005). The BART system of group and organizational analysis: boundary, authority, role and task. Unpublished paper.

Greenfield, D. P., & Hengen, W. K. (2004). Confidentiality in coaching. *Consulting to Management, 15(1)*: 9–14.

Handy, C. B. (1985). *Understanding Organizations*. Harmondsworth: Penguin.

Hanson, B. G. (1995). *General Systems Theory Beginning with Wholes*. Washington, DC: Taylor & Francis.

Hauke, C. (2005). *Human Being Human: Culture and the Soul*. London: Routledge.

Hauser, P. M. (1961). Aspects of sociology for business. *Sociological Inquiry, 31(2)*: 167–179.

Hawkins, P., & Schwenk, G. (2010). The interpersonal relationship in training and supervision of coaches. In: S. Palmer & A. McDowall, *The Coaching Relationship* (pp. 203–221). London: Routledge.

Hecker, L. L., & Wetchler, J. L. (2003). *An Introduction to Marriage and Family Therapy*. New York: Haworth Press.

Heidegger, M. (1962). *Being and Time*. New York: Harper Collins.

Hesse, H. (1984). *Baume: Betractungen und Gedichte*. Frankfurt: Insel.

Hillman, J. (1975). *Revisioning Psychology*. New York: Harper & Row.

Hillman, J. (1983). *Healing Fiction*. New York: Station Hill Press.

Hillman, J. (1989). *A Blue Fire*. New York: Harper & Row.

Hillman, J. (1997). *Archetypal Psychology: A Brief Account*. Dallas: Spring.

Hirsh, S. (1985). *Using the Myers-Briggs Type Indicator in Organizations*. Palo Alto, CA: Consulting Psychological Press.

Hirst, M., Cook, J., & Kahn, M. S. (1996). Shades, witches and somatisation in the narratives of illness and disorder among the Cape Nguni in the Eastern Cape, South Africa. *Curare, 19(2)*: 255–282.

Hofstede, G. (1980). *Culture's Consequences: International Differences in Work-Related Values*. Beverly Hills, CA: Sage.

Hofstede, G. (2001). *Culture's Consequences: Comparing Values, Behaviors, Institutions, and Organizations across Nations*. New York: Sage.

Hofstede, G., Hofstede, G. J., & Minkov, M. (2010). *Cultures and Organizations: Software of the Mind*. New York: McGraw-Hill.

Huffington, C. (2006). A contextualised approach to coaching. In: H. Brunning, *Executive Coaching: Systems-Psychodynamic Perspective*. London: Karnac.

Huffington, C., & Hieker, C. (2006). Reflexive questions in a coaching psychology context. *International Coaching Psychology Review, 1(2)*: 47–56.

Huffington, C., Armstrong, A., Halton, W., Hoyle, L., & Pooley, J. (2004). *Working below the Surface: The Emotional Life of Contemporary Organisations*. London: Karnac.

Hughes, P., & Kerr, I. (2000). Transference and countertransference in communication between doctor and patient. *Advances in Psychiatric Treatment, 6*: 57–64.

Insights® Learning and Development (2005). *Insights Discovery 3.0.1 Profile for (subject's name removed)*. Dundee: Insights Learning and Development Ltd.

International Coach Federation (ICF) (2012). *The 2012 ICF Global Coaching Study*. Retrieved 28 July 2013 from http://www.coachfederation.org/coachingstudy2012/.

Jones, S., Guy, A., & Ormrod, J. A. (2003). A Q-methodological study of hearing voices: a preliminary exploration of voice hearers' understanding of their experiences. *Psychology and Psychotherapy: Theory, Research and Practice, 76*: 189–209.

Jung, C. G. (1965). *Memories, Dreams, Reflections*. New York: Random House.

Jung, C. G. (1996). *The Archetypes and the Collective Unconscious*. London: Routledge.

Kahn, M. S. (2002). The modern male psyche and manhood. *CME, 20(8)*: 531–532.

Kahn, M. S. (2011). Coaching on the Axis: an integrative and systemic approach to business coaching. *International Coaching Psychology Review, 6(2)*: 194–210.

Kahn, M. S., & Kelly, K. J. (2001). Cultural tensions in psychiatric nursing: managing the interface between Western mental health care and Xhosa traditional healing in South Africa. *Transcultural Psychiatry, 38*: 35–50.

Kauth, B. (1992). *A Circle of Men*. New York: St. Martin's Press.

Keen, S. (1991). *Fire in the Belly: On Being a Man*. New York: Bantam Books.

Kelley, A. H. (2007). Coaching executive across cultures. In: F. R. Kets de Vries, K. Korotov, & E. Florent-Treacy (Eds.), *Coach and Couch: The Psychology of Making Better Leaders*. New York: Palgrave Macmillan.

Kemp, T. (2008). Self-management and the coaching relationship: exploring coaching impact beyond models and methods. *International Coaching Psychology Review, 3(1)*: 32–42.

Kets de Vries, M. F. R. (1991). *Organizations on the Couch: Clinical Perspectives on Organizational Behavior and Change*. San Francisco, CA: Jossey-Bass.

Kets de Vries, M. F. R, Korotov, K., & Florent-Treacy, E. (2007). *Coach and Couch: The Psychology of Making Better Leaders*. New York: Palgrave Macmillan.

Kets de Vries, M. F. R., Florent-Treacy, E., Vrignaud, P., & Korotov, K. (2007). Goodbye, Sweet Narcisssus: using 360 feedback for self-reflection. In: F. R. Kets de Vries, K. Korotov, & E. Florent-Treacy (Eds.), *Coach and Couch: The Psychology of Making Better Leaders*. New York: Palgrave Macmillan.

Kilburg, R. R. (2007). Toward a conceptual understanding and definition of executive coaching. In: R. R. Kilburg & R. C. Diedrich (Eds.), *The Wisdom of Coaching*. Washington: American Psychological Association.

Kilburg, R. R., & Diedrich, R. C. (2007). *The Wisdom of Coaching*. Washington: American Psychological Association.

Kolb, A. Y., & Kolb, D. A. (2005). *The Kolb Learning Style Inventory—Version 3.1. 2005 Technical Specifications*. Boston, MA: Hay Group, Hay Resources Direct.

Kolb, D. A. (1984). *Experiential Learning: Experience as the Source of Learning and Development*. New Jersey: Prentice Hall.

Kuttner, R., & Spriggs, W. E. (2008). The color of opportunity: narrowing racial divides and expanding prosperity for all. *The American Prospect, 19(10)*: 1.

Lane, D. A., & Corrie, S. (2006). *The Modern Scientist-Practitioner*. London: Routledge.

Langworth, R. M. (2008). *Churchill by Himself*. London: Ebury Press.

Lao Tzu (2002). *Tao Te Ching*. London: Watkins.

Lencioni, P. (2005). *Overcoming the Five Dysfunctions of a Team*. San Francisco, CA: Jossey-Bass.

Lewin, K. (1938). The conceptual representation and the measurement of psychological forces. In: *Contributions to Psychological Theory*. Durham, NC: Duke University Press.

Lewin, K. (1947a). Group decisions and social change. In: T. M. Newcomb & E. L. Hartley (Eds.), *Reading in Social Psychology*. New York: Henry Holt.

Lewin, K. (1947b). Frontiers in group dynamics. In: D. Cartwright (Ed.), *Field Theory in Social Science*. Chicago: University of Chicago Press.

Lewin, R. (1993). *Complexity: Life at the Edge of Chaos*. London: Phoenix.

Lowman, R. (2013). Coaching ethics. In: J. Passmore, D. B. Peterson, & T. Freire (Eds.), *The Wiley-Blackwell Handbook of the Psychology of Coaching and Mentoring*. West Sussex: Wiley-Blackwell.

Ludden, J. (2011). *Workplace Atmosphere Keeps Many in the Closet*. NPR.org. Downloaded 9 June 2013 from http://www.npr.org/2011/07/03/137560187/workplace-atmosphere-keeps-many-in-the-closet.

Lyubomirsky, S., King, L., & Diener, E. (2005). The benefits of frequent positive affect: does happiness lead to success? *Psychological Bulletin, 131(6)*: 803–855.

Malan, D. (1995). *Individual Psychotherapy and the Science of Psychodynamics*: London: Oxford University Press.

Malcolm, J. (1981). *Psychoanalysis: The Impossible Profession*. London: Random House.

Manzoni, J. F., & Barsoux, J. L. (2009). Setting you up to fail. *MIT Sloan Management Review, 50(4)*: 42–51.

Mathison, J., & Tosey, P. (2010). Exploring inner landscapes through psychophenomenology: the contribution of neuro-linguistic programming to innovations in researching first-person experience. *Qualitative Research in Organizations and Management: An International Journal, 5(1)*: 63–82.

Maturana, H. R., & Varela, F. J. (1987). *The Tree of Knowledge: The Biological Roots of Human Understanding*. Boston, MA: Shambhala.

Maula, M. (2000). The senses and memory of a firm—implications of autopoiesis theory for knowledge management. *Journal of Knowledge Management, 4(2)*: 157–161.

Maxwell, J. C. (1995). *Developing the Leaders Around You*. London: Nelson.

McCrae, R. R., & Costa, P. T. (1987). Validation of the five-factor model of personality across instruments and observers. *Journal of Personality and Social Psychology, 52*: 81–90.

McLean, G. N. (2009). *Organization Development: Principles, Processes, Performance*. San Francisco, CA: Berrett-Koehler.

McLeod, S. A. (2011). *Type A Personality*, retrieved on 23 January 2014 from http://www.simplypsychology.org/personality-a.html.

McNaught, B. (2010). Creating a welcoming environment for gay employees. *The Diversity Factor, 18(4)*: 27–30.

McRae, M. B., & Short, E. L. (2010). *Racial and Cultural Dynamics in Group and Organizational Life*. New York: Sage.

Merriam, S. B., Caffarella, R. S., & Baumgartner, L. M. (2006). *Learning in Adulthood: A Comprehensive Guide*. Indianapolis: Jossey-Bass.

Minahan, M., & Hutton, C. (2004). Group development: meet the theorists. Paper presented at the OD Network Annual Conference.

Mindell, A. (1995). *Sitting in the Fire: Large Group Transformation Using Conflict and Diversity*. Portland: Lao Tse Press.

Mindell, A. (2000). *Quantum Mind: The Edge Between Physics and Psychology*. Portland: Lao Tse Press.

Mindell, A. (2002). *The Deep Democracy of Open Forums: Practical Steps to Conflict Prevention and Resolution for the Family, Workplace, and World*. Charlottseville: Hampton Road Publishing.

Minuchin, S. (1974). *Families and Family Therapy*. London: Harvard University Press.

Moran, C. (1966). *Churchill: The Struggle for Survival, 1940–1965*. London: Houghton Mifflin.

Morden, T. (2004). *Principles of Management*. Aldergate: Ashgate.

Morgan, G. (2006). *Images of Organisation*. London: Sage.

Moyes, B. (2009). Literature review of coaching supervision. *International Coaching Psychology Review, 4(2)*: 162–173.

Muir, H. (2012). Has racial discrimination been eradicated from the workplace? Guardian.co.uk. Retreived on 9 June 2013 from http://www.guardian.co.uk/world/2012/oct/09/racial-discrimination-eradicated-from-workplace.

National Institute of Mental Health (2013). *The Numbers Count: Mental Disorders in America*. USA.gov. Downloaded 21 September 2013 from http://www.nimh.nih.gov/health/publications/the-numbers-count-mental-disorders-in-america/index.shtml.

Newton, J., Long, S., & Sievers, B. (2006). *Coaching in Depth: The Organizational Role Analysis Approach*. London: Karnac.

Norcross, J. C. (2005). A primer on psychotherapy integration. In: J. C. Norcross & M. R. Goldfried (Eds.), *Handbook of Psychotherapy Integration* (2nd edn.). New York: Oxford University Press.

Norcross, J. C., & Goldfried, M. R. (Eds.) (2005). *Handbook of Psychotherapy Integration* (2nd edn.). New York: Oxford University Press.

Northouse, P. G. (2010). *Leadership Theory and Practice* (5th edn.). California: Sage.

O'Brion, A., & Palmer, S. (2010). Reappraising the coach–client relationship. In: S. Palmer & A. Whybrow (Eds.), *Handbook of Coaching Psychology*. London: Routledge.

Obholzer, A., & Roberts, V. Z. (1994). *The Unconscious at Work: Individual and Organizational Stress in the Human Services*. London: Routledge.

Oliver, C. (2010). Reflexive coaching: linking meaning and action in the leadership system. In: S. Palmer & A. McDowall, *The Coaching Relationship*. London: Routledge.

O'Neill, M. B. (2007). *Coaching with Backbone and Heart: A Systems Approach to Engaging Leaders with their Challenges* (2nd edn.). San Francisco, CA: Jossey-Bass.

Page, L., & Rock, D. (2009). *Coaching with the Brain in Mind: Foundations for Practice*. New York: John Wiley.

Palmer, S., & Cavanagh, M. (2006). Coaching psychology: its time has finally come. *International Coaching Psychology Review, 1(1)*: 1–3.

Palmer, S., & McDowall, A. (2010). *The Coaching Relationship*. London: Routledge.

Palmer, S., & Whybrow, A. (2006). The coaching psychology movement and its development within the British Psychological Society. *International Coaching Psychology Review, 1(1)*: 5–10.

Palmer, S., & Whybrow, A. (Eds.) (2007). *Handbook of Coaching Psychology: A Guide for Practitioners*. London: Sage.

Palmer, S., & Woolfe, R. (1999). *Integrative and Eclectic Counselling and Psychotherapy*. London: Sage.

Passmore, J. (2007). An integrative model for executive coaching. *Consulting Psychology Journal: Practice and Research, 59(1)*: 68–78.

Passmore, J., & Mortimer, L. (2011). Ethics in coaching. In: G. Hernez-Broome & L. A. Boyce (Eds.), *Advancing Executive Coaching*. San Francisco, CA: Jossey-Bass.

Passmore, J., Peterson, D. B., & Freire, T. (Eds.) (2013). *The Wiley-Blackwell Handbook of the Psychology of Coaching and Mentoring*. West Sussex: Wiley-Blackwell.

Patton, W., & McMahon, M. (2006). The systems theory framework of career development and counseling: connecting theory and practice. *International Journal for the Advancement of Counselling, 28(2)*: 153–166.

Peltier, B. (2001). *The Psychology of Executive Coaching: Theory and Application*. New York: Brunner-Routledge.

Peterson, C. (2006). *Primer in Positive Psychology*. London: Oxford University Press.

Pope, K. S., & Vetter, V. A. (1992). Ethical dilemmas encountered by members of the American Psychological Association: a national survey. *The American Psychologist, 47(3)*: 397–411.

Popper, K. (1963). *Conjectures and Refutations: The Growth of Scientific Knowledge*. New York: Harper Torchbooks.

Potok, C. (1985). *Davita's Harp*. New York. Random House.

Quotes & Poems.com. (2012). *Top 5 quotes from Leo Burnett*. Retrieved 31 December 2012 from http://www.quotesandpoem.com/quotes/showquotes/author/leo-burnett/81408.

Rachlin, H. (1991). *Introduction to Modern Behaviorism* (3rd edn.). New York: Freeman.

Racker, H. (2002). *Transference and Countertransference*. London: Karnac.

Raeburn, N. C. (2004). *Changing Corporate America from Inside Out: Lesbian and Gay Workplace Rights*. Minneapolis: University of Minnesota Press.

Right Management (2009). *Aligning Leader Coaching to Business Outcomes*. Melbourne: Right Management.

Ringleb, A. H., & Rock, D. R. (2009). Defining NeuroLeadership as a field. *NeuroLeadership Journal. 2*: 1–7.

Rioch, M. J. (1970). The work of Wilfred Bion on groups. *Journal for the Study of Interpersonal Processes, 33(1)*: 56–66.

Roam, D. (2009). *The Back of the Napkin: Solving Problems and Selling Ideas with Pictures*. London: Penguin.

Robbins, R. H. (2011). *Global Problems and the Culture of Capitalism*. Boston: Prentice Hall.

Roberts, V. Z., & Jarrett, M. (2006). What is the difference and what makes the difference? A comparative study of psychodynamic and non-psychodynamic approaches to executive coaching. In: H. Brunning (Ed.), *Executive Coaching: Systems-Psychodynamic Perspective* (pp. 3–39). London: Karnac.

Rodgers, W. M. (2006). *Handbook on the Economics of Discrimination*. North Hampton, MA: Edward Elgar.

Rosinski, P. (2003). *Coaching across Cultures*. London: Nicholas Brealey.

Sandberg, S. (2013). *Lean In: Women, Work, and the Will to Lead*. New York: Knopf Doubleday.

Sarbin, T. R. (Ed.) (1986). *Narrative Psychology: The Storied Nature of Human Conduct*. New York: Praeger.

Sansone, C., Morf, C. C., & Panter, A. T. (2003). *The Sage Handbook of Methods in Social Psychology*. London: Sage.

Scaturo, D. J. (2010). Insight-oriented psychotherapy. In: *The Corsini Encyclopedia of Psychology*. New York: John Wiley.

Schein, E. H. (1999). *Process Consultation Revisited: Building the Helping Relationship*. Prentice Hall Organizational Development Series.

Schein, E. H. (2004). *Organizational Culture and Leadership* (3rd edn.). San Francisco, CA: John Wiley.

Schein, E. H. (2009). *Helping: How to Offer, Give, and Receive Help*. San Francisco, CA: Berrett-Koehler.

Schein, E. H. (2010). *Organizational Culture and Leadership* (4th edn.). San Francisco, CA: John Wiley.

Schneider, K. J. (2008). *Existential-Integrative Psychotherapy: Guideposts to the Core of Practice*. New York: Routledge.

Schneider, K. J., Bugental, J. F. T., & Pierson, J. F. (2001). *The Handbook of Humanistic Psychology: Leading Edges in Theory, Research, and Practice*. Thousand Oaks, CA: Sage.

Schnupp, J., Nelken, I., & King, A. (2011). *Auditory Neuroscience*. Cambridge, MA: MIT Press.

Schultz, M. (1994). *On Studying Organizational Cultures: Diagnosis and Understanding*. Berlin: Walter de Gruyter.

Scott, S. (2009). *Fierce Leadership: A Bold Alternative to the Worst "Best" Practices of Business Today*. London: Piatkus.

Searles, H. F. (1955). The informational value of the supervisor's emotional experience. *Psychiatry, 18*: 135–146.

Seligman, M. (2004). *Authentic Happiness: Using the New Positive Psychology to Realize Your Potential for Lasting Fulfillment*: New York: Simon & Schuster.

Senge, P. (1990). *The Fifth Discipline: The Art and Practice of the Learning Organization*. New York: Doubleday.

Shakespeare, W. (1974). *The Tempest*. The New Folger Library Shakespeare. New York: Washington Square Press.

Sisodia, R., Sheth, J., & Wolfe, D. (2007). *Firms of Endearment*. New Jersey: Wharton School.

Smuts, J. C. (1927). *Holism and Evolution*. London: McMillan.

Spinelli, E. (1989). *The Interpreted World: An Introduction to Phenomenological Psychology*. London: Sage.

Stacey, R. D. (2001). *Complex Responsive Processes in Organizations*. New York: Routlege.

Stapley, L. F. (1996). *The Personality of the Organisation*. London: Free Association Books.

Stapley, L. F. (2006). *Individuals, Groups, and Organisations Beneath the Surface*. London: Karnac.

Stevens, A. (1994). *Jung: A Very Short Introduction*. Oxford: Oxford University Press.

Stokes, J. (1994). The unconscious at work in groups and teams: contributions from the work of Wilfred Bion. In: A. Obholzer & V. Z. Roberts (Eds.), *The Unconscious at Work: Individual and Organizational Stress in the Human Services*. London: Routledge.

Stout-Rostron, S. (2009). *Business Coaching International*. London: Karnac.

Strawbridge, S. (2010). Telling stories. In: S. Corrie & D. A. Lane (Eds.), *Constructing and Telling Stories*. London: Karnac.

Strober, D. R., & Grant, A. M. (Eds.) (2006). *Evidence-Based Coaching Handbook*. New Jersey: John Wiley.

Struwig, H., & Cilliers, F. (2012). Working with boundaries in systems psychodynamic consulting. *SA Journal of Industrial Psychology, 38(2)*: 1–10.

Swedish Institute (2011). *Gender Equality: The Swedish Approach to Fairness*. Retrieved 24 March 2013, from http://www.sweden.se/eng/Home/Society/Equality/Facts/Gender-equality-in-Sweden.

Sylvestre-Williams, R. (2012). *How to Tell if Your Company is Toxic*. Forbes. com. Retrieved 25 September 2013, from http://www.forbes.com/sites/reneesylvestrewilliams/2012/05/07/is-your-company-toxic.

Von Franz, M., & Hillman, J. (1991). *Lectures on Jung's Typology*. New York: Spring Publications.

Walsh, J. (2002). Supervising the countertransference reactions of case managers. *The Clinical Supervisor, 21(2)*: 129–144.

White, M. (2007). *Maps of Narrative Practice*. New York: W. W. Norton.

Whitmore, J. (2009). *Coaching for Performance: Growing Human Potential and Purpose*. London: Nicholas Brealey.

Wilber, K. (2000). *Integral Psychology: Consciousness, Spirit, Psychology, Therapy*. Boston: Shambala.

Wilber, K. (2006). *Integral Spirituality*. Boston: Integral Books.

Woldt, A. L., & Toman, S. M. (2005). *Gestalt Therapy: History, Theory, and Practice*. London: Sage.

Woollard, J. (2010). *Psychology for the Classroom: Behaviourism*. New York: Routledge.

Worldwide Association of Business Coaches (2007). *Business Coaching Definition and Competencies*. Retrieved 2 May 2011, from http://www.wabccoaches.com/includes/popups/definition_and_competencies.html.

INDEX

adult learning theory 3, 106
Alexandrov, A. V. 105
Allen, P. 8, 10
Alleyne, A. 89, 105
Alvesson, M. 22
American Association for Marriage
      and Family Therapy's Code
      of Ethics 138, 140
American Sociological Association 34
Anderson, V. 135
Andreasen, N. C. 103
Antonioni, D. 73, 75
APA Ethics Code 137
Armstrong, A. 20, 64
Armstrong, P. 5, 149
Arneberg, P. 37–38
Art of War, The see Sun Tzu
"Aspects of Sociology of Business"
      34
Auger, R. 37–38
authentic individual action 42

authentic manhood 89
autopoiesis 16
Avens, R. 144
axial notion 6

Bachkirova, T. 34
Baillie, M. G. L. 65
Bandler, R. 105, 143
Bar-On, R. 105
Barsoux, J. L. 66
Bartlett, C. A. 81
Barton, E. R. 89
Bateson, G. 131
Batts, V. A. 89–91, 93–94, 105
Baumgartner, L. M. 106
Beck, A. T. 143
Becvar, D. S. 4
Becvar, R. J. 4
Benoit, S. 118
Benton, S. 106
Bercovici, D. 22, 30

Berglas, S. 124
Berne, E. 127
Best, G. 103
bet-the-company culture 33
Bidlack, J. E. 59
Bion, W. R. 10, 17–19, 23
Blackburn, S. 95
Bly, R. 89
Boroditsky, L. 36
Bowen, M. 7
Breuer, J. 124
Bridges, W. 105
British Psychological Society 146
Brock, V. G. 3
Brooke, R. 144
Brooks-Harris, J. E. 48
Brown, A. 29
Brunning, H. 1, 7, 17–18, 81
Brutus, S. 72
Bugental, J. F. T. 105
Burn, G. 105
Burnett, Leo 9
business coaching, definition of
        practice 2
business models and culture,
        literature 81

C. G. Jung Institute 145
Caffarella, R. S. 106
Callanan, P. 137–138
Capon, B. 65
Cavanagh, M. xviii, 1, 7, 10, 12–14, 81
challenger 18
Chapman, L. 50
Chesbrough, H. W. 81
Cilliers, F. 6, 17
Circle of Men, A 89
circular causality 11–14
circular question 114
client, complexity of 1–20
    duality of client 5
    systems thinking 7

Clutterbuck, D. 42–43
coaching axis 108
    business culture 42, 139
    historical and theoretical
        perspective 3
coaching goal setting 111, 135
coaching interventions 3
coaching on axis 55–58, 143–154, 193
    as iterative and emergent
        learning 149–151
    Jacob's themes 148
    never-ending stories 151–154
    process of working 147–148
    story as formulation 145–146
    story of imagination 144–145
coaching relationship 107–142
    an axial coaching contract
        129–131
    axis connects coaching 115
    boundary management on axis
        132–133
    coaching relationship 108–109
    ethics on the axis 136–137
    goals are compasses not
        destinations 113–114
    pathology-based orientations 117
    success evaluation 134–136
    transference and
        countertransference 123–129
Cohen, J. 146
Collins, J. 81
complexity of theory 45–53
    business culture and 46
    integrative and eclectic
        approaches to 48–50
    modern scientist-practitioner
        50–54
    themes as a framework 52
consensus-creating glue 24
Cook, J. 88
Cooper, A. E. 22
Corbin, H. 145

Corey, G. 137–138, 144
Corey, M. S. 137–138
Corrie, S. 35, 45, 50, 52, 80, 145–146
Corsini, R. J. 105
Costa, P. T. 106
Covey, S. 81
Crowne, D. P. 106
Csikszentmihalyi, M. 105
cultural forces 21
cultural icons 4
culture change 42
culture, complexity of 21–43
    attributes/typologies of 30–31
    coaching business culture 34
    description 22
    emergence of 23
    external adaptation 27
    internal integration 27–28
    leadership and organisational
        culture 29–30
    notion of 22
    organisational culture 26–27
    strength of 28
    view of 22
Cytrynbaum, S. 20

D'Este, C. 103
Davita's Harp 85
de Haan, E. 1, 123–125, 128
Deal, T. E. 22, 28–29, 32, 81
Dembkowski, S. 143
dependence assumption 23
dependency 18–19, 23, 78
Desson, S. 106
Diedrich, R. C. xviii
Diener, E. 99
dual listening 2

Eichinger, B. 152
Eisenberg, L. 30
Eldridge, F. 143
emotional hardness 111

environmental dimension 59–81
    anonymous feedback 72–76
    environmental goals and
        expectations 68–70
    environmental sources of data
        70–71
    environmental sources of theory
        80–81
    individual's relational system
        66–68
    relational map with the client
        78–79
    using open feedback 76–78
Erculj, J. 22
Evans, E. 107
executive coaching, definition of 2
external adaptation 24

Fire in the Belly 89
Fisher, M. A. 137
Flaherty, J. 142
Fleenor, J. W. 72
Florent-Treacy, E. 1, 72
FMCG business 85
Fraher, A. L. 17
Frankl, V. 95, 98–99, 105
Freire, T. 34, 42, 45
Freud, S. 48, 64, 124–126
Friedman, M. 159
Frontiers in Cultural Psychology 37

Geissler, D. 152
Gendlin, E. 33
Global Financial Crisis 120
Global Problems and the Culture of
    Capitalism 34
Gold, J. 3
Goldfried, M. R. 48–49
Goleman, D. 105
Goshal, S. 62, 64, 81
Grandy, G. 22
Grant, A. M. 124, 142

Green, Z. G. 19
Greenfield, D. P. 41
Grinder, J. 105, 143
Guy, A. 88

Halton, W. 20, 64
Handy, C. B. 33
Hanson, B. G. 8
Hauke, C. 105
Hauser, P. M. 34, 46
Hawkins, P. 1, 9, 141
Hecker, L. L. 12, 14
Heidegger, M. 95, 97
Hengen, W. K. 41
Hesse, H. 66
Hieker, C. 114
Hillman, J. 106, 144–145
Hirsh, S. 106
Hirst, M. 88
Hofstede, G. 31–32
Hofstede, G. J. 31
holism 10–11
homeostasis phenomenon 14–16
Hoyle, L. 20, 64
Huffington, C. 1–2, 5, 20, 64, 114
Hughes, P. 123–124, 126–127
Hunter, I. 143
Hutton, C. 19

individual-centric approach 4, 113, 115
individual dimension 83–106
    business coaching at existential level 95–99
    goals and expectations 99–101
    individual below and above the surface 83–85
    individual sources of data 101–102
    individual sources of theory 105
    manage power relations and rank 90–95

psychometrics in business coaching 102–105
    roots of an individual's social and cultural identity 87–88
    visible aspects of an individual's story 85
individual psychology 105
internal integration 23–24, 26–28
internal model of the organisation 149
International Coaching Psychology Review, The 142

Jansky, S. 59
Jarrett, M. 5–6, 149–150
Jones, S. 88
Jung, C. G. 105, 144–145

Kahn, M. S. 1–2, 4, 45, 48, 55, 88–89, 124, 144
Kauth, B. 89
Keen, S. 89
Kelley, A. H. 87–88, 95
Kelly, K. J. 88
Kemp, T. 1, 122
Kennedy, A. A. 22, 28–29, 32, 81
Kerr, I. 123–124, 126–127
Kets de Vries, M. F. R. 1, 72, 124
Kilburg, R. R. 2
King, A. 15
King, L. 99
KLM 88
Kolb, A. Y. 106
Kolb, D. A. 106
Korotov, K. 1, 72
Kuttner, R. 89

Lane, D. A. 35, 45, 50, 52, 80, 145–146
Langworth, R. M. 103
Lao Tzu 8
leadership mindset 109

Lehman Brothers 120
Lencioni, P. 81
Lewin, K. 17, 81
Lewin, R. 17–18, 81
London, M. 72
London Business School 62
Long, S. 5
Lowman, R. 136–137, 142
Ludden, J. 90
Lyubomirsky, S. 99

Maguire, S. 8, 10
maladaptive basic assumptions
    dependency 18–19
    fight–flight 18–19
    pairing 18–19
Malan, D. 105, 124, 143
Malcolm, J. 127
Mankind Project, The 89
Manzoni, J. F. 66
Martone, M. 105
masculinity *vs.* femininity 32
Mathison, J. 105
Maturana, H. R. 16
Maula, M. 16
Maxwell, J. C. 81
McCrae, R. R. 106
McDowall, A. 142
McKelvey, B. 8, 10
McLean, G. N. 64
McLeod, S. A. 159
McMahon, M. 102
McNaught, B. 90
McRae, M. B. 81
Medici Bank 120
Megginson, D. 42–43
Merriam, S. B. 106
Mills, A. J. 22
Minahan, M. 19
Mindell, A. 92–93, 105
Minkov, M. 31
Minuchin, S. 7

modern scientist-practitioner 45,
    50–53, 80
Molenkamp, R. J. 19
Moran, C. 103
Morden, T. 33
Morf, C. C. 17
Morgan, G. 22
Mortimer, L. 136–137, 142
Moyes, B. 141
Muir, H. 89
Mumford, A. 3

Nelken, I. 15
Neverending Story, The 152
Newton, J. 5
Norcross, J. C. 48–49
Northouse, P. G. 81
Noumair, A. 20

O'Brion, A. 34
O'Neill, M. B. 7, 11, 142
Obholzer, A. 124
Oliver, C. 107, 114
organisational culture 26–27
    literature 81
organisational iceberg 65
organisational theory 3
Ormrod, J. A. 88

Page, L. 45, 105
Palmer, S. xvii, 3, 34, 45, 48–49, 124,
    142
Panter, A. T. 17
Parker, J. D. A. 105
Passmore, J. 1, 3, 34, 42, 45, 48,
    136–137, 142
Patton, W. 102
Peltier, B. 3, 124, 142
person-based culture 33
Petersen, W. 152
Peterson, C. 105
Peterson, D. B. 34, 42, 45

Pierson, J. F. 105
Pooley, J. 20, 64
Pope, K. S. 136–137
Popper, K. 35
Potok, C. 85
power distance 31
power-based culture 33
process culture 33
psychoanalytic culture 37
psychotherapeutic approaches 3

Rachlin, H. 105
Racker, H. 123, 142
Raeburn, N. C. 90, 105
reciprocal causality *see* circular
        causality
reflexive awareness 114
relational interface 6
relational wholes 8
rescuer role 18
Ringleb, A. H. 105
Rioch, M. J. 19
Roam, D. 78
Robbins, R. H. 34–35, 40, 81
Roberts, V. Z. 5–6, 124, 149–150
Rock, D. 45, 105
Rock, D. R. 105
Rodgers, W. M. 89
role,
    -based culture 33
    boundaries 6
    concept of 5, 56
    -consultancy approach 5
    environmental dimension 59–61
    in group contexts 18, 20
    organisational 5–6, 10, 17
roots 83, 85, 87
    of individual identity 87–90
Rosinski, P. 81

Sandberg, S. 88, 105
Sansone, C. 17

Sarbin, T. R. 105
Scaturo, D. J. 144
Schein, E. H. 21–29, 36, 81, 142
Schneider, K. J. 105
Schnupp, J. 15
Schultz, M. 23–24
Schurink, C. 106
Schwenk, G. 1, 9, 141
scientist-practitioner *see* modern
        scientist-practitioner
Scott, S. 72
Searles, H. F. 124
Seligman, M. 99, 105
Senge, P. 7, 11–12, 81
Shakespeare, W. 144
Sheth, J. 81
Short, E. L. 81
Sievers, B. 5
Sisodia, R. 81
Smuts, J. C. 10
Spinelli, E. 95, 105
Spriggs, W. E. 89
Stacey, R. D. 9
Stapley, L. F. 7–9, 22, 26, 37, 81
Stern, K. R. 59
Stevens, A. 105
Stevens, J. 105
Stokes, J. 19
Stout-Rostron, S. 2–3, 45, 95, 142, 156
Strawbridge, S. 138
Strober, D. R. 124, 142
Struwig, H. 6
Sun Tzu 8, 63–64
supervision 141–142
Sylvestre-Williams, R. 119
systems theory 8–9
        literature 81

Tao Te Ching 8
task-based culture 33
Terblanche, L. 17
theories of leadership, literature 81

theories of personality 106
Thorpe, R. 3
Toman, S. M. 143
Tosey, P. 105
tough-guy macho culture 32–33
toxic company 119–121
toxic employees 117–118

uncertainty avoidance 31

valence 20
    concept of 17–18
    defined 17
    overview 17
Varela, F. J. 16
Vetter, V. A. 136–137
viability 46, 48, 53, 80, 140
von Bertalanffy, Ludbig. 7–8
Von Franz, M. 106

Walsh, J. 128
way we do things 22, 26, 84
Wedding, D. 105
Westney, D. E. 81
Wetchler, J. L. 12, 14
White, M. 105
Whitmore, J. 42, 143
Whybrow, A. 3, 45, 124, 142
Wilber, K. 50, 105
Woldt, A. L. 143
Wolfe, D. 81
Woolfe, R. 48–49
Woollard, J. 105
work-hard, play-hard culture 33
Worldwide Association of Business
    Coaches 2

PROFESSIONAL COACHING SERIES

This series brings together leading exponents and researchers in the coaching field to provide a definitive set of core texts important to the development of the profession. It aims to meet two needs—a professional series that provides the core texts that are theoretically and experimentally grounded, and a practice series covering forms of coaching based in evidence. Together they provide a complementary framework to introduce, promote and enhance the development of the coaching profession.

"Finally, in this exceptional book, Marc Kahn succeeds in being one of the first to properly plant the emerging service of coaching firmly and commercially in the modern business context. This studied, yet very readable, work uses the concept of a Coaching Axis to expertly meld the fields of psychology and business, and the results are powerful. I particularly like the way real-life examples are used to address the core complexity business coaches face in balancing individual and commercial concerns. With his clear grasp of commerce, Marc Kahn has produced an authoritative and practical work that will, in my opinion, deservedly takes its place in the business canons of the twenty first century."

—*Peter Frampton, President, Accounting Comes Alive International, and co-author of* Accounting Comes Alive *and* Color Accounting, *Geneva, Switzerland*

"A brilliant book. *Coaching on the Axis* is a major contribution to the landscape of executive and business coaching. Marc Kahn draws on his depth in psychology as he masterfully integrates his expertise as a coach with his experience as a corporate executive. This book powerfully articulates the focal 'axis' of attention for business coaches, and ultimately defines the most important factors that determine its success. Highly recommended for those that provide the service and those who procure it."

—*Dr Paddy Pampalis, Executive Director, Centre for Integral Business and Leadership & The Coaching Centre, Cape Town, South Africa*

"Far too many individuals simply 'rebrand' their former selves and services under the rubric of 'business coaching', using the misguided assumption that their 'other qualifications' are all that is needed to competently practice. Unfortunately, this misguided perception all-to-often leads to a fragmented, ineffective, and even unethical service. As a leader in our field, and one who is committed to the highest ethical practice, Marc Kahn speaks to this real-world issue. *Coaching on the Axis* helps the reader grasp and appreciate the context and complexity required to deliver business coaching in an integrated, ethical, and effective manner. A must-read for those who are serious about being professional and ethical business coaches."

—*Wendy Johnson, President and CEO, Worldwide Association of Business Coaches WABC®, Vancouver, Canada*

"I have enjoyed, first-hand, the positive results of working with Marc Kahn, and experienced the way he expertly balances the needs of the organisation with that of the individual in the coaching relationship. His book clearly explains how he does this. *Coaching on the Axis* crystallises coaching theory with engaging and inspirational case studies. A must-read for any executive who wants to develop themselves or their team to deliver incremental value to their company."

—*Laurence Morris, Managing Director, Nando's Grocery, Sydney, Australia*

"I was riveted. I simply couldn't put this book down, which, I must say, is rare for me to experience with texts in this field these days. Very few authors could achieve what Marc Kahn has with *Coaching on the Axis*. The work combines in-depth psychological and organisational theory with real business acumen to arrive at a culturally aligned and very practical framework for business coaching. This remarkable book needs to be read by anyone who is interested in the relationship between psyche and work."

—*Marc Feitelberg, clinical psychologist, executive coach and founder of The South African College of Applied Psychology*

"I welcome this sage and authentic book. It provides a critical and important review of the way business coaching is being applied in organisations today, and reveals that there is much that needs serious attention. *Coaching on the Axis* offers a practical framework for business coaching without compromising the rich theoretical context within which good coaching operates. Marc Kahn makes theory accessible through stories that touch and challenge, and he inspires and stretches the reader. I encourage all human resource practitioners, business leaders, and coaches to read, and heed, the important messages in this book."

—*Bev Cunningham, Vice President, Group Human Resources, Ricoh Europe plc, London, UK*

"In this highly readable and captivating work, Marc Kahn shows how scholarly insights and psychological theory can be seamlessly and engagingly interwoven with practical ideas and entertaining stories, to provide a work that, I predict, will become an essential read for anyone in the field of organisational coaching."

—*Dr Jacqui Farrants, Consultant Psychologist, City University, London, UK*

"*Coaching on the Axis* is an undeniable contribution to the field of business and executive coaching. Regardless the modality you prefer as a coach, this text will add depth and understanding to your practice. The book effectively straightens the tangled rope of ethical and environmental boundaries between the field of coaching and the culture of business in a very practical manner. Marc Kahn does a masterful job of using case studies to clearly describe the role each client's story plays as the prime driver and inspiration for coaching questions. He allows the reader a window into his experience, offering valuable insight into the formulation of coaching questions. The concise, yet adaptive, disciplines described will significantly benefit both coaches and clients. Highly recommended."

—*Craig Bloomstrand, international coach and mentor, author of* Wise Men Look *and* Every Story Casts a Shadow, *Minneapolis, USA*

"This is a marvellous book. It offers so many insightful lessons resulting in 'a-ha' moments. Marc Kahn has finally provided the market with real clarity on the difference between counselling and coaching and the importance of aligning business coaching with the context and reality of business. I was enthralled with the notion of a 'coaching axis' that he uses to work with the duality of client and ensure that coaching aligns with business outcomes and organisational culture. The case study of Des was very revealing, there were parts that I personally identified with and I found this profound. This book is not only for coaches but is a must-have in a leader's reading toolkit."

—*Nokuzola Poswa, GM Human Resources: Organisational Effectiveness & Change, Sasol Limited, Johannesburg, South Africa*

"I recommend *Coaching on the Axis* for coaches and HR practitioners alike. It navigates the coaching process towards business performance, offering practical advice from the author's many years of coaching experience. Of note is that it deals successfully with many thorny issues, such as how coaching needs to serve the interests of both the business and the individual simultaneously; when to ethically terminate coaching; dual client confidentiality; and who has right of access to coaching data. A great read."

—*Radi Anguelova, Human Resources Director, Asia Pacific Group, The Coca-Cola Company, Istanbul, Turkey*

"This book is a testament to the author's depth of knowledge and incisive wisdom. It demonstrates his ability to merge the complex worlds of psychology, coaching, and business in a remarkable way. I've been fortunate enough to work with Marc Kahn and experience the benefits of his rare acumen. He helped me deal with some serious executive challenges. As much as *Coaching on the Axis* is a comprehensive academic work, it also has a compelling narrative and cogency that makes it a fantastic read, providing a really good sense of the amazing benefits business coaching can bring to an executive when it is delivered properly—on the 'axis'."

—Brett Morris, Group CEO, FCB South Africa

"*Coaching on the Axis* is a brilliant and inspired work. Marc Kahn has masterfully integrated leading edge theory in a practical and powerful book that is a must-read for both coaches and executives. His case examples are often profound and moving."

—Sacha Sorrell, International Franchise Coach and former Fortune Franchise 100 Senior Executive, London, UK

"This is one of the most insightful books on business coaching I have ever read. Marc Kahn expertly bridges the theory underlying coaching with real and very practical business application, something most other authors on the subject have tried but failed. Also, *Coaching on the Axis* is thoughtfully constructed in way that makes its complex arguments easy to follow and understand. Essential reading for coaches working with business executives."

—Allon Raiz, CEO, Raizcorp and bestselling author of Lose the Business Plan *and* What to Do When You Want to Give Up, *Johannesburg, South Africa*

"Marc Kahn's extensive experience as a leading business coach and psychologist, alongside his years as an executive in a multinational corporation, position him perfectly to write this important book. While he writes with academic rigour, his use of story immerses the reader in real-life coaching interactions that are moving and profoundly insightful. Mandatory reading for coaches and those who hire them."

—Justin Cohen, international speaker and author of The Astonishing Power of Story, *Johannesburg and New York*

"I run an intensive human capital business and truly appreciate the value of mechanisms, such as coaching, that help my organisation function across its specialisations, geographies, and stakeholders. *Coaching on the Axis* is an incisive and significant contribution to this end. The author is both a psychologist and experienced executive coach, but more importantly, he is an accomplished businessman. This means he really understands the complex task at hand from all sides of the equation and is uniquely positioned to see what others, without his background, do not. The text addresses fundamental blind spots and gaps in the approach that coaching has historically taken in the business world. Marc Kahn's book is undoubtedly a major contribution to the coaching industry."

—Alon Davidov, CEO, Shaft Sinkers Holdings plc, London, UK

"In any field there are those that develop theories and those that actually do the work. Marc Kahn is the latter, which makes this book, with its many real cases, an invaluable resource. This is especially true for those coaches that have realised their work must expand beyond the individual. The *Coaching on the Axis* framework provides a much-needed practical approach for coaches to achieve this. The book challenges many traditional paradigms around the ideal boundaries for coaching, and offers practical examples that assist in navigating the complex set of relationships coaches encounter in the multiple client reality of business. An absolute must for all coaches, especially for those working with individuals in an organisational context."

—John Brodie, Managing Director, Mindcor Group,
Johannesburg, South Africa

"This is a tremendous book. A product of real range and depth in its author: top executive coach and supervisor, HR executive, clinical psychologist, businessman, and martial artist. Marc Kahn brings this powerful combination of perspectives to bear upon the landscape of business coaching and the results are profound. *Coaching on the Axis* is academically rigorous, captivating, and very practical."

—Edwin Edelstein, Managing Director,
Martial Art Education, London, UK

"I recommend *Coaching on the Axis* by Marc Kahn. I found it replete with engaging exemplars and case studies from the lived worlds of organisational culture and the marketplace. The book is clearly and usefully grounded in both theory and the author's experience. It skilfully presents, explores, and uses the living interface between individual and business, explicit and implicit, conscious and unconscious, and it invites the reader into the dialectic between individual and business needs in a very useful and practical manner."

—Dr Chris Milton, Training Analyst of the Australian and New Zealand Society of Jungian Analysts, Auckland, New Zealand

"*Coaching on the Axis* is groundbreaking, not only for coaches, but also for business leaders. It's the first text I have seen that skilfully weaves strategy, performance, and organisational culture into the conversation about executive and business coaching. Marc Kahn's book is well-crafted, combining practical tools with insightful theory. He masterfully explains the complexity involved in managing a 'duality of client' in business coaching practice. It is an important read for both organisations and individuals who are committed to using business coaching for learning and development. This seminal text will, no doubt, be used to steer coaching practices going forward in the corporate world."

—Lesley-Ann Gatter, Head of Learning and Development, Investec Limited, Johannesburg, South Africa

"*Coaching on the Axis* provides both critical insight and practical approaches to enable coaches with an individual, clinical, or personal health focus to coach effectively within the complex reality of the organisational context."

—Pauline Willis, BPS Chartered Psychologist and Director, Lauriate Business Psychology, Coaching & Consulting, Oxford, UK

"In this text, Marc Kahn concretises his passion and gravitas in the field of business and executive coaching. The book integrates both theory and practice, and manages a great deal of knowledge and experience in providing readers a rich and complex approach to this work. *Coaching on the Axis* offers a systemic stance that covers individual behaviour, the nature and dynamics of the coaching relationship, and relevant organisational constructs. It includes a well-thought-through background to coaching and offers a framework, based in the notion of a 'coaching axis', which students and professionals alike can use to explore the depths of this service to the business world."

—Professor Frans Cilliers, Professor of Industrial & Organisational Psychology, University of South Africa

"At last, a sophisticated and business-savvy account of business and executive coaching. Marc Kahn's book represents an important shift of understanding in the world of business coaching. His keen understanding of complexity theory, psychology, and the business context challenges many of the hidden (and not so hidden) assumptions imported into business coaching from counselling. *Coaching on the Axis* is a welcome and important contribution to the business coaching literature. A book that should be on every coach's bookshelf, and, more importantly, a book that should inform every coach's practice."

—Dr Michael Cavanagh, Deputy Director, Coaching Psychology Unit, Sydney University, Australia

"This is a masterful contribution to the literature on business coaching. Drawing on his depth of experience as a clinical psychologist, coach practitioner, and organisational business consultant, Marc Kahn creates a paradigm shift for business coaches. He integrates insights from the worlds of psychology, business science, and organisational systems. The Coaching Axis is offered as a practical model to understand the complex relationship between individual client, coach practitioner, and organisational culture. Instead of emphasising one or the other, Marc weaves individuals' stories with that of the organisation as a way to deliver results and enhance performance. Grappling with the indefatigable concerns of business—his book offers a new approach to align multiple and complex perspectives. Addressing the reality of coaching on the axis—between an individual's goals and the organisational agenda, this book is a must-have. Not just in every coach's library—but in every leader's."

—Dr Sunny Stout-Rostron, Founding Fellow, Institute of Coaching at McLean Hospital, a Harvard Medical School Affiliate

Printed in the United States
by Baker & Taylor Publisher Services